FIRST COURSE

IN

NUMERICAL METHODS

FIRST COURSE

IN

NUMERICAL METHODS

WALTER JENNINGS

Professor of Mathematics
United States Naval Postgraduate School

THE MACMILLAN COMPANY, *New York*
COLLIER–MACMILLAN LIMITED, *London*

© WALTER JENNINGS 1964

First Printing

Based upon a preliminary edition published by the author, © Walter Jennings 1962.

Library of Congress catalog card number: 63-15284

THE MACMILLAN COMPANY, NEW YORK

COLLIER-MACMILLAN CANADA, LTD., TORONTO, ONTARIO

Printed in the United States of America

To Mausita

Preface

This little text is intended as an introduction to scientific computing, to the basic ideas of numerical mathematics. I have written it for advanced undergraduate students of science and engineering who either have had or will have some experience with a digital computer. However, all of the numerical problems are sufficiently small-scale to make their solution on a desk calculator entirely practicable, if not preferable. Instructors with large-scale computers available will, of course, make liberal use of illustrative problems from their files.

The text is based on courses given by the author in recent years to students of science and engineering at the United States Naval Postgraduate School, Monterey, California. It must be emphasized that this is a *first* course. It is hoped that some students will be stimulated to pursue further courses in this area, but for many students this will be a terminal course. For this reason the coverage is more in breadth than in depth—without, it is hoped, being superficial. I have tried to make this not a dull collection of favorite recipes but rather a logical piece of applied mathematics—the mathematics of scientific computing. I have used a multilithed version of the text in a course of thirty lectures and ten two-hour laboratory periods.

This introductory course is centered around the basic problems of approximation of functions, numerical integration of ordinary differential equations, and numerical solution of polynomial equations and systems of linear algebraic equations. Other topics are introduced as preparatory to these basic problems or as a natural outgrowth of them. The specific techniques discussed are, for the most part, relatively simple methods that have been found useful in modern computing laboratories. It is hoped that an adequate groundwork has been laid for the study of the more sophisticated problems of numerical analysis.

Only a modest level of attainment in mathematics is presupposed, namely, the calculus and differential equations; in the final chapters an understanding of the algebra of matrices, as summarized in Appendix B, is required.

Most existing texts are far too voluminous for a short introductory course, and most place far too much emphasis on the difference calculus. I have emphasized the so-called Lagrangian or differenceless methods of interpolation, differentiation, and integration. In keeping with modern trends in numerical work, there is considerably more emphasis on the polynomials of Čebyšev than has been customary in past elementary texts. There is an introduction to the vast and still growing field of matrix computational methods.

The bibliographies found at the end of most chapters indicate some of the sources that have influenced the author. It is hoped that students will be intrigued to follow up some of these. Individual class reports on some of the simpler papers—such as those found, for example, in the *American Mathematical Monthly* and in the *Journal of the Association of Computing Machinery*—often stimulate interest.

Much of the literature of the eighteenth and nineteenth centuries has not been readily available to me. And so I have probably contributed my share to the confusion about credits for various classical results. I have used what appear to be the most frequently used names for various formulas. I hope that I may be forgiven if I have failed at times to give adequate acknowledgment for the ultimate source of ideas and methods used. I simply do not know who first published some of the procedures that have since become standard.

My own introduction to the field was via the classic text of Whittaker and Robinson. But my first real interest was stimulated by the novel lectures of Henry Blumberg at the Ohio State University, based on his association with Runge at Göttingen. Among the recent books that have influenced the present text are Ralston and Wilf's *Mathematical Methods for Digital Computers*, Lance's *Numerical Methods for High-Speed Computers*, and the National Physical Laboratory's *Modern Computing Methods*. Detailed references to these are made in the pertinent chapters.

It is a pleasure to thank my students at the Naval Postgraduate School for their constructive criticisms of several preliminary versions of this text. My sincere thanks go also to B. J. Lockhart and E. H. Hanson of the Naval Postgraduate School's Department of Mathematics for their critical reading of the manuscript while using it with their classes. Finally, I should like to thank other friends who read various portions of the manuscript and made many helpful suggestions. The production staff at Macmillan has also been helpful and constructive.

Monterey, California   WALTER JENNINGS

Contents

FIRST COURSE
IN
NUMERICAL METHODS

INTRODUCTION

Forsythe [1] has defined numerical analysis as "the branch of applied mathematics which uses mathematical ideas to devise and evaluate numerical techniques for employing computers to solve problems, and to study their convergence and errors." From this point of view it is, then, absolutely essential that any course in numerical methods provide for experience in a computing laboratory. Ideally this laboratory would have a desk calculator for each student, a library, and a digital computer.

For students with no previous machine experience the book by Varner [2] might be made available for individual study.

If a digital computer with a compiler is available, some laboratory time might be devoted to the study of one of McCracken's Guides [3,4].

It is not our intent to dwell on the controversial subject of desk calculators versus digital computers in teaching numerical methods. But let us emphasize the desirability of giving all students of science and engineering some experience with each. Originally I planned to include full-page display giving detailed printouts of the solutions to a few illustrative problems on a large-scale digital computer. It was soon realized, however, that simple examples which the student could check through with a desk calculator would be considerably more instructive. The methods discussed are for the most part appropriate for use with digital computers. Some, like Bernoulli's method for obtaining the zeros of polynomials, are inappropriate for use with desk calculators. But even here most beginning students will profit from doing a few lines of an example "by hand."

Digital computers appeared on the mathematical scene less than two decades ago. The intelligent use of these machines demands continued study and research in the relevant mathematics. They are not "giant brains" but rather "dimwitted slaves" whose principal assets are speed, accuracy, and

1

indefatigability. They are completely automatic only if their masters can foresee every possible contingency that can arise in the course of a calculation. Thus, rather than replacing mathematics, they are creating the need for more study of mathematics.

REFERENCES

1. G. E. Forsythe. *Contemporary State of Numerical Analysis* (Surveys in Applied Mathematics, V). New York: Wiley, 1958.
2. W. W. Varner. *Computing with Desk Calculators*. New York: Rinehart, 1957.
3. D. D. McCracken. *A Guide to Fortran Programming*. New York: Wiley, 1961.
4. ———. *A Guide to Algol Programming*. New York: Wiley, 1962.

POLYNOMIALS

It is not unusual for the exact solutions of mathematical problems to involve functions of such complexity as to make such solutions of little interest in numerical work. Specific examples will be given in later chapters in connection with the problems of evaluating integrals and finding solutions of initial and boundary problems in differential equations. In such cases we replace the complicated exact solutions by simple, approximate solutions. The problem of function approximation is one of fundamental importance in all numerical work.

Linear interpolation, familiar to all users of tables of the elementary functions, depends on the possibility of approximating any continuous function by a polygonal arc, that is, of locally approximating a continuous function by a first degree polynomial. Analytic functions—those that can be expressed as convergent power series—can be approximated as accurately as desired by polynomials, the initial segments of those power series. But Weierstrass has shown that a much larger class, namely, the class of all continuous functions, can be approximated by polynomials on any finite interval with arbitrarily small (nonzero) error.

Polynomials are the simplest of finite mathematical structures used to represent functions. We shall develop systematic procedures for evaluating them with ease. The derivative and integral of a polynomial are polynomials.

Numerical procedures will be developed for the approximate evaluation of integrals and for obtaining approximate particular solutions in tabular form of differential equations. These solutions depend on the possibility of obtaining suitable polynomial approximations. Thus, as we shall see, polynomials play a basic role in numerical work.

Other approximations, notably rational functions (quotients of polynomials) and trigonometric polynomials, have been used with considerable success, but cannot be handled with the same ease as polynomials. The integral of a rational function need not be itself a rational function, but may, for example, involve the logarithm. In the present text we shall use only polynomials to approximate continuous functions. A major part of our concern will be with the problem of obtaining polynomial approximations which are in some sense "best" and in showing how such approximations can be used to evaluate integrals and obtain solutions of differential equations.

2

EVALUATION OF

POLYNOMIALS

AND THEIR

DERIVATIVES

2.1 POLYNOMIALS

The value of the polynomial

$$p(x) = a_0x^n + a_1x^{n-1} + \cdots + a_{n-1}x + a_n \qquad (2.1)$$

at x_0 may be found using a computing routine involving a succession of multiplications and additions as indicated:

$$\{[(a_0x_0 + a_1)x_0 + a_2]x_0 + a_3\}x_0 + \cdots . \qquad (2.2)$$

This procedure, known as *nested multiplication*, is actually equivalent to Horner's algorithm. For let

$$
\begin{aligned}
b_0 &= a_0 + 0x_0 \\
b_1 &= a_1 + b_0 x_0 \\
b_2 &= a_2 + b_1 x_0 \\
&\cdots\cdots\cdots\cdots \\
b_i &= a_i + b_{i-1} x_0 \\
&\cdots\cdots\cdots\cdots \\
b_n &= a_n + b_{n-1} x_0 = p(x_0).
\end{aligned}
\tag{2.3}
$$

In the days of hand calculations these relations were displayed in a form due to W. G. Horner (1773–1827):

1	a_0	a_1	a_2	$\cdots$	a_{n-1}		a_n
x_0		$b_0 x_0$	$b_1 x_0$	$\cdots$	$b_{n-2} x_0$		$b_{n-1} x_0$
	b_0	b_1	b_2	$\cdots$	b_{n-1}		$b_n = p(x_0)$

While the method of nested multiplication and the Horner algorithm are equivalent, they differ appreciably in the amount of recording of intermediate results indicated. The method of nested multiplication when used with a desk calculator requires no recording of intermediate results (storage in a high-speed digital computer), provided that only values of $p(x)$ are required. We shall see, however, that some storage of intermediate results will facilitate the calculation of values of $p'(x)$.

The Horner scheme is often referred to as *synthetic division*. For note that

$$
\begin{aligned}
p(x) &= \sum_{i=0}^{n} a_i x^{n-i} \\
&= b_0 x^n + \sum_{i=1}^{n} (b_i - b_{i-1} x_0) x^{n-1} \\
&= (x - x_0) \sum_{i=0}^{n-1} b_i x^{n-1-i} + b_n.
\end{aligned}
\tag{2.4}
$$

Thus

$$
q_1(x) = \sum_{i=0}^{n-1} b_i x^{n-1-i}
$$

is the quotient obtained by dividing $p(x)$ by $x - x_0$, and the remainder b_n is equal to $p(x_0)$. Hence the familiar

REMAINDER THEOREM. If a polynomial $p(x)$ be divided by $x - x_0$ until a remainder independent of x is obtained, this remainder is equal to $p(x_0)$.

The method of nested multiplication gives us a systematic procedure for calculating not only $p(x_0)$ but also the coefficients of the quotient of $p(x)$ by $x - x_0$. It requires n multiplications and n additions. An alternative scheme of calculating first the powers of x and storing them would require $2n - 1$ multiplications and n additions. If the values of $p(x)$ are desired for many equally spaced values of x it may be desirable to work with a difference table (Chap. 9). Motzkin [1] has suggested a process based on evaluation of a sequence of nonlinear polynomials. But, because of its simplicity and generality, the method of nested multiplication is usually to be preferred.

2.2 DERIVATIVES

According to Taylor's formula (A-6)* the polynomial $p(x)$ can be written as follows in power of $x - x_0$:

$$p(x) = p(x_0) + p'(x_0)(x - x_0) + \frac{p''(x_0)}{2!}(x - x_0)^2$$

$$+ \frac{p'''(x_0)}{3!}(x - x_0)^3 + \cdots + \frac{p^{(n)}(x_0)}{n!}(x - x_0)^n. \tag{2.5}$$

Thus

$$p(x) = (x - x_0)q_1(x) + p(x_0)$$

where

$$q_1(x) = p'(x_0) + \frac{p''(x_0)}{2!}(x - x_0) + \cdots + \frac{p^{(n)}(x_0)}{n!}(x - x_0)^{n-1}.$$

Thus $p'(x_0) = q_1(x_0)$ and is therefore the remainder obtained by dividing $q_1(x)$ by $x - x_0$.

This process extends to higher derivatives as follows:

Let

$$p(x) = (x - x_0)q_1(x) + r_0$$

$$q_1(x) = (x - x_0)q_2(x) + r_1$$

$$q_2(x) = (x - x_0)q_3(x) + r_2 \tag{2.6}$$

$$\cdots \cdots \cdots \cdots \cdots \cdots \cdots \cdots$$

$$q_{n-1}(x) = (x - x_0)q_n(x) + r_{n-1}$$

$$q_n(x) = r_n.$$

* Theorem 6 of Appendix A.

Using the above relations for successive substitutions we obtain

$$p(x) = r_n(x - x_0)^n + r_{n-1}(x - x_0)^{n-1} + \cdots$$
$$+ r_1(x - x_0) + r_0. \tag{2.7}$$

A comparison of this with the Taylor formula for $p(x)$ shows that

$$p^{(k)}(x_0) = k! \, r_k. \tag{2.8}$$

EXAMPLE 2.1. Write the polynomial

$$p(x) = 6x^4 - 53x^3 + 184x^2 - 295x + 186$$

in powers of $x - 2$. This can be done by evaluating $p(x)$ and its derivatives at $x = 2$ by successive application of iteration described above. The coefficients of $p(x)$ and successive quotients are:

6	6	6	6	6	$6 = p^{\mathrm{IV}}(2)/4!$
−53	−41	−29	−17	$-5 = p'''(2)/3!$	
184	102	44	$10 = p''(2)/2!$		
−295	−91	$-3 = p'(2)$			
186	$4 = p(2)$				

Hence

$$p(x) = 4 - 3(x - 2) + 10(x - 2)^2 - 5(x - 2)^3 + 6(x - 2)^4.$$

2.3 POLYNOMIALS AT COMPLEX VALUES

While Horner's algorithm might be used for evaluating a polynomial at a complex value of the variable, the multiplications involved are somewhat awkward. For polynomials with real coefficients such multiplications can be avoided by a procedure based on division by a real quadratic.

The real quadratic—that is, the quadratic with real coefficients,

$$x^2 - 2\alpha x + \alpha^2 + \beta^2 = x^2 - rx - s \tag{2.9}$$

may be thought of as corresponding to the complex number $\alpha + \beta i$, it being simply

$$[x - (\alpha + \beta i)][x - (\alpha - \beta i)].$$

The division of a polynomial $p(x) = \sum_{i=0}^{n} a_i x^{n-i}$ of degree n with real coefficients by this real quadratic will give a quotient and remainder having real coefficients. Thus

$$p(x) = (x^2 - rx - s)q(x) + Rx + S. \tag{2.10}$$

Furthermore,

$$p(\alpha + \beta i) = R\alpha + S + R\beta i.$$

The quotient $q(x)$ is a real polynomial of degree $n - 2$ which we write as

$$q(x) = \sum_{k=0}^{n-2} b_k x^{n-2-k}.$$

Multiplication of $q(x)$ by $x^2 - rx - s$, addition of $Rx + S$ and rearrangement into descending powers of x shows that

$$b_k = a_k + rb_{k-1} + sb_{k-2}, \qquad k = 0, 1, 2, \ldots, n, \tag{2.11}$$

where

$$b_{-2} = b_{-1} = 0$$

and

$$R = b_{n-1}, \qquad S = b_n - rb_{n-1}.$$

Hence

$$p(\alpha + \beta i) = b_n - \alpha b_{n-1} + \beta b_{n-1} i. \tag{2.12}$$

2.4 DERIVATIVES AT COMPLEX VALUES

Again we write

$$p(x) = (x^2 - rx - s)q(x) + Rx + S$$

where

$$r = 2\alpha, \qquad s = -(\alpha^2 + \beta^2).$$

Then

$$p'(x) = (2x - r)q(x) + (x^2 - rx - s)q'(x) + R$$

and hence

$$p'(\alpha + \beta i) = 2\beta i \, q(\alpha + \beta i) + R.$$

The evaluation of $q(\alpha + \beta i)$ is accomplished by the algorithm:

$$c_k = b_k + rc_{k-1} + sc_{k-2},$$

$$k = 0, 1, 2, \ldots, n - 2,$$

where

$$c_{-2} = c_{-1} = 0.$$

Then

$$q(\alpha + \beta i) = c_{n-2} - \alpha c_{n-3} + \beta c_{n-3} i$$

and

$$p'(\alpha + \beta i) = b_{n-1} - 2c_{n-3}\beta^2$$

$$+ 2(c_{n-2} - \alpha c_{n-3})\beta i. \tag{2.13}$$

It is, of course, assumed that the original polynomial is of degree 4 or more.

EXAMPLE 2.2. Evaluate the polynomial

$$p(x) = 3x^5 - 2x^3 + x^2 - 4x + 3$$

and its derivative at $x = 3 - 2i$. The coefficients of $p(x)$ and its successive quotients upon division by the real quadratic

$$x^2 - 6x + 13$$

are:

a_k	b_k	c_k
	0	0
	0	0
3	3	3
0	18	36
−2	67	244
1	169	1165
−4	139	
3	−1360	

Hence

$$p(3 - 2i) = -1777 - 278i,$$
$$p'(3 - 2i) = -1813 - 1732i.$$

As a check, note that

$$p'(x) = 15x^4 - 6x^2 + 2x - 4.$$

Dividing this by same real quadratic we obtain:

a_k	b_k
	0
	0
15	15
0	90
−6	339
2	866
−4	785

$$p'(3 - 2i) = -1813 - 1732i.$$

2.5 SUMMARY

The evaluation of a polynomial

$$p(x) = \sum_{i=0}^{n} a_i x^{n-i}$$

having real coefficients and its derivative at x_0 can be effected as follows:

CASE I: x_0 real

Record (store) the following numbers:

	0	0
a_0	b_0	c_0
a_1	b_1	c_1
.	.	.
.	.	.
.	.	.
a_{n-1}	b_{n-1}	c_{n-1}
a_n	b_n	

where

$$b_i = a_i + b_{i-1}x_0, \qquad i = 0, 1, 2, \ldots, n,$$
$$c_i = b_i + c_{i-1}x_0, \qquad i = 0, 1, 2, \ldots, n-1,$$
$$b_{-1} = c_{-1} = 0.$$

Then

$$p(x_0) = b_n, \qquad p'(x_0) = c_{n-1}.$$

CASE II: x_0 complex

Let

$$x_0 = \alpha + \beta i,$$
$$r = 2\alpha, \qquad s = -(\alpha^2 + \beta^2).$$

Record (store) the following real numbers:

	0	0
	0	0
a_0	b_0	c_0
a_1	b_1	c_1
.	.	.
.	.	.
.	.	.
a_{n-2}	b_{n-2}	c_{n-2}
a_{n-1}	b_{n-1}	
a_n	b_n	

where

$$b_k = a_k + rb_{k-1} + sb_{k-2}, \qquad k = 0, 1, \ldots, n,$$
$$b_{-2} = b_{-1} = 0$$
$$c_k = b_k + rc_{k-1} + sc_{k-2}, \qquad k = 0, 1, \ldots, n-2,$$
$$c_{-2} = c_{-1} = 0.$$

Then

$$p(\alpha + \beta i) = b_n - \alpha b_{n-1} + \beta b_{n-1} i$$
$$p'(\alpha + \beta i) = b_{n-1} - 2c_{n-3}\beta^2 + 2\beta(c_{n-2} - \alpha c_{n-3})i.$$

EXERCISES

1. Evaluate the polynomial

$$p(x) = 2x^3 - 6x^2 + 3$$

and its first derivative at $x = -2$. Check latter calculation by first differentiating $p(x)$.

2. Evaluate the polynomial

$$p(x) = x^4 + 3x^2 - 3$$

and its first derivative at $x = 2 + i$ using the method suggested for x_0 real. Check by direct substitution.

3. Evaluate the polynomial of Ex. 2 and its derivative at $x = 2 + i$, using the algorithm suggested for x_0 complex.

4. Suppose a polynomial is divided by $(x - x_0)^2$ obtaining a quotient $q(x)$ and a linear remainder $r(x)$. How can the results of this division be used to calculate $p'(x_0)$?

5. Verify the values in the following table:

x	$p(x)$	$p'(x)$	$p''(x)$
2.7	0.7601	−23.428	−18.12
2.8	−1.6704	−25.152	−16.32

where

$$p(x) = x^4 - 8x^3 + 12x^2 + 8x - 4.$$

REFERENCE

1. J. Todd. "Motivation for Working in Numerical Analysis," *Com. Pure Appl. Math.** **8:** 97–116 (1955). Reprinted in J. Todd, ed., *A Survey of Numerical Analysis*, New York: McGraw-Hill, 1962.

* Journal abbreviations are those suggested by *Mathematical Reviews* **19:** 1417–1430 (1958).

3

LINEAR APPROXIMATIONS

3.1 INTRODUCTION

Any continuous function $f(x)$ can be locally approximated by a linear function (polynomial of the first degree):

$$l(x) = a_0 x + a_1.$$

Since $l(x)$ has two coefficients it seems reasonable to require that $l(x)$ and $f(x)$ "agree" in two ways. We consider two examples that have had wide application.

3.2 LINEAR TAYLOR POLYNOMIAL

The linear polynomial

$$t_1(x) = f(x_0) + f'(x_0)(x - x_0), \tag{3.1}$$

given by Brook Taylor (1685–1731), is such that

$$t_1(x_0) = f(x_0)$$

and

$$t_1'(x_0) = f'(x_0).$$

The remainder term (A.6) is

$$R_2(x) = f(x) - t_1(x) = \int_{x_0}^{x} (x - s) f''(s) \, ds.$$

13

Since $x - s$ does not change sign for $x_0 \leq s \leq x$, the second law of the mean for integrals (A.5) applies. Thus there exists at least one number ξ between x_0 and x such that

$$R_2(x) = f''(\xi) \int_{x_0}^{x} (x - s) \, ds$$

$$= f''(\xi) \frac{(x - x_0)^2}{2}.$$

3.3 LINEAR INTERPOLATING POLYNOMIAL

The first degree polynomial

$$I_1(x) = A_0 + A_1 x$$

where A_0 and A_1 are chosen so that

$$I_1(x_0) = f(x_0) = f_0$$

and

$$I_1(x_1) = f(x_1) = f_1, \qquad x_0 \neq x_1,$$

will be called the *linear interpolating polynomial for* $f(x)$ *with collocation points* x_0, x_1. An explicit expression can be obtained for $I(x)$ by noting that

$$A_0 + A_1 x = I_1(x)$$
$$A_0 + A_1 x_0 = f_0$$
$$A_0 + A_1 x_1 = f_1$$

form three consistent equations in the two unknowns A_0 and A_1. Hence (D.1.1):

$$\begin{vmatrix} 1 & x & I_1(x) \\ 1 & x_0 & f_0 \\ 1 & x_1 & f_1 \end{vmatrix} = 0. \tag{3.2}$$

The linear interpolating polynomial is usually written in other forms. We shall consider three of particular interest. They will all be seen to be but various ways of writing $I_1(x)$.

3.31 *LAGRANGE FORM.* Expanding determinant (3.2) by the elements of its last column gives:

$$I_1(x) = \frac{x_1 - x}{x_1 - x_0} f_0 + \frac{x_0 - x}{x_0 - x_1} f_1, \tag{3.3}$$

which is known as *Lagrange* form of the linear interpolating polynomial.

3.32 *COMPUTING FORM.* Equation (3.3) can be written in the following more useful form:

$$I_1(x) = \frac{1}{x_1 - x_0} \begin{vmatrix} f_0 & x_0 - x \\ f_1 & x_1 - x \end{vmatrix}. \tag{3.4}$$

This form is especially useful with a desk calculator since it can be calculated in one machine operation. Note that any factor common to $x_0 - x$, $x_1 - x$, and $x_1 - x_0$ can be removed. Further simplifications are possible, some of which are illustrated in

EXAMPLE 3.1. Given $\sinh U = 0.52186$, find $\cosh U$.
From a table we obtain:

$x_i = \sinh U_i$	$y_i = \cosh U_i$	$x_i - x$
0.52110	1.12763	−0.00076
0.53240	1.13289	0.01054

$$\cosh U = \frac{1}{0.01130} \begin{vmatrix} 1.12763 & -0.00076 \\ 1.13289 & 0.01054 \end{vmatrix}$$

$$= 1.1 + \frac{10^{-5}}{1130} \begin{vmatrix} 2763 & -76 \\ 3289 & 1054 \end{vmatrix}$$

$$= 1.12798.$$

3.33 *NEWTON FORM.* Starting with three distinct numbers x, x_0, x_1 we define, after Newton, the numbers $f(x, x_0)$ and $f(x, x_0, x_1)$ by the equations

$$f(x, x_0) = \frac{f(x_0) - f(x)}{x_0 - x},$$

$$f(x, x_0, x_1) = \frac{f(x_0, x_1) - f(x, x_0)}{x_1 - x}. \text{ *} \tag{3.5}$$

These equations may be rewritten in the following form:

$$f(x) = f(x_0) + (x - x_0)f(x, x_0),$$
$$f(x, x_0) = f(x_0, x_1) + (x - x_1)f(x, x_0, x_1). \tag{3.6}$$

The numbers $f(x, x_0)$ and $f(x, x_0, x_1)$ are called, respectively, the first and second order *divided differences of* $f(x)$. Combining the two Eqs. (3.6) we obtain

$$f(x) = f(x_0) + (x - x_0)f(x_0, x_1) + (x - x_0)(x - x_1)f(x, x_0, x_1)$$
$$= N_1(x) + R_2(x). \tag{3.7}$$

* Among the many other notations that have been used for these divided differences are:
1. $[x, x_0]$, $[x, x_0, x_1]$,
2. $\Delta(x, x_0)$, $\Delta^2(x, x_0, x_1)$.

We note that the linear polynomial $N_1(x)$ is identical with $I_1(x)$. It is known as *Newton's* form of the linear interpolating polynomial.

3.4 REMAINDER IN LINEAR INTERPOLATION

From the Newton form of the linear interpolating polynomial we note that the remainder term is

$$R_2(x) = (x - x_0)(x - x_1)f(x, x_0, x_1). \tag{3.8}$$

We now proceed to recast this in a form more suitable for numerical work.

Letting x' denote any number other than x_0 and x_1, we define

$$\phi(x) = f(x) - N_1(x) - (x - x_0)(x - x_1)f(x', x_0, x_1).$$

Since $\phi(x_0) = \phi(x_1) = \phi(x') = 0$, it follows from a generalization of Rolle's theorem (A.3) that there exists at least one number ξ, between the least and greatest of the three numbers x_0, x_1 and x' such that $\phi''(\xi) = 0$.

But

$$\phi''(x) = f''(x) - 2f(x', x_0, x_1)$$

and hence

$$f(x', x_0, x_1) = \tfrac{1}{2}f''(\xi).$$

provided only that this second derivative exist. Thus

$$0 = f(x') - N_1(x') - (x' - x_0)(x' - x_1)\frac{f''(\xi)}{2}.$$

But $N_1(x) \equiv I_1(x)$. Hence, on dropping the prime:

Remainder in Linear Interpolation (Cauchy form):

$$R_2(x) = (x - x_0)(x - x_1)\frac{f''(\xi)}{2}, \tag{3.9}$$

where

$$min\ (x_0, x_1, x) < \xi < max\ (x_0, x_1, x)$$

3.41 *BOUND ON REMAINDER.* We write

$$R_2(x) = \Pi_2(x)\frac{f''(\xi)}{2}$$

where

$$\Pi_2(x) = (x - x_0)(x - x_1).$$

We shall speak of this as the Π-factor in the remainder term. Since $|\Pi_2(x)|$

attains its maximum value for $x_0 \leq x \leq x_1$ at $x = \frac{1}{2}(x_0 + x_1)$ and this maximum value is $\frac{1}{4}(x_1 - x_0)^2$, we may write

$$|R_2(x)|_{x_0 < x < x_1} \leq \tfrac{1}{8}(x_1 - x_0)^2 M_2, \tag{3.10}$$

where M_2 is an upper bound for $|f''(x)|$ on the closed interval $[x_0, x_1]$.

EXAMPLE 3.2.   Given:

x_i	$\sinh x_i$
3.210	12.369 36
3.220	12.494 08

Interpolating linearly we find

$$\sinh 3.217 = \frac{1}{0.010} \begin{vmatrix} 12.369\ 36 & -0.007 \\ 12.494\ 08 & 0.003 \end{vmatrix} + R_2$$
$$= 12.456\ 66 + R_2.$$

Using Cauchy form of the remainder, Eq. (3.9), we find:

$$-1312 \times 10^{-7} \leq R_2(3.217) \leq -1298 \times 10^{-7}.$$

Thus by subtracting 13×10^{-5} from the interpolated value we obtain $\sinh 3.217 = 12.456\ 53$. The table value is $12.456\ 54$. The disagreement is due to the inevitable rounding.

From Eq. (3.10) we obtain a bound on remainder for any linear interpolation between 3.21 and 3.22:

$$|R_2(x)|_{3.21 < x < 3.22} \leq 1562 \times 10^{-7}.$$

Hummel [1] has given other bounds on the remainder in linear interpolation.

3.5   ERROR IN LINEAR INTERPOLATION

We define:

   error = exact value − interpolated value.

We designate the error at x by $E(x)$. This is not to be confused with the *remainder* in linear interpolation. All remainder formulas were developed under the assumption that f_0 and f_1 were exact, which is, of course, almost never the case, owing to the inevitable rounding. The error is a combination of that due to the lack of linearity of the function considered and that due to rounding.

Let f_0 and f_1 designate, as before, the exact values of $f(x)$ at x_0 and x_1, while $f_0^\star$ and $f_1^\star$ the values actually used in the interpolation, where

$$f_0 = f_0^\star + \epsilon_0$$

and

$$f_1 = f_1^\star + \epsilon_1.$$

Letting

$$I_1(x) = \frac{1}{x_1 - x_0} \begin{vmatrix} f_0 & x_0 - x \\ f_1 & x_1 - x \end{vmatrix}$$

we have seen that there exists at least one number ξ such that

$$f(x) - I_1(x) = (x - x_0)(x - x_1)\frac{f''(\xi)}{2}$$

where $\min(x_0, x_1, x) < \xi < \max(x_0, x_1, x)$.

But we actually used

$$I_1^\star(x) = \frac{1}{x_1 - x_0} \begin{vmatrix} f_0^\star & x_0 - x \\ f_1^\star & x_1 - x \end{vmatrix}$$

$$= I_1(x) - \frac{1}{x_1 - x_0} \begin{vmatrix} \epsilon_0 & x_0 - x \\ \epsilon_1 & x_1 - x \end{vmatrix}.$$

Hence

$$E(x) = f(x) - I_1^\star(x)$$

$$= (x - x_0)(x - x_1)\frac{f''(\xi)}{2} + \frac{1}{x_1 - x_0} \begin{vmatrix} \epsilon_0 & x_0 - x \\ \epsilon_1 & x_1 - x \end{vmatrix}.$$

Thus the contribution to the error of the interpolated value due to rounding of the f_i is

$$r(x) = \frac{x_1 - x}{x_1 - x_0} \epsilon_0 + \frac{x - x_0}{x_1 - x_0} \epsilon_1.$$

Denoting the larger of $|\epsilon_0|$ and $|\epsilon_1|$ by ϵ we find

$$|r(x)| \leq \left\{ \left| \frac{x_1 - x}{x_1 - x_0} \right| + \left| \frac{x - x_0}{x_1 - x_0} \right| \right\} \epsilon = \epsilon$$

if $x_0 < x < x_1$. Thus, for example, in linear interpolation in a six-place table the contribution to the error of the interpolated value due to rounding is not greater than 5×10^{-7}. However, in a borderline case, the error due to rounding combined with even a very small remainder can produce an error in the interpolated value.

3.6 REMARKS

Most tables of the elementary functions relate the number of digits in the functional values to the spacing of the argument so that linear interpolation will give results whose last digit will be in error by not more than 1. For many of the functions of higher mathematics such a practice could lead to uncomfortably voluminous tables. In such tables more sophisticated interpolation procedures are required, some of which we shall describe in later chapters.

Another approach to table making, especially well-adapted to slowly changing functions, is that of the so-called *critical tables*. In these no interpolation is necessary. Each distinct rounded value of the function (to as many digits as desired) is entered together with corresponding value of the argument. The latter will not, in general, be equally spaced.

As a brief example we quote an extract from a table of Bessel coefficients:

p	B_2
0.0000	
	0.000
0.0020	
	0.001
0.0060	
	0.002
0.0101	

Here, for example,

$$B_2(p) = 0.002$$

for

$$0.0060 < p \le 0.0101.$$

The equality on the right is usually described by the phrase "in critical cases, ascend."

3.7   OTHER TYPES OF LINEAR APPROXIMATIONS

There are two other types of polynomial approximations having an extensive literature. We shall here content ourselves with merely describing them in the linear case. The subject is developed further in Chap. 12.

3.71   *LINEAR LEAST-SQUARES APPROXIMATIONS.*   If the linear function

$$l(x) = a_0 x + a_1$$

is so chosen that

$$F(a_0, a_1) = \int_{x_0}^{x_1} [f(x) - l(x)]^2 \, dx$$

is minimum, then that polynomial is called the *linear least-squares approximation* to $f(x)$ on the interval $[x_0, x_1]$. The coefficients of $l(x)$ can be found by solving the equations obtained by setting the first partial derivatives of F equal to zero. Thus the equations

$$F_{a_0}(a_0, a_1) = 0, \qquad F_{a_1}(a_0, a_1) = 0$$

are solved for a_0 and a_1.

3.72 *LINEAR MINIMAX APPROXIMATIONS.* If the linear function

$$l(x) = a_0 x + a_1$$

is so chosen that

$$\max_{x_0 \leq x \leq x_1} |f(x) - l(x)|$$

is a minimum, then that polynomial is called the *linear minimax approximation* to $f(x)$ on the interval $[x_0, x_1]$. It is known that such a function exists and is unique if $f(x)$ is continuous [2].

The problem of how to compute the coefficients of the approximating polynomial, even in the linear case, has no simple solution. See Refs. [3,4] of this chapter and Ref. [7] of Chap. 12.

3.8 TAYLOR POLYNOMIAL AS LIMITING FORM OF THE INTERPOLATING POLYNOMIAL

According to the mean value theorem of the differential calculus (A.1) if $f(x)$ is differentiable on the interval (x_0, x_1) then there exists at least one number η of this interval for which

$$f(x_0, x_1) = f'(\eta).$$

Thus for any function $f(x)$ having a second derivative we may rewrite Newton's divided difference linear interpolation formula with remainder (Secs. 3.33 and 3.4) as

$$f(x) = f(x_0) + (x - x_0)f'(\eta) + (x - x_0)(x - x_1)\frac{f''(\xi)}{2}$$

where

$$x_0 < \eta < x_1$$

and

$$\min(x_0, x_1, x) < \xi < \max(x_0, x_1, x).$$

The limiting form of this as x_1 approaches x_0 is the linear Taylor formula:

$$f(x) = f(x_0) + (x - x_0)f'(x_0) + (x - x_0)^2 \frac{f''(\xi^\star)}{2}$$

where

$$\min(x, x_0) < \xi^\star < \max(x, x_0).$$

If the linear Taylor polynomial and linear interpolating polynomials are used to approximate $f(x)$ in the interval $x_0 < x < x_0 + h$ the coefficients of $\frac{1}{2}f''$ in the remainders attain maximum values of h^2 and $\frac{1}{4}h^2$ respectively. Thus, unless $f''(\xi^\star)$ is appreciably different from $f''(\xi)$, the linear interpolating polynomial will be a better approximation to $f(x)$ throughout the interval $(x_0, x_0 + h)$ than will the linear Taylor polynomial. Similar results hold for Taylor polynomials and interpolating polynomials of higher degree.

EXERCISES

1. Write the Lagrange and computing forms of the linear interpolating polynomial $I_1(x)$ for $\ln(1 + x)$ with collocation points 0.5, 0.6. Calculate $I_1(0.57)$ and compare with a tabled value of $\ln 1.57$.

2. The polynomial

$$p(y) = y^3 - 2y - 5$$

has opposite signs at 2.0 and 2.1 and hence has at least one zero in this interval. Since $p'(y)$ is of constant sign in this interval the portion of the graph of $x = p(y)$ lying between $(2.0, p(2.0))$ and $(2.1, p(2.1))$ defines y as a single-valued function of x, say, $y = f(x)$. Use linear interpolation to find approximate value $I_1(0)$ of $f(0)$. Calculate $p(I_1(0))$.

3. Use Cauchy form of remainder to obtain bounds for the remainder in linear interpolation of Exercise 1. Compare with the known error of interpolated value.

4. A table of natural sines is given with entries for every degree. Use Eq. (3.9) to obtain an upper bound on the absolute value of remainder in any linear interpolation between any two consecutive entries in table.

5. Repeat Exercise 3.4 for a table whose entries are for every minute.

6. Find the linear least squares approximation to $\ln(1 + x)$ on the interval [0, 1].

7. Determine the "best" choice of collocation points for linear interpolation on the closed interval $[-1, 1]$ in the sense that

(1) $-1 \le x_0 < x_1 \le 1$
(2) $\max |(x - x_0)(x - x_1)|$ on the interval $[-1, 1]$ is minimum.
HINT: It is sufficient to choose x_0 and x_1 so that the largest of the three numbers

$$\tfrac{1}{4}(x_1 - x_0)^2, \quad (1 - x_0)(1 - x_1), \quad (1 + x_0)(1 + x_1)$$

is minimum.

REFERENCES

1. P. M. Hummel. "The Accuracy of Linear Interpolation," *Am. Math. Monthly* **53:** 364–366 (1946).

2. C. J. de la Vallée Poussin. *Leçons sur l'approximation des fonctions d'une variable réelle.* Paris: Gauthier-Villars, 1919.

3. R. G. Selfridge. "Approximations with Least Maximum Error," *Pacific J. Math.* **3:** 247–255 (1953).

4. R. E. Langer (ed.). *On Numerical Approximation.* Madison: U. Wisconsin P., 1959.

5. J. Kunzmann. *Méthodes numériques, interpolation-dérivées.* Paris: Dunod, 1959

4

ZEROS OF FUNCTIONS

4.1 INTRODUCTION

We shall refer to a number x_0 such that $f(x_0) = 0$ as a *zero* of $f(x)$. It is often referred to as a *root* of the equation $f(x) = 0$. The two methods of calculating zeros of given functions which we shall describe both depend on the possibility of locally approximating $f(x)$ by a linear function. One method is based on the linear interpolating polynomial and the other on the linear Taylor polynomial.

4.2 METHOD OF LINEAR INTERPOLATION*

We consider the linear interpolating polynomial $I_1(x)$ for $f(x)$ with two distinct collocation points x_{n-1} and x_n and calculate the number x_{n+1} for which $I_1(x_{n+1}) = 0$. Instead of considering this unique line as determined by the points (x_{n-1}, f_{n-1}) and (x_n, f_n) of the xy-plane, it is simpler to consider it as determined by the points (f_{n-1}, x_{n-1}) and (f_n, x_n) of the yx-plane. The point $(0, x_{n+1})$ on this line is given by

$$x_{n+1} = \frac{1}{f_n - f_{n-1}} \begin{vmatrix} x_{n-1} & f_{n-1} \\ x_n & f_n \end{vmatrix}. \tag{4.1}$$

* Often referred to as method of *false position* or *regula falsi*.

This is, of course, inverse linear interpolation. We have here an iterative procedure for producing a sequence of numbers $\{x_i\}$, $i = 2, 3, 4, \ldots$, once an initial pair of estimates x_0 and x_1 have been found. If $f(x_0)$ and $f(x_1)$ differ in sign and $f(x)$ is continuous, then there is at least one zero in the interval (x_0, x_1) (A.8). In the next section we discuss a set of conditions that are sufficient to ensure the convergence of the process.

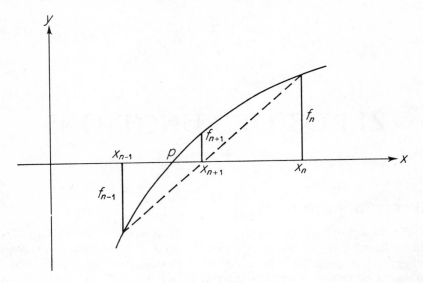

Fig. 4.1.

4.21 *CONVERGENCE OF THE METHOD OF LINEAR INTER-POLATION.* We shall limit our discussion to the situation depicted in the graph of Fig. 4.2. Specifically, we suppose the function $f(x)$ and the initial interval (x_0, x_1) to be such that

(1) $f(x_0)f(x_1) < 0$,

(2) $f(x_0)f''(x_0) > 0$,

(3) $f''(x) \neq 0$, $x_0 < x < x_1$.

We shall refer to these three conditions as the *Fourier conditions.*

The method of linear interpolation produces a sequence of successive approximations to the unique zero, p, lying in the interval (x_0, x_1). We shall use the iteration equation

$$x_{n+1} = \frac{1}{f_n - f_0} \begin{vmatrix} x_0 & f_0 \\ x_n & f_n \end{vmatrix} \tag{4.2}$$

in order to maintain an interval containing p. We shall show that the sequence $\{x_n\}$ necessarily converges to p and obtain a relation between the errors of successive iterates.

To prove the convergence we note that the sequence $x_1, x_2, \ldots, x_n, \ldots$ is monotone decreasing and bounded below by p. The sequence must therefore converge to a unique number, say $p_0 \geq p$. Subtracting p_0 from both

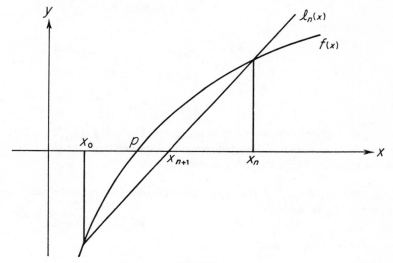

Fig. 4.2.

sides of Eq. (4.2) and taking limits as $n \to \infty$ we obtain

$$0 = \frac{1}{f(p_0) - f(x_0)} \begin{vmatrix} x_0 & f(x_0) \\ p_0 & f(p_0) \end{vmatrix} - p_0$$

$$= -\frac{p_0 - x_0}{f(p_0) - f(x_0)} f(p_0).$$

Since $p_0 \neq x_0$, $f(p_0) = 0$. But since p is the unique zero of $f(x)$ in the interval (x_0, x_1), $p_0 = p$. Thus the conditions of Fourier are sufficient to ensure the convergence of the method of linear interpolation.

We now investigate the rate of convergence. We let $l_n(x)$ denote the linear interpolating polynomial through the points (x_0, f_0) and (x_n, f_n), and use the Cauchy form of the remainder in linear interpolation to write

$$0 = f(p) = l_n(p) + (x_0 - p)(x_n - p)\frac{f''(\xi_n)}{2}, \qquad x_0 < \xi_n < x_n. \quad (4.3)$$

The line $l_n(x)$ is also determined by the points (x_0, f_0) and $(x_{n+1}, 0)$. So its equation may be written

$$l_n(p) = \frac{1}{x_{n+1} - x_0} \begin{vmatrix} f_0 & x_0 - p \\ 0 & x_{n+1} - p \end{vmatrix}.$$

Substituting this in Eq. (4.3) and rearranging we obtain

$$x_{n+1} - p = (x_{n+1} - x_0)(x_0 - p)(x_n - p) \frac{f''(\xi_n)}{-2f_0}.$$

But

$$\frac{-f_0}{x_{n+1} - x_0} = \frac{f_n - f_0}{x_n - x_0} = f'(\xi_n^\star), \qquad x_0 < \xi_n^\star < x_n.$$

Hence

$$x_{n+1} - p = (x_0 - p)(x_n - p) \frac{f''(\xi_n)}{2f'(\xi_n^\star)} \tag{4.4}$$

where ξ_n and $\xi_n^\star$ both lie in the interval (x_0, x_n). Thus if $[f''(\xi_n)/2f'(\xi_n^\star)] < 1$, then the error of the $(n + 1)$st approximation is less than the product of the errors of the initial and the nth approximations.

EXAMPLE 4.1. We illustrate the method of linear interpolation by applying it to the cubic

$$f(x) = x^3 - 2x - 5,$$

once considered by Newton.

i	x_i	$f(x_i)$
0	2	-1
1	3	16
2	2.058 824	$-0.390\ 795$
3	2.081 264	$-0.147\ 200$
4	2.094 824	$0.003\ 042$
5	2.094 549	$-0.000\ 028$
6	2.094 551 5	$0.000\ 000$

4.3 NEWTON-RAPHSON METHOD

We consider the linear Taylor polynomial $t_1(x)$ which approximates $f(x)$ in some neighborhood of x_n and use its zero x_{n+1} as next approximation to zero of $f(x)$. Thus

$$t_1(x) = f(x_n) + (x - x_n)f'(x_n)$$

and x_{n+1} is defined by the equation

$$f(x_n) + (x_{n+1} - x_n)f'(x_n) = 0.$$

Thus

$$x_{n+1} = x_n - \frac{f(x_n)}{f'(x_n)} . \qquad (4.5)$$

This, again, is an iterative procedure for producing a sequence of numbers $\{x_i\}$, $i = 1, 2, 3, \ldots$ once an initial estimate x_0 has been obtained.

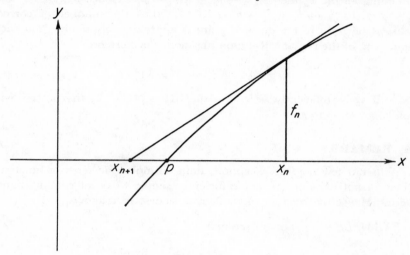

Fig. 4.3.

4.31 *CONVERGENCE OF NEWTON-RAPHSON METHOD.* Let p designate a zero of $f(x)$. Then by Taylor formula:

$$0 = f(p) = f(x_n) + (p - x_n) f'(x_n) + (p - x_n)^2 \frac{f''(\xi_n)}{2}$$

where ξ_n lies between x_n and p. Hence

$$p = x_n - \frac{f(x_n)}{f'(x_n)} - (p - x_n)^2 \frac{f''(\xi_n)}{2f'(x_n)}$$

$$= x_{n-1} - (p - x_n)^2 \frac{f''(\xi_n)}{2f'(x_n)} .$$

Hence

$$x_{n+1} - p = (x_n - p)^2 \frac{f''(\xi_n)}{2f'(x_n)} . \qquad (4.6)$$

Thus the error of the $(n + 1)$st iterate is "proportional" to the square of the error in the nth iterate. A comparison of Eqs. (4.4) and (4.6) shows the superiority of the Newton-Raphson method over the method of linear interpolation as far as rate of convergence is concerned. But note that one iteration of the method of linear interpolation requires but one evaluation of $f(x)$, while the Newton-Raphson requires one evaluation of $f(x)$ and $f'(x)$.

If $|f''(\xi_n)/2f'(x_n)|$ is bounded by a number K in a neighborhood of p containing all the x_i, then $|x_{n+1} - p| \leq K(x_n - p)^2$. Hence if $K \leq 10^\alpha$ and $|x_n - p| \leq 10^{-\beta}$, then $|x_{n+1} - p| \leq 10^{\alpha - 2\beta}$. Thus the number of correct digits to the right of the decimal point is approximately doubled on each application of the Newton-Raphson iteration. Furthermore

$$|x_n - p| \leq K^{-1}[(x_0 - p)K]^{2^n}.$$

Hence if x_0 is sufficiently near to p that $|x_0 - p| \, K < 1$, the process will rapidly converge to p.

4.4 REMARKS

With but few notable exceptions finite formulas for zeros of functions either do not exist or are not sufficiently simple to be of computational interest. Hence the need for methods such as described above.

EXAMPLE 4.2.   The polynomial

$$p(x) = x^4 - 8x^3 + 12x^2 + 8x - 4$$

has a zero between the limits 2.7 and 2.8. Confining our attention to the interval $2.7 \leq x \leq 2.8$ we find (Exercise 2.5):

$$|p'(x)| \geq 23.42, \qquad |p''(x)| \leq 18.12$$

and hence $K < 0.4$. Thus

$$|x_n - p| < 2.5(0.04)^{2^n}$$

and x_n approaches p rapidly.

EXAMPLE 4.3.   We apply the Newton-Raphson method to the cubic $f(x) = x^3 - 2x - 5$:

i	x_i	$f(x_i)$	$f'(x_i)$
0	2	-1	10
1	2.1	0.061	11.23
2	2.094 568	0.000 184	11.161 645
3	2.094 552	0.000 006	11.161 444
4	2.094 551	$-0.000\ 005$	11.161 432

Comparing with Example 4.1, we see the convergence is somewhat more rapid.

EXAMPLE 4.4. We use the Newton-Raphson method to locate more accurately the zero of the quartic

$$p(x) = x^4 - 8x^3 + 23x^2 + 16x - 50$$

which lies near $3.5 + 3.5i$.

i	x_i	$p(x_i)$	$p'(x_i)$
0	$3.50 + 3.50i$	$91.75 - 66.50i$	$-166.00 - 84.00i$
1	$3.78 + 2.96i$	$30.16 + 1.82i$	$-124.15 + 2.88i$
2	$4.02 + 2.98i$	$-2.22 + 3.50i$	$-142.33 + 34.10i$
3	$4.00 + 3.00i$	$0 + 0i$	

EXERCISES

1. Apply the Newton-Raphson iteration equation to the functions $x^2 - N$ and $x^3 - N$ to obtain

$$x_{n+1} = \frac{1}{2}\left(\frac{N}{x_n} + x_n\right) \quad \text{and} \quad x_{n+1} = \frac{1}{3}\left(\frac{N}{x_n^2} + 2x_n\right)$$

as iterations for calculating, respectively, $\sqrt{N}$ and $\sqrt[3]{N}$.

2. Complex zeros by Newton-Raphson method. Show that if $x_n = \alpha_n + i\beta_n, f(x_n) = A_n + iB_n, f'(x_n) = C_n + iD_n$, then

$$\alpha_{n+1} = \alpha_n - \frac{A_n C_n + B_n D_n}{C_n^2 + D_n^2},$$

$$\beta_{n+1} = \beta_n + \frac{A_n D_n - B_n C_n}{C_n^2 + D_n^2}.$$

3. The polynomial

$$p(x) = x^4 - 3x^3 + 20x^2 + 44x + 54$$

considered by Milne [1], has no real zeros. Use Newton-Raphson method to locate correctly to three places of decimals the zero near $2.5 + 4.5i$.

4. Use a five-place table to locate zero of the function

$$f(x) = \log_{10} x - 0.25681.$$

Find a more precise value of this zero using: (*a*) method of linear interpolation; (*b*) Newton-Raphson method.

5. Show that Eq. (4.1) can be written as

$$x_{n+1} = x_n - \frac{f(x_n)}{f'(\xi_n)}, \qquad x_{n-1} < \xi_n < x_n.$$

Note similarity to Newton-Raphson algorithm.

6. (a) Apply the Newton-Raphson iteration equation to the function $(1/x) - a$ to obtain a process for computing the reciprocal of the nonzero number a. (The resulting process is commonly used by high-speed digital computers.)

(b) Show that the sequence of numbers defined by the iteration equation

$$x_{n+1} = x_n(2 - ax_n), \qquad a \neq 0,$$

converges to $1/a$ if and only if x_0 is chosen so that $|1 - ax_0| < 1$.
HINT: Let $y_n = 1 - ax_n$ and show that $y_n = y_0^{2^n}$.

REFERENCES

1. W. E. Milne. *Numerical Calculus*. Princeton: Princeton U.P., 1949.
2. E. J. Putzer. "A Numerical Method for Solving Scalar Equations," *Am. Math. Monthly* **69**: 408–411 (1962).

5

ZEROS OF POLYNOMIALS

5.1 INTRODUCTION

The methods of Chap. 4 are, of course, applicable to polynomials as well as transcendental functions. But those methods are at their best only once reasonably accurate first approximations have been found. For polynomials there is an extensive literature giving bounds on their zeros and methods for their actual calculation [1,2]. Within the last decade at least three important new methods have been devised which are especially appropriate for use with digital computers [3,4,5].

After a few basic preliminaries we shall describe the method of D. Bernoulli (1728). While this method will produce zeros of any polynomial, it has the disadvantage of being at times rather slowly convergent. It can, however, be used to advantage to obtain a first approximation to a zero. The method is particularly useful when only complex zeros are present, since then approximate zeros are not readily obtainable. The approximate zeros obtained by the Bernoulli method can be further improved by applying, say, the Newton-Raphson method. Tables are available for finding approximate zeros of cubics [9,10].

5.2 PRELIMINARIES

The fundamental theorem of algebra (first proved by Gauss in 1799) assures us that every polynomial having complex coefficients has at least one complex zero [6]. This, in turn, implies that a polynomial of degree n can be factored into n linear factors and that it cannot have more than n zeros.

While procedures are known for expressing all the zeros of polynomials of degree 4 or less in terms of radicals, only the quadratic formula is of sufficient simplicity to be of much computational interest. No such formulas can exist for arbitrary polynomials of degree greater than 4, as was first shown by N. H. Abel (1824). Thus for polynomials of degree 3 or more numerical procedures are a practical necessity.

5.3 RELATIONS BETWEEN ZEROS AND COEFFICIENTS

Let $\alpha_1, \alpha_2, \alpha_3, \ldots, \alpha_n$, be the n zeros (distinct or not) of the polynomial

$$f(x) = a_0 x^n + a_1 x^{n-1} + \cdots + a_{n-1} x + a_n \tag{5.1}$$

with $a_0 \neq 0$. Then

$$f(x) = a_0(x - \alpha_1)(x - \alpha_2) \cdots (x - \alpha_n). \tag{5.2}$$

If we multiply the factors of Eq. (5.2) and compare coefficients of powers of x with those of corresponding powers in (5.1) we obtain, among others, the relations

$$\alpha_1 \alpha_2 \cdots \alpha_n = (-1)^n \frac{a_n}{a_0} \tag{5.3}$$

and

$$\alpha_1 + \alpha_2 + \cdots + \alpha_n = -\frac{a_1}{a_0}. \tag{5.4}$$

Equation (5.4) is a special case of the

THEOREM OF NEWTON. If $\alpha_1, \alpha_2, \alpha_3, \ldots, \alpha_n$ are the zeros of the polynomial

$$f(x) = x^n + a_1 x^{n-1} + \cdots + a_{n-1} x + a_n$$

and if

$$S_p = \alpha_1^p + \alpha_2^p + \cdots + \alpha_n^p,$$

then for any positive integer k between 1 and n inclusive

$$S_k = -a_1 S_{k-1} - a_2 S_{k-2} - \cdots - a_{k-1} S_1 - a_k k$$

and

$$S_{n+j} = -a_1 S_{n+j-1} - \cdots - a_n S_j, \qquad j = 1, 2, 3, \ldots.$$

The theorem results from identifying the coefficients in two expressions for the derivative of $f(x)$. One of these is

$$f'(x) = nx^{n-1} + (n-1)a_1x^{n-2} + \cdots + 2a_{n-2}x + a_{n-1}. \qquad (5.5)$$

The other is derived from

$$f'(x) = \frac{f(x)}{x-\alpha_1} + \frac{f(x)}{x-\alpha_2} + \cdots + \frac{f(x)}{x-\alpha_n} \qquad (5.6)$$

as follows: If α is any one of the zeros of $f(x)$, then

$$\frac{f(x)}{x-\alpha} = \frac{f(x) - f(\alpha)}{x-\alpha}$$

$$= \frac{x^n - \alpha^n}{x-\alpha} + a_1\frac{x^{n-1} - \alpha^{n-1}}{x-\alpha} + \cdots + a_{n-1}\frac{x-\alpha}{x-\alpha}$$

$$= x^{n-1} + \alpha x^{n-2} + \alpha^2 x^{n-3} + \cdots + \alpha^{n-1}$$

$$+ a_1(x^{n-2} + \alpha x^{n-3} + \cdots + \alpha^{n-2})$$

$$+ \cdots + a_{n-2}(x + \alpha) + a_{n-1}.$$

Taking α to be in turn $\alpha_1, \alpha_2, \ldots, \alpha_n$ and adding results we have

$$f'(x) = nx^{n-1} + S_1 x^{n-2} + S_2 x^{n-3} + \cdots + S_{n-1}$$

$$+ a_1(nx^{n-2} + S_1 x^{n-3} + \cdots + S_{n-2}) \qquad (5.7)$$

$$+ \cdots + a_{n-2}(nx + S_1) + na_{n-1}.$$

$$= nx^{n-1} + (S_1 + na_1)x^{n-2} + (S_2 + S_1a_1 + na_2)x^{n-3} + \cdots$$

$$+ (S_{n-2} + S_{n-3}a_1 + \cdots + na_{n-2})x \qquad (5.8)$$

$$+ (S_{n-1} + S_{n-2}a_1 + \cdots + na_{n-1}).$$

Comparing coefficients in Eqs. (5.5) and (5.8) we have

$$(n-1)a_1 = S_1 + na_1,$$

$$(n-2)a_2 = S_2 + S_1a_1 + na_2,$$

$$\cdots \cdots \cdots \cdots \cdots \cdots$$

$$2a_{n-2} = S_{n-2} + S_{n-3}a_1 + \cdots + na_{n-2},$$

$$a_{n-1} = S_{n-1} + S_{n-2}a_1 + \cdots + na_{n-1}.$$

Whence

$$S_1 + a_1 = 0,$$

$$S_2 + S_1a_1 + 2a_2 = 0,$$

$$\cdots \cdots \cdots \cdots \cdots \cdots \cdots \qquad (5.9)$$

$$S_{n-2} + S_{n-3}a_1 + \cdots + (n-2)a_{n-2} = 0,$$

$$S_{n-1} + S_{n-2}a_1 + \cdots + (n-1)a_{n-1} = 0.$$

To find S_n note that

$$0 = f(\alpha_1) + \cdots + f(\alpha_n)$$
$$= S_n + a_1 S_{n-1} + \cdots + a_{n-1} S_1 + n a_n.$$

To find S_i for $i > n$ note that

$$0 = \alpha_1^{i-n} f(\alpha_1) + \alpha_2^{i-n} f(\alpha_2) + \cdots + \alpha_n^{i-n} f(\alpha_n)$$
$$= S_i + a_1 S_{i-1} + \cdots + a_{n-1} S_{i+1-n} + a_n S_{i-n}.$$

5.4 BERNOULLI'S METHOD

We suppose

$$f(x) = x^n + a_1 x^{n-1} + \cdots + a_{n-1} x + a_n$$
$$= (x - \alpha_1)(x - \alpha_2) \cdots (x - \alpha_n),$$

where the a_i are all real and

$$|\alpha_1| \geq |\alpha_2| \geq |\alpha_3| \geq \cdots \geq |\alpha_n|.$$

We shall here limit our discussion of the method of Bernoulli to the following two cases:

CASE I: $|\alpha_1| > |\alpha_2|$

CASE II: $\alpha_2 = \bar{\alpha}_1$ and $|\alpha_2| > |\alpha_3|$.

In Case I the method produces the *dominant zero* α_1. The polynomial $f(x)$ is then divided by $x - \alpha_1$, giving a polynomial of degree $n - 1$ whose zeros are the remaining zeros of $f(x)$ and to which the method is then applied. In Case II the method produces the two dominant zeros α_1 and α_2. The polynomial is then divided by the real quadratic factor $(x - \alpha_1)(x - \alpha_2)$ giving a polynomial of degree $n - 2$ to which the method is then applied.

The remaining cases are included in Exercise 5.5. In all cases the sequence $\{S_k\}$ is calculated from the recurrence formulas given in the theorem of Newton (Sec. 5.3). The dominant zeros are then obtained from sequences derived from this one.

In Case I we write

$$S_p = \alpha_1^p \left\{ 1 + \left(\frac{\alpha_2}{\alpha_1} \right)^p + \cdots + \left(\frac{\alpha_n}{\alpha_1} \right)^p \right\}.$$

Hence

$$\frac{S_p}{S_{p-1}} \xrightarrow[p \to \infty]{} \alpha_1.$$

In Case II we write

$$\alpha_k = r_k(\cos \theta_k + i \sin \theta_k),$$

$$k = 1, 2, \ldots, n.$$

Then

$$S_p = \sum_{k=1}^{n} r_k^p(\cos p\theta_k + i \sin p\theta_k)$$

$$= 2r_1^p \cos p\theta_1 + \sum_{k=3}^{n} r_k^p(\cos p\theta_k + i \sin p\theta_k)$$

and hence

$$\frac{S_p}{r_1^p} - 2 \cos p\theta_1 = \sum_{k=3}^{n} \left(\frac{r_k}{r_1}\right)^p (\cos p\theta_k + i \sin p\theta_k) \xrightarrow[p \to \infty]{} 0.$$

Thus for large p

$$\frac{S_p}{r_1^p} - 2 \cos p\theta_1 \doteq 0. \tag{5.10}$$

If the left member of the above were precisely 0 it would imply that

$$S_p - 2r_1 \cos \theta_1 S_{p-1} + r_1^2 S_{p-2} = 0,$$
$$S_{p-1} - 2r_1 \cos \theta_1 S_{p-2} + r_1^2 S_{p-3} = 0. \tag{5.11}$$

This system of two equations, linear in r_1^2 and $2r_1 \cos \theta_1$, has the solution

$$r_1^2 = \frac{S_p S_{p-2} - S_{p-1}^2}{S_{p-1} S_{p-3} - S_{p-2}^2},$$

$$2r_1 \cos \theta_1 = \frac{S_p S_{p-3} - S_{p-1} S_{p-2}}{S_{p-1} S_{p-3} - S_{p-2}^2}. \tag{5.12}$$

Let

$$T_p = S_p S_{p-2} - S_{p-1}^2,$$
$$U_p = S_p S_{p-3} - S_{p-1} S_{p-2}. \tag{5.13}$$

Then, since (5.10) is in reality a limit relation we can but say that

$$\frac{T_p}{T_{p-1}} \xrightarrow[p \to \infty]{} r_1^2,$$

$$\frac{U_p}{T_{p-1}} \xrightarrow[p \to \infty]{} 2r_1 \cos \theta_1. \tag{5.14}$$

Once approximations to these limits have been obtained, we solve for approximate values of r_1 and θ_1, from which we obtain estimates of the pair of complex conjugate zeros α_1 and α_2.

EXAMPLE 5.1. We use Bernoulli's method to locate that zero of the cubic

$$x^3 - 11x^2 + 32x - 22$$

which is largest in absolute value. Here

$$S_1 = 11$$
$$S_2 = 11S_1 - 64$$
$$S_3 = 11S_2 - 32S_1 + 66$$
$$\cdots \cdots \cdots \cdots$$
$$S_i = 11S_{i-1} - 32S_{i-2} + 22S_{i-3}$$
$$i = 4, 5, 6, \ldots.$$

From these we calculate:

i	S_i	S_i/S_{i-1}
1	11	
2	57	5.181 81
3	341	5.982 45
4	2 169	6.360 70
5	14 201	6.547 25
6	94 305	6.640 72
7	630 641	6.687 24
8	4 231 713	6.710 17
9	28 443 041	6.721 40
10	191 332 737	6.726 87

We take 6.73 as our estimate of the zero. Applying the Newton-Raphson method we obtain:

x_i	$f(x_i)$	$f'(x_i)$
6.73	−0.04068	19.8187
6.73205	−0.00002	

Thus we obtain 6.732 05, which can, of course, be further improved if desired.

EXAMPLE 5.2. As an example of a polynomial whose dominant zeros are complex conjugates we take that one cited by Hildebrand [7]:

$$x^4 - 8x^3 + 23x^2 + 16x - 50.$$

Here

$$S_1 = 8$$

$$S_2 = 8S_1 - 46$$

$$S_3 = 8S_2 - 23S_1 - 48$$

$$S_4 = 8S_3 - 23S_2 - 16S_1 + 200$$

$$. \quad . \quad . \quad . \quad . \quad . \quad . \quad . \quad .$$

$$S_i = 8S_{i-1} - 23S_{i-2} - 16S_{i-3} + 50S_{i-4},$$

$$i \geq 5.$$

From these we calculate the following:

i	S_i	S_i/S_{i-1}
1	8	
2	18	2.25
3	−88	−4.89
4	−1046	11.89
5	−6232	5.96
6	-2349×10	3.77
7	-3225×10	1.37
8	3297×10^2	−10.22
9	3444×10^3	10.45
10	1931×10^4	5.61

The failure of S_i/S_{i-1} to converge is an indication that the dominant zero(s) may be complex. Hence we calculate:

i	T_i	T_i/T_{i-1}
3	−1028	
4	-2657×10	25.85
5	-5457×10^2	20.54
6	-1427×10^4	26.15
7	-3508×10^5	24.58
8	-8785×10^6	25.04
9	-2198×10^8	25.02
10	-5495×10^9	25.00

i	U_i	U_i/T_{i-1}
4	-6784	6.60
5	-2042×10^2	7.69
6	-4452×10^3	8.16
7	-1127×10^5	7.90
8	-2812×10^6	8.02
9	-7027×10^7	8.00
10	-1738×10^9	8.00

Thus we estimate:
$$r_1^2 = 25.00, \qquad 2r_1 \cos \theta_1 = 8.00.$$
From these we find
$$r_1 = 5.00, \qquad \cos \theta_1 = 0.80, \qquad \sin \theta_1 = 0.60.$$
Whence
$$\alpha_1 = 4 + 3i, \qquad \alpha_2 = 4 - 3i.$$

These happen to be exact. If they were not, they could be improved by applying the Newton-Raphson method.

EXERCISES

1. (*a*) Use Newton's theorem to calculate S_1, S_2, S_3, S_4 for the polynomial
$$f(x) = x^2 - 2x + 5.$$

(*b*) Use quadratic formula to calculate the zeros of $f(x)$. From these zeros obtain S_1, S_2, S_3 and S_4.

2. Bernoulli's method was applied to the polynomial
$$2x^3 - 11x^2 + 37.98x - 16.49$$
and it was found that
$$r_1^2 = 16.49, \qquad 2r_1 \cos \theta_1 = 5.00.$$

Find all zeros of this polynomial.

3. Use Bernoulli's method to locate dominant zero(s) of the polynomial
$$p(x) = x^4 - 3x^3 + 20x^2 + 44x + 54.$$

See Exercise 4.3.

4. Use Bernoulli's method to locate dominant zero(s) of the polynomial
$$p(x) = x^3 - 5x^2 - x + 5.$$

As a check note that
$$p(x) = (x - 1)(x + 1)(x - 5).$$

5. Cases I and II of the method of Bernoulli discussed in the text may be considered as the basic cases. Show what adjustments, if any, must be made to apply the method to the following cases:

CASE III: $\alpha_1 = \alpha_2 = \cdots = \alpha_k$, $|\alpha_k| > |\alpha_{k+1}|$.

CASE IV: $\alpha_1 = \alpha_2 = \cdots = \alpha_k = r(\cos \theta + i \sin \theta)$,

$\alpha_{k+1} = \alpha_{k+2} = \cdots = \alpha_{2k} = r(\cos \theta - i \sin \theta)$, $|\alpha_{2k}| > |\alpha_{2k+1}|$.

CASE V: $\alpha_1 = \alpha_2 = \cdots = \alpha_k > 0$, $\alpha_{k+1} = \alpha_{k+2} = \cdots = \alpha_{k+l}$,
$\alpha_1 = -\alpha_{k+1}$, $|\alpha_{k+l}| > |\alpha_{k+l+1}|$.

If $f(x)$ has three or more distinct zeros having same absolute value the method of Bernoulli fails. However, the substitution $x = y - a$, $a \neq 0$ and real, will usually result in a polynomial in y, no three of whose zeros have same absolute value. A zero of the transformed polynomial is, of course, a zero of original polynomial increased by a.

REFERENCES

1. L. E. Dickson. *New First Course in Theory of Equations.* New York: Wiley, 1952.
2. A. Ralston, and H. S. Wilf (eds.). *Mathematical Methods for Digital Computers.* New York: Wiley, 1960.
3. D. H. Lehmer. "A Machine Method for Solving Polynomial Equations," *J. Assoc. Comput. Mach.* **8:** 151–161 (1961).
4. D. E. Muller. "A Method for Solving Algebraic Equations Using an Automatic Computer," *Math. Tables Aids Comput.* **10:** 208–215 (1956).
5. P. Henrici. "The Quotient-Difference Algorithm," *Appl. Math. Ser. U.S. Bur. Standards* **49:** 23–46 (1958).
6. P. C. Rosenbloom. "An Elementary Constructive Proof of the Fundamental Theorem of Algebra," *Am. Math. Monthly* **52:** 562–570 (1945).
7. F. B. Hildebrand. *An Introduction to Numerical Analysis.* New York: McGraw-Hill, 1956.
8. G. N. Lance. *Numerical Methods for High Speed Computers,* London: Iliffe and Sons, 1960.
9. V. L. Zaguskin. *Handbook of Numerical Methods for the Solution of Algebraic and Transcendental Equations.* New York, Pergamon, 1961, translated from the Russian edition of 1960.
10. H. E. Salzer, C. H. Richards and I. Arsham. *Table for the Solution of Cubic Equations.* New York: McGraw-Hill, 1958.

BASIC SETS OF

POLYNOMIALS

6.1 INTRODUCTION

Sets of polynomials containing exactly one of each and every degree will be used in the sequel. While each set has some special property that makes it of interest, all have the fundamental property that any polynomial can be uniquely expressed as a linear combination of polynomials of any given set. This fact will be called the

6.2 EXPANSION THEOREM

The sequence of polynomials

$$B_0(x) = b_{00}$$
$$B_1(x) = b_{11}x + b_{10}$$
$$B_2(x) = b_{22}x^2 + b_{21}x + b_{20}$$
$$B_3(x) = b_{33}x^3 + b_{32}x^2 + b_{31}x + b_{30}$$

$$\cdot \quad \cdot \quad \cdot \quad \cdot \quad \cdot \quad \cdot \quad \cdot \quad \cdot$$

$$B_k(x) = b_{kk}x^k + b_{k,k-1}x^{k-1} + \cdots + b_{k0}$$

$$\cdot \quad \cdot \quad \cdot \quad \cdot \quad \cdot \quad \cdot \quad \cdot \quad \cdot$$

where the B_{kj} are completely unrestricted except that $b_{kk} \neq 0$, is said to form a *basic set of polynomials.*

THEOREM.   *Any polynomial*

$$P_n(x) = a_n x^n + a_{n-1} x^{n-1} + \cdots + a_1 x + a_0$$

has an unique expression of the form

$$P_n(x) = c_n B_n(x) + c_{n-1} B_{n-1}(x) + \cdots + c_0 B_0(x).$$

The proof is constructive. Define the following sequence of polynomials:

$$P_{n-1}(x) = P_n(x) - \frac{a_n}{b_{n,n}} B_n(x) = a_{n-1}^{(1)} x^{n-1} + \cdots$$

$$P_{n-2}(x) = P_{n-1}(x) - \frac{a_{n-1}^{(1)}}{b_{n-1,n-1}} B_{n-1}(x) = a_{n-2}^{(2)} x^{n-2} + \cdots$$

$$\cdot \quad \cdot \quad \cdot \qquad \cdot \quad \cdot \quad \cdot \quad \cdot$$

$$P_{n-i}(x) = P_{n-i+1}(x) - \frac{a_{n-i+1}^{(i-1)}}{b_{n-i+1,n-i+1}} B_{n-i+1}(x) = a_{n-i}^{(i)} x^{n-i} + \cdots$$

$$\cdot \quad \cdot \quad \cdot \qquad \cdot \quad \cdot \quad \cdot \quad \cdot$$

$$P_1(x) = P_2(x) - \frac{a_2^{(n-2)}}{b_{22}} B_2(x) = a_1^{(n-1)} x + \cdots$$

$$P_0(x) = P_1(x) - \frac{a_1^{(n-1)}}{b_{11}} B_1(x) = a_0^{(n)}.$$

Then

$$P_n(x) = \frac{a_n}{b_{n,n}} B_n(x) + \frac{a_{n-1}^{(1)}}{b_{n-1,n-1}} B_{n-1}(x) + \cdots$$

$$+ \frac{a_2^{(n-2)}}{b_{22}} B_2(x) + \frac{a_1^{(n-1)}}{b_{11}} B_1(x) + a_0^{(n)},$$

and hence

$$c_{n-i} = \frac{a_{n-i}^{(i)}}{b_{n-i,n-i}}, \qquad i = 0, 1, \ldots, n.$$

Thus the coefficients c_{n-i} may be determined by successively subtracting from $P_n(x)$ appropriate multiples of the polynomials of our basic set. We shall see, however, that some basic sets have certain special properties that can be used to advantage to determine the coefficients c_{n-i}. But in any case the expansion is unique. For otherwise the difference of two such expansions would be a polynomial of degree $\leq n$ having more than n distinct zeros.

EXAMPLE 6.1. We write the polynomial

$$P_4(x) = 2x^4 - 7x^3 + 8x^2 - 2x + 9$$

as a linear combination of polynomials of the basic set $B_k(x) = (x + 1)^k$. Here

$$B_0(x) = 1$$
$$B_1(x) = x + 1$$
$$B_2(x) = x^2 + 2x + 1$$
$$B_3(x) = x^3 + 3x^2 + 3x + 1$$
$$B_4(x) = x^4 + 4x^3 + 6x^2 + 4x + 1.$$

We need list only the coefficients of the P_{4-i} obtained by successive subtractions:

$P_4(x)$	$P_3(x)$	$P_2(x)$	$P_1(x)$	$P_0(x)$
[2]				
−7	[−15]			
8	−4	[41]		
−2	−10	35	[−47]	
9	7	22	−19	[28]

Thus

$$P_4(x) = 2B_4(x) - 15B_3(x) + 41B_2(x) - 47B_1(x) + 28B_0(x).$$

Among the basic sets used in this text are:

1. binomial: $(x - x_0)^k$, $x_0 \neq 0$;

2. factorial: $x^{[k]} = x(x - 1)(x - 2) \cdots (x - k + 1)$;

3. binomial coefficient: $\binom{x}{k} = \dfrac{x^{[k]}}{k!}$;

4. Bernstein;

5. Legendre;

6. Čebyšev.

The polynomials of Bernstein will be introduced in Chap. 7. Those of Legendre and Čebyšev will be briefly described in following sections.

6.3 LEGENDRE POLYNOMIALS

The polynomials of A. M. Legendre (1752–1833) may be defined in a variety of equivalent ways [1]. For our purposes it seems sufficient merely to say that the *Legendre polynomial* of degree n is

$$P_n(x) = \sum_{i=0}^{[n/2]} (-1)^i \frac{1 \cdot 3 \cdot 5 \cdots (2n - 2i - 1)}{2^i i! \, (n - 2i)!} x^{n-2i}$$

where $[n/2] = n/2$ if n is even and $[n/2] = (n-1)/2$ if n is odd. Thus, for example,

$$P_0(x) = 1$$
$$P_1(x) = x$$
$$P_2(x) = \tfrac{3}{2}x^2 - \tfrac{1}{2}$$
$$P_3(x) = \tfrac{5}{2}x^3 - \tfrac{3}{2}x.$$

PROPERTY 1. The Legendre polynomial $P_n(x)$ is a solution of the linear second-order homogeneous differential equation

$$(1 - x^2)y'' - 2xy' + n(n+1)y = 0.$$

This can be verified by direct substitution.

PROPERTY 2. Any two Legendre polynomials are orthogonal on the interval $(-1, 1)$, that is,

$$\int_{-1}^{1} P_m(x)P_n(x)\, dx = 0, \qquad m \neq n.$$

For, from Property 1,

$$P_n(x)[(1 - x^2)P_m''(x) - 2xP_m'(x) + m(m+1)P_m(x)] = 0$$

and

$$P_m(x)[(1 - x^2)P_n''(x) - 2xP_n'(x) + n(n+1)P_n(x)] = 0.$$

Let

$$W(x) = P_m'(x)P_n(x) - P_m(x)P_n'(x).$$

Then

$$W'(x) = P_m''(x)P_n(x) - P_m(x)P_n''(x),$$

and subtraction of the first two equations gives

$$(1 - x^2)W'(x) - 2xW(x) + [m(m+1) - n(n+1)]P_m(x)P_n(x) = 0.$$

Hence

$$\frac{d}{dx}[(1 - x^2)W(x)] = [n(n+1) - m(m+1)]P_m(x)P_n(x).$$

Integrating both sides from -1 to $+1$ we have

$$[n(n+1) - m(m+1)]\int_{-1}^{1} P_m(x)P_n(x)\, dx = \left[(1 - x^2)W(x)\right]_{-1}^{1} = 0.$$

Since $m \neq n$ it follows that

$$\int_{-1}^{1} P_m(x)P_n(x)\, dx = 0.$$

PROPERTY 3.   Any three successive Legendre polynomials satisfy the recurrence relation

$$(n + 1)P_{n+1}(x) - (2n + 1)xP_n(x) + nP_{n-1}(x) = 0.$$

The proof is left as an exercise (Exercise 3 at end of chapter).

PROPERTY 4.   The Legendre polynomial $P_n(x)$ is orthogonal on the interval $(-1, 1)$ to every polynomial of lower degree.

We have but to note that any polynomial $p(x)$ of degree $< n$ can be written as a linear combination of Legendre polynomials of degree $< n$ (Sec. 6.2).

PROPERTY 5

$$\int_{-1}^{1} [P_n(x)]^2 \, dx = \frac{2}{2n + 1}.$$

Let

$$c_n = \int_{-1}^{1} [P_n(x)]^2 \, dx,$$

and let A_k denote the leading coefficient of $P_k(x)$. Then

$$P_n(x) - \frac{A_n}{A_{n-1}} xP_{n-1}(x) = r(x)$$

is a polynomial of degree $< n$ and hence orthogonal to $P_n(x)$. Hence

$$c_n = \int_{-1}^{1} P_n(x) \left[\frac{A_n}{A_{n-1}} xP_{n-1}(x) + r(x) \right] dx$$

$$= \frac{A_n}{A_{n-1}} \int_{-1}^{1} xP_n(x)P_{n-1}(x) \, dx.$$

By Property 3,

$$xP_n(x) = \frac{n + 1}{2n + 1} P_{n+1}(x) + \frac{n}{2n + 1} P_{n-1}(x),$$

and hence

$$c_n = \frac{A_n}{A_{n-1}} \frac{n}{2n + 1} \int_{-1}^{1} [P_{n-1}(x)]^2 \, dx.$$

From the definition of the Legendre polynomials

$$\frac{A_n}{A_{n-1}} = \frac{2n - 1}{n}$$

and hence

$$c_n = \frac{2n - 1}{2n + 1} c_{n-1}.$$

By direct evaluation we find that $c_0 = 2$. Thus it follows that $c_n = 2/(2n + 1)$.

PROPERTY 6. Except for a constant factor, $P_{n+1}(x)$ is the only polynomial of degree $n + 1$ which is orthogonal on the interval $(-1, 1)$ to all polynomials of degree $\leq n$.

Let $\psi_{n+1}(x)$ designate any polynomial of degree $n + 1$ which is orthogonal on the interval $(-1, 1)$ to all polynomials of degree $\leq n$. Thus if $\phi_n(x)$ is any polynomial of degree $\leq n$, then

$$\int_{-1}^{1} \phi_n(x)\psi_{n+1}(x) \, dx = 0.$$

According to our expansion theorem we may write

$$\phi_n(x) = \sum_{i=0}^{n} a_i P_i(x),$$

and

$$\psi_{n+1}(x) = \sum_{j=0}^{n+1} b_j P_j(x),$$

and hence

$$\int_{-1}^{1} \phi_n(x)\psi_{n+1}(x) \, dx = \sum_{i=0}^{n} a_i b_i \int_{-1}^{1} [P_i(x)]^2 \, dx = 0.$$

Since the a_i are completely arbitrary, it follows that $b_i = 0$, $i = 0, 1, \ldots, n$. Hence

$$\psi_{n+1}(x) = b_{n+1} P_{n+1}(x).$$

PROPERTY 7. The zeros of any Legendre polynomial are all real, all distinct and all interior to the interval $(-1, 1)$.

Any Legendre polynomial $P_n(x)$, $n \geq 1$, is orthogonal on the interval $(-1, 1)$ to $P_0(x)$. Thus

$$\int_{-1}^{1} P_n(x) \, dx = 0$$

and $P_n(x)$ must necessarily change sign at least once between -1 and 1. We suppose $P_n(x)$ changes sign at just m points $x_1, x_2, \ldots, x_m$ of this interval. Let

$$\Pi_m(x) = (x - x_1)(x - x_2) \cdots (x - x_m).$$

Then $\Pi_m(x)P_n(x)$ must be of constant sign on the interval and hence

$$\int_{-1}^{1} \Pi_m(x)P_n(x) \neq 0.$$

In view of Property 4, $m \geq n$. But $P_n(x)$ can change sign at most n times and hence $m = n$. Thus $P_n(x)$ changes sign at precisely n points of the interval and hence has precisely n real distinct zeros all lying in the interval $(-1, 1)$.

Table 6.1

LEGENDRE POLYNOMIALS

$P_0(x) = 1$

$P_1(x) = x$

$P_2(x) = 2^{-1}[3x^2 - 1]$

$P_3(x) = 2^{-1}[5x^3 - 3x]$

$P_4(x) = 2^{-3}[35x^4 - 30x^2 + 3]$

$P_5(x) = 2^{-3}[63x^5 - 70x^3 + 15x]$

$P_6(x) = 2^{-4}[231x^6 - 315x^4 + 105x^2 - 5]$

$P_7(x) = 2^{-4}[429x^7 - 693x^5 + 315x^3 - 35x]$

$P_8(x) = 2^{-7}[6435x^8 - 12012x^6 + 6930x^4 - 1260x^2 + 35]$

$P_9(x) = 2^{-7}[12155x^9 - 25740x^7 + 18018x^5 - 4620x^3 + 315x]$

$P_{10}(x) = 2^{-8}[46189x^{10} - 109395x^8 + 90090x^6$
$$- 30030x^4 + 3465x^2 - 63]$$

Table 6.2

LEGENDRE EXPANSIONS OF POWERS OF x

$1 = P_0(x)$

$x = P_1(x)$

$x^2 = \frac{1}{3}[2P_2(x) + P_0(x)]$

$x^3 = \frac{1}{5}[2P_3(x) + 3P_1(x)]$

$x^4 = \frac{1}{35}[8P_4(x) + 20P_2(x) + 7P_0(x)]$

$x^5 = \frac{1}{63}[8P_5(x) + 28P_3(x) + 27P_1(x)]$

$x^6 = \frac{1}{693}[48P_6 + 216P_4(x) + 330P_2(x) + 99P_0(x)]$

6.4 ČEBYŠEV POLYNOMIALS*

Since

$$\cos (k + 1)\theta = 2 \cos \theta \cos k\theta - \cos (k - 1)\theta, \qquad (6.1)$$

$\cos n\theta$ can be written as a polynomial of degree n in $\cos \theta$. For example,

$$\cos 2\theta = 2 \cos^2 \theta - 1,$$

$$\cos 3\theta = 4 \cos^3 \theta - 3 \cos \theta,$$

$$\cos 4\theta = 8 \cos^4 \theta - 8 \cos^2 \theta + 1.$$

* We use the transliteration from the Russian Чебышев adopted by *Mathematical Reviews*. Other popular spellings are Chebyshev and Tchebysheff.

Replacing $\cos \theta$ by x, we obtain examples of Čebyšev polynomials of the first kind:

$$T_2(x) = 2x^2 - 1,$$
$$T_3(x) = 4x^3 - 3x,$$
$$T_4(x) = 8x^4 - 8x^2 + 1.$$

We are thus led to the following

DEFINITION. The nth degree polynomial

$$T_n(x) = \cos (n \text{ arc } \cos x), \qquad -1 \leq x \leq 1,$$

is called the *Čebyšev polynomial of the first kind of degree n.*

We now list some of the more fundamental properties of these polynomials. Most proofs are either omitted or only briefly outlined.

PROPERTY 1. ZEROS. The zeros of $T_{n+1}(x)$ are

$$x_i = \cos \frac{2i + 1}{n + 1} \frac{\pi}{2}, \qquad i = 0, 1, 2, \ldots, n.$$

They are all real and lie in the interval $(-1, 1)$.

PROPERTY 2. RECURRENCE FORMULA

$$T_{n+1}(x) = 2x T_n(x) - T_{n-1}(x).$$

This results from replacing $\cos n\theta$ in Eq. (6.1) by $T_n(x)$.

PROPERTY 3. DIFFERENTIAL EQUATION. The Čebyšev polynomial $T_n(x)$ is a solution of the differential equation

$$(1 - x^2)y'' - xy' + n^2 y = 0.$$

If we use θ, where $x = \cos \theta$, as independent variable this differential equation becomes

$$\frac{d^2 y}{d\theta^2} + n^2 y = 0,$$

one solution of which is $\cos n\theta$.

PROPERTY 4. EXPLICIT EXPRESSION

$$T_n(x) = \sum_{k=0}^{[n/2]} (-1)^k \frac{n}{n - k} \binom{n - k}{k} 2^{n-2k-1} x^{n-2k},$$

where $[\nu]$ means the largest integer in ν.

$T_n(x)$ is a polynomial of degree n with leading coefficient 2^{n-1} which satisfies the differential equation given in Property 3. Hence if we substitute

$$T_n(x) = \sum_{k=0}^{n} a_k x^{n-k}$$

in this differential equation we find $a_1 = 0$ and

$$a_k = -\frac{(n-k+2)(n-k+1)}{k(2n-k)}\,a_{k-2}.$$

The expression listed for $T_n(x)$ results upon replacing k by $2k$.

PROPERTY 5.   EXPANSION OF x^n

$$x^n = \frac{1}{2^{n-1}} \sum_{k=0}^{[n/2]} \binom{n}{k} T_{n-2k}(x)$$

where the coefficient of $T_0(x)$, if present, must be halved and $[\nu]$ means the largest integer in ν.

PROPERTY 6.   INTEGRAL ORTHOGONAL PROPERTY. The Čebyšev polynomials of the first kind are orthogonal on the interval $(-1, 1)$ with respect to the weight function $(1 - x^2)^{-1/2}$, that is,

$$\int_{-1}^{1} (1 - x^2)^{-1/2} T_m(x) T_n(x)\,dx = \begin{cases} 0, & m \neq n \\ \pi/2, & m = n \neq 0. \\ \pi, & m = n = 0 \end{cases}$$

This is a consequence of the orthogonality of the cosine functions on the interval $(0, \pi)$.

PROPERTY 7.   FINITE ORTHOGONAL PROPERTY.   Letting

$$x_i = \cos \frac{2i+1}{n+1}\frac{\pi}{2}, \qquad i = 0, 1, 2, \ldots, n,$$

designate the zeros of $T_{n+1}(x)$,

$$\sum_{i=0}^{n} T_r(x_i) T_s(x_i) = \begin{cases} 0, & r \neq s \\ \dfrac{n+1}{2}, & r = s \neq 0 \\ n+1, & r = s = 0 \end{cases}$$

provided r and s are nonnegative integers not exceeding n.

A proof may be based on the following:

1. $\cos r\theta_i \cos s\theta_i = \frac{1}{2}[\cos (r - s)\theta_i + \cos (r + s)\theta_i]$,

2. $\sum\limits_{i=0}^{n} \cos m\theta_i = \begin{cases} 0, & m \neq 2\nu(n + 1) \\ (-1)^\nu(n + 1), & m = 2\nu(n + 1), \end{cases}$

where

$$\theta_i = \frac{2i + 1}{n + 1} \frac{\pi}{2}.$$

PROPERTY 8. MINIMAX PROPERTY. If $P_n(x)$ is any polynomial of degree $\leq n$ having leading coefficient 1, then

$$\max_{-1 \leq x \leq 1} |2^{1-n} T_n(x)| \leq \max_{-1 \leq x \leq 1} |P_n(x)|.*$$

We suppose $P_n(x)$ to be of degree n. The leading coefficient of $T_n(x)$ is 2^{n-1} and hence

$$f_{n-1}(x) = 2^{1-n} T_n(x) - P_n(x)$$

is a polynomial of degree $n - 1$ or less. Since

$$T_n(x) = \cos (n \text{ arc cos } x),$$

it follows that $T_n(x)$ attains its bounds ± 1 at

$$x = x_k = \cos \frac{k\pi}{n}, \qquad k = 0, 1, 2, \ldots, n.$$

Furthermore

$$T_n(x_k) = (-1)^k.$$

If the deviation from zero of the polynomial $P_n(x)$ in the interval $-1 \leq x \leq 1$ were less than that of $2^{1-n} T_n(x)$ then it would follow that

$$2^{1-n} T_n(x_0) - P_n(x_0) > 0,$$

$$2^{1-n} T_n(x_1) - P_n(x_1) < 0,$$

$$2^{1-n} T_n(x_2) - P_n(x_2) > 0, \quad \text{etc.}$$

Thus the polynomial $f_{n-1}(x)$ would be alternately positive and negative at the $n + 1$ successive points x_k. Hence $f_{n-1}(x)$ would have at least n zeros in the interval $(-1, 1)$, which is, of course, impossible since $f_{n-1}(x)$ is of degree $\leq n - 1$ and may be assumed to be not identically 0.

* Figures 11.1 and 11.2 illustrate this property.

If $P_n(x)$ were of degree $m < n$, then

$$\max_{-1 \le x \le 1} |P_n(x)| \ge \max_{-1 \le x \le 1} |2^{1-m} T_m(x)| > \max_{-1 \le x \le 1} |2^{1-n} T_n(x)|.$$

The stated property thus holds for all polynomials $P_n(x)$ of degree $\le n$.

Table 6.3

ČEBYŠEV POLYNOMIALS OF THE FIRST KIND

$$T_0(x) = 1$$
$$T_1(x) = x$$
$$T_2(x) = 2x^2 - 1$$
$$T_3(x) = 4x^3 - 3x$$
$$T_4(x) = 8x^4 - 8x^2 + 1$$
$$T_5(x) = 16x^5 - 20x^3 + 5x$$
$$T_6(x) = 32x^6 - 48x^4 + 18x^2 - 1$$
$$T_7(x) = 64x^7 - 112x^5 + 56x^3 - 7x$$
$$T_8(x) = 128x^8 - 256x^6 + 160x^4 - 32x^2 + 1$$
$$T_9(x) = 256x^9 - 576x^7 + 432x^5 - 120x^3 + 9x$$
$$T_{10}(x) = 512x^{10} - 1280x^8 + 1120x^6 - 400x^4 + 50x^2 - 1$$

Table 6.4

ČEBYŠEV EXPANSIONS OF POWERS OF x

$$1 = T_0$$
$$x = T_1$$
$$x^2 = 2^{-1}[T_0 + T_2]$$
$$x^3 = 2^{-2}[3T_1 + T_3]$$
$$x^4 = 2^{-3}[3T_0 + 4T_2 + T_4]$$
$$x^5 = 2^{-4}[10T_1 + 5T_3 + T_5]$$
$$x^6 = 2^{-5}[10T_0 + 15T_2 + 6T_4 + T_6]$$
$$x^7 = 2^{-6}[35T_1 + 21T_3 + 7T_5 + T_7]$$
$$x^8 = 2^{-7}[35T_0 + 56T_2 + 28T_4 + 8T_6 + T_8]$$
$$x^9 = 2^{-8}[126T_1 + 84T_3 + 36T_5 + 9T_7 + T_9]$$
$$x^{10} = 2^{-9}[126T_0 + 210T_2 + 120T_4 + 45T_6 + 10T_8 + T_{10}]$$

EXERCISES

1. Show that differences of the factorial polynomials are like derivatives of powers of x, that is,

$$\Delta x^{[r]} = r x^{[r-1]}$$

. . . . . .

$$\Delta^i x^{[r]} = r(r-1) \cdots (r-i+1) x^{[r-i]}$$

. . . .

$$\Delta^r x^{[r]} = r!$$

if $h = 1$. (See Sec. 9.1 for definition of differences.)

2. Show that

$$P_n(x) = P_n(0) + \Delta P_n(0) x^{[1]} + \frac{\Delta^2 P_n(0)}{2!} x^{[2]} + \cdots + \frac{\Delta^n P_n(0)}{n!} x^{[n]},$$

by writing $P_n(x)$ as a linear combination of factorial polynomials with coefficients determined by taking successive ordinary differences. We thus obtain Newton's forward difference interpolation formula (See Sec. 9.5).

3. Establish Property 3 of the Legendre polynomials.

4. Show that if

$$p(x) = \sum_{i=0}^{n} b_i P_i(x)$$

where $P_i(x)$ is the Legendre polynomial of degree i, then

$$b_i = \frac{2i+1}{2} \int_{-1}^{1} p(x) \, P_i(x) \, dx.$$

5. Write x^4 as a linear combination of Legendre polynomials.

6. If $P(x) = \sum_{k=0}^{n} A_k P_k(x)$, where $P_k(x)$ is Legendre polynomial of degree k, show that $P(x_0)$ may be evaluated by the following recurrence process: Calculate numbers $B_n, B_{n-1}, \ldots, B_1, B_0$ by the recurrence formula

$$B_k = A_k + \frac{2k+1}{k+1} x_0 B_{k+1} - \frac{k+1}{k+2} B_{k+2}$$

with $B_{n+2} = B_{n+1} = 0$. Then $P(x_0) = B_0$.

7. Use quadratic formula to calculate, correct to six places of decimals, the smallest positive zero of the Čebyšev polynomial of the first kind of degree 5. As a check note that answer is

$$\cos 3\pi/10 = 0.587785.$$

8. If $P(x) = \sum_{k=0}^{n} A_k T_k(x)$ where $T_k(x)$ is the Čebyšev polynomial of degree k, show that $P(x_0)$ can be calculated by the following recurrence process [3]:

Calculate the sequence of numbers $B_n, B_{n-1}, \ldots, B_1, B_0$ by the recurrence formula

$$B_k = A_k + 2x_0 B_{k+1} - B_{k+2}$$

with $B_{n+2} = B_{n+1} = 0$. Then $P(x_0) = B_0 - x_0 B_1$.

9. Use the method of preceding exercise to evaluate $T_{10}(0.873)$. Compare with tabled value [4], or with a direct evaluation.

REFERENCES

1. D. Jackson. *Fourier Series and Orthogonal Polynomials.* Kenasha: Mathematical Association of America, 1941.

2. G. Szegö. *Orthogonal Polynomials.* New York: American Mathematical Society, 1939, revised 1959.

3. C. W. Clenshaw. "A Note on Summation of Chebyshev Series," *Math. Tables Aids Comput.* **9:** 118–120 (1955).

4. National Bureau of Standards, *Tables of Chebyshev Polynomials.* Washington, D.C.: U.S. Government Printing Office, 1952.

7

POLYNOMIAL

APPROXIMATIONS

7.1 INTRODUCTION

One of the principal problems of numerical analysis is that of finding adequate simple approximations for mathematical functions, whatever their source, but especially those defined by integrals and differential equations. Although an explicit expression may in some cases be desired, more frequently we require a procedure for evaluating it with a prescribed accuracy for some set of values of the argument. Of the simple functions that have been used for approximating more complicated functions, none are simpler than polynomials. They may be evaluated with comparative ease. Furthermore, derivatives and integrals of polynomials are polynomials.

Fortunately, continuous functions defined on closed intervals may be approximated with any specified precision by polynomials. In 1885, K. T. Weierstrass published a fundamental paper proving the existence of such polynomial approximations. We shall describe briefly the proof given by S. N. Bernstein and shall give details of an elementary proof due to Lebesgue.

7.2 WEIERSTRASS POLYNOMIAL APPROXIMATION THEOREM

Corresponding to a function $f(x)$ defined and continuous on a finite closed interval $[a, b]$ and to an arbitrary $\epsilon > 0$ there is a polynomial $P(x)$ such that $|f(x) - P(x)| < \epsilon$ for all x of $[a, b]$.

7.21   *BERNSTEIN'S PROOF*   Of the known proofs of this theorem one of the more elegant is that given in 1912 by S. N. Bernstein [4,5] who exhibited a sequence of polynomials converging uniformly to a given continuous function.

BERNSTEIN POLYNOMIALS: Each of the $n + 1$ polynomials

$$B_{n,k}(x) = \binom{n}{k} x^k (1 - x)^{n-k},$$

$k = 0, 1, 2, \ldots, n$ is called a *Bernstein Polynomial* of degree n. The polynomial

$$B_n(x) = \sum_{k=0}^{n} f\left(\frac{k}{n}\right) B_{n,k}(x), \qquad 0 \leq x \leq 1,$$

is called the *Bernstein polynomial of degree n associated with $f(x)$.*

BERNSTEIN POLYNOMIAL APPROXIMATION THEOREM. If $f(x)$ is defined and continuous on the closed interval $[0,1]$ and $\epsilon > 0$ then there exists an integer N_ϵ such that $|B_n(x) - f(x)| < \epsilon$ for all $n > N_\epsilon$ and all x of $[0, 1]$.

7.22   *LEBESGUE'S PROOF*   In 1898 H. L. Lebesgue published a proof of the Weierstrass theorem [6] which depends essentially on the possibility of closely approximating a continuous graph by a polygonal arc, a consequence of the uniform continuity of any continuous function on a finite closed interval. We state without proof the basic

LEMMA: [1] *If $f(x)$ is continuous for $a \leq x \leq b$ then for arbitrary $\epsilon > 0$ there exists a $\delta > 0$ such that $|f(\beta) - f(\alpha)| < \epsilon$ if $\beta - \alpha < \delta$ and $a \leq \alpha \leq \beta \leq b$.*

If then corresponding to the δ of the lemma we divide the interval $[a, b]$ into n subintervals, each of length $\leq \delta$ by the points $a = x_0 < x_1 < x_2 < \cdots < x_n = b$ and let the points $(x_i, f(x_i))$, $i = 0, 1, 2, \ldots, n$, be the vertices of a polygonal arc, $y = L(x)$, then $|f(x) - L(x)| < \epsilon$ for all $a \leq x \leq b$. We now show that $L(x)$ can be written as a finite sum of functions for each of which the Weierstrass theorem is true. To this end consider the functions

$$\phi_i(x) = |x - x_i| + (x - x_i), \qquad i = 0, 1, \ldots, n - 1.$$

That is,

$$\phi_i(x) = \begin{cases} 0, & x \leq x_i \\ 2(x - x_i), & x \geq x_i \end{cases}.$$

Then let

$$\Phi(x) = f(x_0) + \sum_{i=0}^{n-1} a_i \phi_i(x),$$

where the a_i are uniquely determined by the n conditions

$$f(x_1) = \Phi(x_1) = f(x_0) + a_0\phi_0(x_1)$$
$$f(x_2) = \Phi(x_2) = f(x_0) + a_0\phi_0(x_2) + a_1\phi_1(x_2)$$
$$\cdot \quad \cdot \quad \cdot \quad \cdot \quad \cdot \quad \cdot \quad \cdot \quad \cdot$$
$$f(x_i) = \Phi(x_i) = f(x_0) + a_0\phi_0(x_i) + \cdots + a_{i-1}\phi_{i-1}(x_i)$$
$$\cdot \quad \cdot \quad \cdot \quad \cdot \quad \cdot \quad \cdot \quad \cdot \quad \cdot$$
$$f(x_n) = \Phi(x_n) = f(x_0) + a_0\phi_0(x_n) + \cdots + a_{n-1}\phi_{n-1}(x_n).$$

Since $\Phi(x)$ is linear in each subinterval $x_{i-1} \leq x \leq x_i$ and $\Phi(x_i) = f(x_i)$, it follows that $\Phi(x) = L(x)$, $a \leq x \leq b$. The binomial series

$$1 - \frac{1}{2}u - \frac{1}{2^2 2!}u^2 - \frac{1 \cdot 3}{2^3 3!}u^3 - \cdots$$

converges uniformly to $\sqrt{1 - u} = |x|$ if $u = 1 - x^2$, $|x| < \lambda < 1$. Thus the theorem of Weierstrass is true for the function $|x|$ on the interval $[-\lambda, \lambda]$. By linear transformations of variables the theorem is true for each $|x - x_i|$ on interval $[a, b]$ and hence for $\phi_i(x)$. Thus $f(x)$ differs by at most ϵ from a linear combination of functions for each of which the Weierstrass theorem is true. The theorem is then necessarily true of $f(x)$. See Exercise 7.2.

7.3　REMARKS

Although the proof of Bernstein is constructive in that it actually exhibits a sequence of polynomials converging uniformly to the given continuous function, the construction is of little practical value for purpose of numerical work. The construction suggested by the proof of Lebesgue is also of no use in actual numerical work. For all practical purposes it merely shows the existence of excellent polynomial approximations to all continuous functions.

We shall consider the problem of finding polynomial approximations to given functions. First, detailed consideration will be given to procedures of obtaining the so-called interpolating polynomials. The procedures here are well established and straightforward. Interpolating polynomials play a fundamental role in classical numerical methods. Less detailed consideration must be given to the incompletely resolved problems of obtaining polynomial approximations which are in some sense "best" [2,3].

EXERCISES

1. Make graphs of the functions $a_0\phi_0(x)$, $a_1\phi_1(x)$ and $\Phi(x)$, $x_0 \leq x \leq x_2$, as defined in Sec. 7.22.

2. Show in detail that if $f_1(x)$ and $f_2(x)$ are functions for which the Weierstrass theorem is true for $a \leq x \leq b$, and if c_1 and c_2 are arbitrary constants, then the Weierstrass theorem is true for the function

$$F(x) = c_1 f_1(x) + c_2 f_2(x).$$

REFERENCES

1. C. Goffman. *Real Functions*. New York: Rinehart, 1953.

2. C. Hastings, Jr. *Approximations for Digital Computers*. Princeton: Princeton U.P., 1955.

3. R. E. Langer (ed.). *On Numerical Approximations*. Madison: U. Wisconsin P., 1959.

4. G. G. Lorentz. *Bernstein Polynomials*. U. Toronto P., 1953.

5. I. P. Natanson. *Konstructive Funktionentheorie*. Berlin: Akademie-Verlag, 1955. Translated from the Russian edition of 1951. Also available in English translation from the Office of Technical Services, Department of Commerce, Washington 25, D.C., AEC-tr-4503.

6. C. J. de la Vallée Poussin. *Leçons sur l'approximation des fonctions d'une variable réelle.* Paris: Gauthier-Villars, 1919.

8

DIVIDED DIFFERENCES

8.1 DEFINITION

In Sec. 3.33 we defined first and second order divided differences of a function $f(x)$. We now extend that discussion to divided differences of any integral order.

Let $x_0, x_1, x_2, \ldots, x_n$ be any set of $n + 1$ distinct numbers. We defined the first order divided difference of x_0, x_1 to be the difference quotient

$$\frac{f(x_1) - f(x_0)}{x_1 - x_0} \tag{8.1}$$

and denoted it by $f(x_0, x_1)$. The second order divided difference $f(x_0, x_1, x_2)$ was defined in terms of first order divided differences. Thus

$$f(x_0, x_1, x_2) = \frac{f(x_1, x_2) - f(x_0, x_1)}{x_2 - x_0} . \tag{8.2}$$

In general the $(i + 1)$st divided difference $f(x_0, x_1, x_2, \ldots, x_{i+1})$ is now defined in terms of divided differences of order i. Thus

$$f(x_0, x_1, x_2, \ldots, x_i, x_{i+1}) = \frac{f(x_1, x_2, \ldots, x_{i+1}) - f(x_0, x_1, \ldots, x_i)}{x_{i+1} - x_0} . \tag{8.3}$$

Divided differences may be displayed in the form of a table:

x_0 $f(x_0)$

        $f(x_0, x_1)$

x_1 $f(x_1)$ $f(x_0, x_1, x_2)$

        $f(x_1, x_2)$ $f(x_0, x_1, x_2, x_3)$

x_2 $f(x_2)$ $f(x_1, x_2, x_3)$ $f(x_0, x_1, x_2, x_3, x_4)$

        $f(x_2, x_3)$ $f(x_1, x_2, x_3, x_4)$

x_3 $f(x_3)$ $f(x_2, x_3, x_4)$

        $f(x_3, x_4)$

x_4 $f(x_4)$

EXAMPLE 8.1. The following is an example of a divided difference table. The given points are taken from the graph of the quartic

$$f(x) = x^4 - 3x^3 + x^2 - x + 1.$$

x	$f(x)$				
-4	469				
		-211			
-2	47		57		
		-40		-10	
-1	7		17		1
		-6		-4	
0	1		1		1
		-3		3	
2	-5		19		1
		92		14	
5	271		159		
		1364			
10	7091				

8.2 SYMMETRY

Consider $n + 1$ distinct numbers $x_0, x_1, x_2, x_3, \ldots, x_n$. Note that

$$f(x_0, x_1) = \frac{f_0}{x_0 - x_1} + \frac{f_1}{x_1 - x_0}$$

and

$$f(x_0, x_1, x_2) = \frac{f_0}{(x_0 - x_1)(x_0 - x_2)} + \frac{f_1}{(x_1 - x_0)(x_1 - x_2)} + \frac{f_2}{(x_2 - x_0)(x_2 - x_1)}.$$

It is possible to show by induction that

$$f(x_0, x_1, \ldots, x_\alpha) = \sum_{i=0}^{\alpha} \frac{f_i}{\Pi_{(i)}(x_i)} \tag{8.4}$$

$$\alpha = 1, 2, \ldots, n$$

where

$$\Pi_{(i)}(x_i) = (x_i - x_1) \cdots (x_i) - (x_i - x_{i-1})(x_i - x_{i+1}) \cdots (x_i - x_\alpha).$$

From this it is clear that the interchange of any two arguments in a divided difference does not change its value. Thus if $\nu_0, \nu_1, \ldots, \nu_n$ is any permutation of the first $n + 1$ integers including 0 then

$$f(x_{\nu_0}, x_{\nu_1}, \ldots, x_{\nu_n}) = f(x_0, x_1, \ldots, x_n). \tag{8.5}$$

8.3　NEWTON'S FORMULA

We now consider a set of $n + 2$ distinct numbers $x, x_0, x_1, \ldots, x_n$ and form the divided difference of order $i + 1$ associated with the first $i + 2$ of these numbers. Thus

$$f(x, x_0, x_1, \ldots, x_i) = \frac{f(x_0, x_1, \ldots, x_i) - f(x, x_0, \ldots, x_{i-1})}{x_i - x}, \tag{8.6}$$

which may be written in the following form:

$$f(x, x_0, \ldots, x_{i-1}) = f(x_0, x_1, \ldots, x_i) + (x - x_i) f(x, x_0, \ldots, x_i). \tag{8.7}$$

Taking $i = 0, 1, 2, \ldots, n$ we obtain the $n + 1$ equations

$$f(x) = f(x_0) + (x - x_0) f(x, x_0)$$
$$f(x, x_0) = f(x_0, x_1) + (x - x_1) f(x, x_0, x_1)$$
$$f(x, x_0, x_1) = f(x_0, x_1, x_2) + (x - x_2) f(x, x_0, x_1, x_2)$$
$$\cdot \qquad \cdot \qquad \cdot \qquad \cdot \qquad \cdot \qquad \cdot \qquad \cdot \qquad \cdot \tag{8.8}$$
$$f(x, x_0, x_1, \ldots, x_{n-1}) = f(x_0, x_1, \ldots, x_n) + (x - x_n) f(x, x_0, \ldots, x_n).$$

Substituting the expression for $f(x, x_0)$ as given by the second of Eqs. (8.8) into the first we obtain

$$f(x) = f(x_0) + (x - x_0) f(x_0, x_1) + (x - x_0)(x - x_1) f(x, x_0, x_1).$$

We may then substitute into this equation the expression for $f(x, x_0, x_1)$ as given by the third of Eqs. (8.8). Continuing in this manner we obtain

$$\begin{aligned} f(x) &= f(x_0) + (x - x_0) f(x_0, x_1) \\ &\quad + (x - x_0)(x - x_1) f(x_0, x_1, x_2) + \cdots \\ &\quad + (x - x_0)(x - x_1) \cdots (x - x_k) f(x, x_0, \ldots, x_k) \\ &= N_k(x) + R_{k+1}(x), \qquad k = 0, 1, 2, \ldots, n, \end{aligned} \tag{8.9}$$

where
$$R_{k+1}(x) = (x - x_0)(x - x_1) \cdots (x - x_k) f(x, x_0, x_1, \ldots, x_k).$$

Then $N_n(x)$ is Newton's form of the *interpolating polynomial of degree n or less* for $f(x)$ *with collocation points* $x_0, x_1, \ldots, x_n$ and

$$R_{n+1}(x) = (x - x_0)(x - x_1) \cdots (x - x_n) f(x, x_0, \ldots, x_n)$$

is the *remainder*. For observe that

$$f(x_i) = N_0(x_i), \qquad i = 0,$$
$$f(x_i) = N_1(x_i), \qquad i = 0, 1.$$

Using mathematical induction we can show that

$$f(x_i) = N_n(x_i), \qquad i = 0, 1, 2, \ldots, n.$$

The proof depends on the fact that

$$N_{k+1}(x_i) = N_k(x_i), \qquad i = 0, 1, 2, \ldots, k$$

and that since the divided differences are symmetric functions,

$$f(x_{k+1}) = N_k(x_{k+1}) + R_{k+1}(x_{k+1}) = N_{k+1}(x_{k+1}).$$

8.4 UNIQUE INTERPOLATING POLYNOMIAL

If $I_n(x)$ is any polynomial of degree n or less such that $I_n(x_i) = f(x_i)$, $i = 0, 1, \ldots, n$, then we refer to $I_n(x)$ as the *interpolating polynomial for* $f(x)$ *with collocation points** $x_0, x_1, \ldots, x_n$. This statement implies uniqueness, and such is, indeed, the case.

> For a given function $f(x)$ and a given set of $n + 1$ distinct collocation points x_i, $i = 0, 1, \ldots, n$ there is precisely one interpolating polynominal. Its degree is $\leq n$.

Newton's formula $N_n(x)$, Eq. (8.9), is one such. We now show that it is unique. For if there were another, say $P_n(x)$, of degree $\leq n$, then $N_n(x) - P_n(x)$ would be a polynomial of degree $\leq n$ having $n + 1$ zeros, which is impossible (Sec. 5.2).

We shall see in the next chapter that there are many ways of obtaining and forms for writing an interpolating polynomial. But no matter how different two polynomials each of degree $\leq n$ may look, if their graphs have at least $n + 1$ points in common then their graphs are identical.

* Also referred to as *sample points* and as *interpolating points*.

EXAMPLE 8.2. We may use the divided difference table of Example 8.1 to write down Newton's form of the interpolating polynomial associated with the first five points.

$$I_4(x) = 469 + (x + 4)(-211) + (x + 4)(x + 2)57$$
$$+ (x + 4)(x + 2)(x + 1)(-10) + (x + 4)(x + 2)(x + 1)x.$$

Using the last five points we obtain:

$$I_4(x) = 7 + (x + 1)(-6) + (x + 1)x$$
$$+ (x + 1)x(x - 2)3 + (x + 1)x(x - 2)(x - 5).$$

Each of the above polynomials is, of course, identical to

$$f(x) = x^4 - 3x^3 + x^2 - x + 1.$$

8.5   REMAINDER IN POLYNOMIAL INTERPOLATION

Newton's form of the remainder is, as we have seen,

$$R_{n+1}(x) = (x - x_0)(x - x_1) \cdots (x - x_n) f(x, x_0, \ldots, x_n).$$

This is, of course, of no computational interest since its evaluation requires knowledge of $f(x)$ at the value where the interpolation is to be made. It is, however, of considerable use as a starting point for producing other forms of the remainder which are of computational interest. This is especially true in the integration problems to be considered in a later chapter.

We now extend the argument of Sec. 3.4 to the interpolating polynomial of arbitrary degree. Letting x' denote any number other than $x_0, x_1, \ldots, x_n$, we define

$$\phi(x) = f(x) - N_n(x) - (x - x_0) \cdots (x - x_n) f(x', x_0, \ldots, x_n).$$

Since $\phi(x') = 0$ and $\phi(x_i) = 0$ for $i = 0, 1, 2, \ldots, n$, it follows from a generalization of Rolle's theorem (A.3) that there exists at least one number ξ such that $\phi^{(n+1)}(\xi) = 0$ where

$$\min (x', x_0, \ldots, x_n) < \xi < \max (x', x_0, \ldots, x_n).$$

This, in turn, implies that

$$0 = f^{(n+1)}(\xi) - (n + 1)! f(x', x_0, \ldots, x_n).$$

Dropping the prime we obtain two basic formulas:

> **Remainder in Polynomial Interpolation (Cauchy form):**
> *There exists at least one number ξ such that*
> $$R_{n+1}(x) = (x - x_0) \cdots (x - x_n) \frac{f^{(n+1)}(\xi)}{(n+1)!}$$ (8.10)
> *where*
> $$min\,(x, x_0, \ldots, x_n) < \xi < max\,(x, x_0, \ldots, x_n).$$

> *If $x_0, x_1, \ldots, x_n$ are any $n + 1$ distinct numbers, then there exists at least one number ξ such that*
> $$f(x_0, x_1, \ldots, x_n) = \frac{f^{(n)}(\xi)}{n!}$$ (8.11)
> *where*
> $$min\,(x_0, x_1, \ldots, x_n) < \xi < max\,(x_0, x_1, \ldots, x_n).$$

In each of the above cases we suppose, of course, the existence of the derivatives involved.

If $f(x)$ is a polynomial of degree n with leading coefficient a_0 then $f^{(n)}(x) = n!\, a_0$ and hence $f(x_0, x_1, \ldots, x_n) = a_0$. Thus all the nth order differences of a polynomial of degree n are constant (equal to the coefficient of x^n). Conversely, if the nth order differences of a function are constant or approximately so, then it may be that that function can be closely approximated by a polynomial of degree n, but not necessarily so.

There is danger in using any interpolating polynomial without due consideration of the remainder. Without additional information about two functions we cannot assume they are even approximately the same throughout an interval just because they are identical at n points of this interval, *no matter how big n may be.* For example, the functions

$$e^x \qquad \text{and} \qquad e^x + 10^6 \sin 100\pi x$$

are identical at $x = 0.00, 0.01, 0.02, \ldots$, but differ by 10^6 at $x = 0.005$, $0.015, 0.025, \ldots$. In a later chapter we shall consider very briefly the meaning and possibility of *divergence* of interpolating polynomials.

8.6 DIFFERENTIATION OF DIVIDED DIFFERENCES

Consider the divided difference

$$f(x, x_0, x_1, \ldots, x_n, x + h) = \frac{f(x_0, x_1, \ldots, x_n, x + h) - f(x, x_0, \ldots, x_n)}{h}.$$

In view of the symmetry of divided differences we may then write

$$f(x, x_0, x_1, \ldots, x_n, x + h) = \frac{f(x + h, x_0, x_1, \ldots, x_n) - f(x, x_0, \ldots, x_n)}{h}.$$

(8.12)

We have seen (Sec. 8.5) that there exists at least one number ξ such that

$$f(x, x_0, x_1, \ldots, x_n, x + h) = \frac{f^{(n+2)}(\xi)}{(n + 2)!}$$

(8.13)

where

$$\min (x, x_0, \ldots, x_n, x + h) < \xi < \max (x, x_0, \ldots, x_n, x + h),$$

provided, of course, that $f^{(n+2)}(x)$ exists. If we consider fixed values of $x, x_0, x_1, \ldots, x_n$, then ξ is a function of h alone. Combining Eqs. (8.12) and (8.13) we find

$$\frac{f(x + h, x_0, x_1, \ldots, x_n) - f(x, x_0, x_1, \ldots, x_n)}{h} = \frac{f^{(n+2)}(\xi(h))}{(n + 2)!}.$$

(8.14)

We now suppose that $f^{(n+2)}(x)$ is continuous. If we let $h \to 0$ we obtain the following:

If $f^{(n+2)}(x)$ is continuous then there exists at least one number ξ such that

$$\frac{d}{dx} f(x, x_0, x_1, \ldots, x_n) = \frac{f^{(n+2)}(\xi)}{(n + 2)!}.$$

(8.15)

where

$$min (x, x_0, \ldots, x_n) < \xi < max (x, x_0, \ldots, x_n).$$

EXERCISES

1. Find Newton's form of the interpolating polynomial for $\ln (1 + x)$ with collocation point 2.0, 2.1, 2.2, 2.5, 3.0. Evaluate this polynomial at $x = 2.37$. Compare with published table value.

2. Form a divided difference table for the data of Example 8.1 taking the values of x in the order $-1, -2, -4, 10, 5, 2, 0$. Note the numerical verifications of the symmetry property (Eq. 8.5).

3. Calculate bounds for the remainder in Exercise 1.

4. Write the polynomial $p(x)$ of minimum degree for which:

x:	0	1	3	4	6
$p(x)$:	3	0	18	63	285

5. Write Newton's formula for the four collocation points x_0, $x_0 + \epsilon$, x_1, $x_1 + \eta$. Show that its limiting forms as $\epsilon \to 0$, $\eta \to 0$ is

$$f(x_0 + uh) = [1 - u^2(3 - 2u)]f_0 + u^2(3 - 2u)f_1$$
$$+ h\{u(u - 1)^2 f_0' + u^2(u - 1)f_1'\}$$
$$+ u^2(u - 1)^2 h^4 \frac{f^{(4)}(\xi)}{4!},$$

where

$$x_1 - x_0 = h, \quad u = \frac{1}{h}(x - x_0), \qquad f_i = f(x_0 + ih), \quad f_i' = \frac{d}{dx}f(x)\Big]_{x = x_0 + ih}$$

and

$$\min(x, x_0, x_1) < \xi < \max(x, x_0, x_1).$$

This formula is known as the *two-point osculatory interpolation formula* [1].

6. Make a divided difference table for the following data [2]:

x:	-1.941	-1.000	0.061	1.248	2.567
$f(x)$:	1.9	2.0	2.1	2.2	2.3

Use Newton's formula to calculate approximate value of $f(0)$.

The above table gives five points on the graph of $x = y^3 - 2y - 5$. Thus Newton's formula can be used to approximate a zero of a function once an interval (here [2.0, 2.1]) has been found in which it is located. This amounts to a generalization of the method of false position using nonlinear approximating polynomials. See Exercise 3.2 and Examples 4.1 and 4.3.

REFERENCES

1. H. E. Salzer. *Tables of Osculatory Interpolation Coefficients.* Washington, D.C.: National Bureau of Standards, U.S. Government Printing Office, 1959.
2. L. M. Milne-Thomson. *The Calculus of Finite Differences.* London: Macmillan, 1933, 1951.

9

ORDINARY DIFFERENCES

9.1 DEFINITION

If values of a function $f(x)$ are available for a set of values of x which are equally spaced it is customary to use ordinary differences or differences of the functional values rather than divided differences. Thus if $f_i = f(x_i)$, $i = 0, 1, 2, \ldots, n$, are known and $x_i = x_0 + ih$, $h > 0$, we may form a

FORWARD DIFFERENCE TABLE

$$
\begin{array}{cccccc}
x_0 & f_0 & & & & \\
 & & \Delta f_0 & & & \\
x_1 & f_1 & & \Delta^2 f_0 & & \\
 & & \Delta f_1 & & \Delta^3 f_0 & \\
x_2 & f_2 & & \Delta^2 f_1 & & — \\
 & & \Delta f_2 & & — & \\
x_3 & f_3 & & — & & \\
 & & — & & & \\
 & & — & — & &
\end{array}
$$

Here

$\Delta f_i = f_{i+1} - f_i$ is the *first forward difference,*

$\Delta^2 f_i = \Delta f_{i+1} - \Delta f_i$ is the *second forward difference,*

$\Delta^3 f_i = \Delta^2 f_{i+1} - \Delta^2 f_i$ is the *third forward difference,*

etc.

EXAMPLE 9.1. We form an ordinary difference table for the quartic

$$p(x) = x^4 - 3x^3 + x^2 - x + 1,$$

considered in Example 8.1:

x	$p(x)$			
−4	469			
		−422		
−2	47		376	
		−46		−336
0	1		40		384
		−6		48
2	−5		88		384
		82		432
4	77		520	
		602		
6	679			

9.2 DIFFERENCES OF POLYNOMIALS

Comparing the definitions of ordinary and divided differences we see that if $x_i = x_0 + ih,$ $i = 0, 1, 2, \ldots, n$, then

$$\Delta f_j = h f(x_j, x_{j+1}),$$
$$\Delta^2 f_j = 2h^2 f(x_j, x_{j+1}, x_{j+2})$$
$$\Delta^3 f_j = 3!\, h^3 f(x_j, x_{j+1}, x_{j+2}, x_{j+3})$$

and in general

$$\Delta^n f_j = n!\, h^n f(x_j, x_{j+1}, \ldots, x_{j+n}).$$

We have previously noted that the nth order divided differences of a polynomial of degree n are equal to the coefficient a_0 of x^n. Hence if

$$P(x) = a_0 x^n + a_1 x^{n-1} + \cdots + a_{n-1}x + a_n$$

then

$$\Delta^n P_j = n!\, h^n a_0. \tag{9.1}$$

Thus in Example 9.1 we could have predicted that

$$\Delta^4 P_j = 4!\, 2^4 = 384.$$

The fact that nth order differences of a polynomial of degree n are equal is of primary importance in the calculus of ordinary differences. If the nth order differences of a function are essentially constant then this can be taken as a strong indication of the possibility of adequately approximating that function over the interval of the data by a polynomial of degree n.

EXAMPLE 9.2

x	$\ln(1+x)$	Δ	Δ^2
2.00	1.098 612		
		6 645	
2.02	1.105 257		-44
		6 601	
2.04	1.111 858		-44
		6 557	
2.06	1.118 415		-42
		6 515	
2.08	1.124 930		-43
		6 472	
2.10	1.131 402		

Since ordinary differences usually involve appreciably fewer significant digits than the given ordinates, it is customary not to write them as decimals. Thus, for example, we have written -44 instead of $-0.000\,044$. Since the second order differences are approximately constant, there is a strong indication that the function $\ln(1+x)$ to six places of decimals can be approximated on the interval $2.00 \leq x \leq 2.10$ by a quadratic polynomial.

The evidence in this example is not conclusive for again note that if

$$f(x) = F(x) + G(x),$$

where $F(x)$ is arbitrary and $G(x)$ is a continuous function which is periodic of period h, then

$$\Delta f(x) \equiv \Delta F(x).$$

In particular, if $F(x)$ is a polynomial of degree n, then $\Delta^n f(x)$ is constant but $f(x)$ need not be a polynomial.

9.3 RELATIONS BETWEEN ORDINATES AND DIFFERENCES

Since any difference is defined as a difference of two differences of order one lower it can be expressed in terms of the ordinates. Thus, for example,

$$\Delta f_0 = f_1 - f_0,$$
$$\Delta^2 f_0 = f_2 - 2f_1 + f_0,$$
$$\Delta^3 f_0 = f_3 - 3f_2 + 3f_1 - f_0.$$

Conversely, any ordinate of a set of ordinates corresponding to equally spaced values of the argument can be expressed in terms of one ordinate and a set of differences. For example,

$$f_1 = f_0 + \Delta f_0,$$
$$f_2 = f_0 + 2\Delta f_0 + \Delta^2 f_0,$$
$$f_3 = f_0 + 3\Delta f_0 + 3\Delta^2 f_0 + \Delta^3 f_0.$$

Note in each of the above relations the appearance of the binomial coefficients. We use the notation $\binom{u}{k}$ for the *binomial coefficient function.* Thus for any number u and any positive integer k.

$$\binom{u}{k} = \frac{u(u-1)(u-2)\cdots(u-k+1)}{k!},$$

a polynomial of degree k in u. As a matter of convenience we agree that $\binom{u}{0} = 1$. Using this notation we may write

$$\Delta^3 f_0 = \binom{3}{0} f_3 - \binom{3}{1} f_2 + \binom{3}{2} f_1 - \binom{3}{3} f_0$$

and

$$f_3 = \binom{3}{0} \Delta^0 f_0 + \binom{3}{1} \Delta^1 f_0 + \binom{3}{2} \Delta^2 f_0 + \binom{3}{3} \Delta^3 f_0$$

where

$$\Delta^0 f_0 = f_0, \qquad \Delta^1 f_0 = \Delta f_0.$$

These suggest the following:

$$\Delta^j f_0 = \sum_{k=0}^{j} (-1)^k \binom{j}{k} f_{j-k}, \tag{9.2}$$

$$f_j = \sum_{k=0}^{j} \binom{j}{k} \Delta^k f_0. \tag{9.3}$$

Each of these relations can be established by mathematical induction. For example, we know that Eq. (9.2) is true for $j = 1$. Suppose now that it is true for all positive integers $j < n$. Then

$$\Delta^n f_0 = \Delta^{n-1} f_1 - \Delta^{n-1} f_0$$

$$= \sum_{k=0}^{n-1} (-1)^k \binom{n-1}{k} f_{n-k} - \sum_{k=0}^{n-1} (-1)^k \binom{n-1}{k} f_{n-1-k}$$

$$= \sum_{k=0}^{n-1} (-1)^k \binom{n-1}{k} f_{n-k} - \sum_{k=1}^{n} (-1)^{k-1} \binom{n-1}{k-1} f_{n-k}$$

$$= f_n + \sum_{k=1}^{n-1} (-1)^k \left[\binom{n-1}{k} + \binom{n-1}{k-1} \right] f_{n-k} + (-1)^n f_0.$$

We then use the result stated in Exercise 9.1 to obtain

$$\Delta^n f_0 = f_n + \sum_{k=1}^{n-1} (-1)^k \binom{n}{k} f_{n-k} + (-1)^n f_0 = \sum_{k=0}^{n} (-1)^k \binom{n}{k} f_{n-k}.$$

Thus Eq. (9.2) is true for $j = n$. It is then true for j any positive integer.

9.4 BACKWARD DIFFERENCES AND CENTRAL DIFFERENCES

Various notations are used for the numbers occurring in a difference table. Thus the table of Sec. 9.1 may be written as a

TABLE OF BACKWARD DIFFERENCES

x_0	f_0			
		∇f_1		
x_1	f_1		$\nabla^2 f_2$	
		∇f_2		$\nabla^3 f_3$
x_2	f_2		$\nabla^2 f_3$	
		∇f_3		
x_3	f_3			

or as a

TABLE OF CENTRAL DIFFERENCES

x_0	f_0			
		$\delta f_{1/2}$		
x_1	f_1		$\delta^2 f_1$	
		$\delta f_{3/2}$		$\delta^3 f_{3/2}$
x_2	f_2		$\delta^2 f_2$	
		$\delta f_{5/2}$		
x_3	f_3			

For any given numerical example each of the above three tables would be precisely the same. The different notations are useful for elegance of writing certain interpolating polynomials. A comparison of the three tables shows that

$$\nabla^i f_j = \Delta^i f_{j-i}$$
$$i = 1, 2, 3, \ldots \tag{9.4}$$
$$j = 1, 2, 3, \ldots$$

and

$$\delta^i f_{j/2} = \Delta^i f_{(j-i)/2}, \tag{9.5}$$

i and j both odd or both even.

We shall see that formulas involving central differences are usually used near the middle of the range of x's involved in the formula and that the middle or left of middle value is labeled x_0. For this reason a central difference table is usually extended below x_0 and looks like that given in Exercise 9.5.

9.5 POLYNOMIAL INTERPOLATION FORMULAS

The unique interpolating polynomial of degree $\leq n$ for a function $f(x)$ with $n + 1$ equally spaced collocation points can be written in a wide variety of ways in terms of differences. All the differences—out to and including the single one of order n—that can be formed from $n + 1$ consecutive ordinates form a triangle. A knowledge of only one number from each column of this triangle, for example, is sufficient to completely determine the triangle. It is not unreasonable then to suppose that the interpolating polynomial could be written in terms of any such selection of differences. We list, without proof, a selection of classical interpolation formulas in terms of differences. (Derivations may be found in [1] and [2].)

NEWTON'S FORWARD INTERPOLATION FORMULA:

$$f(x_0 + uh) = f_0 + u\,\Delta f_0 + \binom{u}{2}\Delta^2 f_0 + \binom{u}{3}\Delta^3 f_0 + \cdots$$
$$+ \binom{u}{n}\Delta^n f_0 + R_{n+1}(u). \quad (9.6)$$

NEWTON'S BACKWARD INTERPOLATION FORMULA:

$$f(x_n - uh) = f_n - u\,\nabla f_n + \binom{u}{2}\nabla^2 f_n - \binom{u}{3}\nabla^3 f_n + \cdots$$
$$+ (-1)^n \binom{u}{n}\nabla^n f_n + R_{n+1}(u). \quad (9.7)$$

BESSEL'S FORMULA:

$$f(x_0 + uh) = \frac{f_0 + f_1}{2} + B_1\,\delta f_{1/2} + B_2\frac{\delta^2 f_0 + \delta^2 f_1}{2} + B_3\,\delta^3 f_{1/2}$$
$$+ B_4\frac{\delta^4 f_0 + \delta^4 f_1}{2} + B_5\,\delta^5 f_{1/2} + \cdots + R_{n+1}(u), \quad (9.8)$$

where

$$B_1 = u - \frac{1}{2}, \qquad B_2 = \frac{u(u-1)}{2}, \qquad B_3 = \frac{u(u-1)(u-\frac{1}{2})}{3!},$$

$$B_{2k} = \binom{u+k-1}{2k}, \qquad B_{2k+1} = \frac{u - \frac{1}{2}}{2k+1} B_{2k}.$$

STIRLING'S FORMULA:

$$f(x_0 + uh) = f_0 + u\frac{\delta f_{-1/2} + \delta f_{1/2}}{2} + S_2\,\delta^2 f_0 + S_3\frac{\delta^3 f_{-1/2} + \delta^3 f_{1/2}}{2} + S_4\,\delta^4 f_0$$

$$+ S_5\frac{\delta^5 f_{-1/2} + \delta^5 f_{1/2}}{2} + S_6\,\delta^6 f_0 + \cdots + R_{n+1}(u), \qquad (9.9)$$

where

$$S_{2k} = \frac{u}{2k}\binom{u + k - 1}{2k - 1}, \qquad S_{2k+1} = \binom{u + k}{2k + 1}.$$

EVERETT'S FORMULA:

$$f(x_0 + uh) = vf_0 + E_2(v)\,\delta^2 f_0 + E_4(v)\,\delta^4 f_0 + \cdots$$

$$+ uf_1 + E_2(u)\,\delta^2 f_1 + E_4(u)\,\delta^4 f_1 + \cdots \qquad (9.10)$$

$$+ R_{n+1}(u),$$

where

$$v = 1 - u$$

and

$$E_{2k}(t) = \binom{t + k}{2k + 1}.$$

Appendix E is a brief table of interpolation coefficients. For more extensive tables see [3] and [4].

Bessel's formula should always be used out to and including a term of odd degree. For example, if $\delta^4 f_0$ and $\delta^4 f_1$ are known, then $\delta^5 f_{1/2}$ is necessarily known. For a similar reason Stirling's formula should be used to an even degree. Everett's formula is necessarily of odd degree. The two formulas of Newton may be used to any degree.

Each formula listed above is polynomial of degree n and based on $n + 1$ collocation points. For the formulas of Newton the collocation points are labeled $x_0, x_1, x_2, \ldots, x_n$. The formulas of Bessel and Everett are based on an even number of collocation points which are labeled $x_{-(n-1)/2}, \ldots, x_{-1}$, $x_0, x_1, \ldots, x_{(n+1)/2}$. The formula of Stirling is based on an odd number of collocation points which are labeled $x_{-n/2}, \ldots, x_{-1}, x_0, x_1, \ldots, x_{n/2}$.

It must be emphasized that although these formulas look very different indeed, any two of the same degree and based on the same difference triangle are identical. The form of a given formula may, however, make it especially appropriate for a given interpolation. Newton's forward and backward formulas are designed for ease of interpolation at the beginning and end of a table. The other formulas listed are especially convenient for use near the middle of a set of values from a table. Some tables of mathematical functions list second and fourth differences so that Everett's formula may be used for interpolation. We illustrate with an example from a table of Bessel functions [5]:

EXAMPLE 9.3.   Given $x = 8.103\,64$, to find the value of $I_{3/4}(x)$. From the table of $I_{3/4}(x)$ we find the following:

x	$I_{3/4}(x)$	δ^2	δ^4
8.10	452.358 980 927 0	40 368 753 0	3 689 0
8.11	456.636 004 124 7	40 755 626 1	3 724 2

Here $u = 0.364,\quad v = 0.636,$

$$E_2(u) = 0.052\,628\,576\ 0 \qquad E_2(v) = 0.063\,123\,424\,0$$

$$E_4(u) = 0.010\,177 \qquad\qquad E_4(v) = 0.011\,348$$

Then

$$uf_1 = 166.215\,505\,501\,39$$
$$vf_0 = 287.700\,311\,869\,57$$
$$E_2(u)\ \delta^2 f_1 = -0.002\,144\,910\,56$$
$$E_2(v)\ \delta^2 f_0 = -0.002\,548\,213\,91$$
$$E_4(u)\ \delta^4 f_1 = \ \ 0.000\,000\,037\,90$$
$$E_4(v)\ \delta^4 f_0 = \ \ 0.000\,000\,041\,86$$
$$I_{3/4}(x) = 453.911\,124\,326\,3$$

The various products listed above should, of course be cumulated in the machine.

9.6 CUBIC INTERPOLATION WITH MODIFIED DIFFERENCES (THROWBACK)

It has been noted that in some interpolation formulas certain coefficients are in essentially constant ratio. For example, for Everett's interpolation formula

$$\frac{E_4(t)}{E_2(t)} = \frac{t^2 - 4}{20}.$$

This ratio does not vary appreciably in the range $0 \le t \le 1$ in which the formula is normally used. This may have suggested to L. J. Comrie (1931) the possibility of using modified differences to obtain accuracy comparable to that which would be obtained using certain higher order differences [6]. This, of course, amounts to approximating polynomials by polynomials of lower degree. We shall describe only the case of most practical interest: Everett's cubic interpolation formula with modified second differences.

Everett's expression for the fifth degree interpolating polynomial is

$$p_5(x_0 + uh) = vf_0 + E_2(v)\, \delta^2 f_0 + E_4(v)\, \delta^4 f_0$$
$$+ uf_1 + E_2(u)\, \delta^2 f_1 + E_4(u)\, \delta^4 f_1,$$

where

$$v = 1 - u, \qquad E_{2k}(t) = \binom{t + k}{2k + 1}.$$

If we let C be some average value of $E_4(t)/E_2(t)$, $0 \leq t \leq 1$, and replace $E_4(t)$ by $CE_2(t)$, we obtain a cubic

$$p_3(x_0 + uh) = vf_0 + E_2(v)\, \delta_m^2 f_0$$
$$+ uf_1 + E_2(u)\, \delta_m^2 f_1$$

where

$$\delta_m^2 f_i = \delta^2 f_i + C\, \delta^4 f_i, \qquad i = 0, 1.$$

The difference between these two polynomials is

$$p_5 - p_3 = [E_4(v) - CE_2(v)]\, \delta^4 f_0 + [E_4(u) - CE_2(u)]\, \delta^4 f_1.$$

While we would like to choose C so that

$$\max_{x_0 \leq x \leq x_1} |p_5(x) - p_3(x)|$$

is a minimum, such a choice would in general depend on the fourth differences and hence is inappropriate. It has been found that (to three decimals) the value $C = -0.181$ makes

$$\max_{0 \leq t \leq 1} |E_4(t) - CE_2(t)|$$

a minimum. But since the coefficients of $\delta^4 f_0$ and $\delta^4 f_1$ in $p_5(x) - p_3(x)$ attain their maxima at different points, a compromise value of $C = -0.184$ is used. This happens to be the constant that would be obtained if modified second differences were to be used with Bessel's formula.

Some tables of the less frequently used mathematical functions, for example [7], include second differences and where fourth differences would influence the interpolated value, modified second differences. This appreciably reduces the size of printed tables.

Table V of Appendix E is a table of $E_2(t)$, $0 \le t \le 1$, to facilitate the use of Everett's cubic interpolation formula, either with or without modified second differences. We illustrate using a part of a table of the cosine integral

$$C_i(x) = -\int_x^\infty \frac{\cos u}{u}\, du$$

x	$C_i(x)$	δ	δ^2	δ^3	δ^4
15.5	0.01719				
		−3139			
16.0	−0.01420		528		
		−2611		590	
16.5	−0.04031		1118		−301
		−1493		289	
17.0	−0.05524		1407		−348
		−86		−59	
17.5	−0.05610		1348		
		1262			
18.0	−0.04348				

From the above table two modified second differences $\delta_m^2 = \delta^2 - 0.184\,\delta^4$, can be obtained:

x	$C_i(x)$	δ_m^2
16.5	−0.04031	1173
17.0	−0.05524	1471

The printed table, of course, contains only the modified second differences.

Using Everett's cubic interpolation formula and modified second differences listed above we obtain:

$$C_i(16.7) = 0.6 \times (-0.04031) - 0.0640 \times 0.01173$$
$$+ 0.4 \times (-0.05524) - 0.0560 \times 0.01471$$
$$= -0.047\,86.$$

This is what would be obtained using Everett's quintic interpolation formula with unmodified differences and is correct to number of decimals listed. On the other hand, Everett's cubic interpolation formula used with unmodified second-order differences gives $-0.047\,79$.

9.7 REMARKS

Formerly the calculus of finite differences dominated the field of numerical analysis. Many older texts contain the phrase "finite differences" in their titles. In the days of extensive hand calculations interpolation formulas involving differences were widely used, primarily because they normally involve fewer significant digits than the ordinates. In machine calculation this is of little or no advantage. In Chap. 10 we shall discuss the method of Lagrange, a method involving only the ordinates. But since so much of the extensive literature of numerical analysis is written in terms of differences, it seems desirable to include this brief introduction to the difference calculus.

EXERCISES

1. Show that

$$\binom{u}{k} + \binom{u}{k-1} = \binom{u+1}{k}.$$

2. Prove relation (9.3) using mathematical induction.

HINT: Suppose formula true for all positive integers $j < n$. Then

$$f_{n-1} = \sum_{k=0}^{n-1} \binom{n-1}{k} \Delta^k f_0,$$

$$f_n = \sum_{k=0}^{n-1} \binom{n-1}{k} \Delta^k f_1 = \sum_{k=0}^{n-1} \binom{n-1}{k} [\Delta^{k+1} f_0 + \Delta^k f_0].$$

3. Derive Newton's forward interpolation formula from Newton's divided difference interpolation formula (Sec. 8.3).

4. Use Eq. (9.3) to show that Newton's forward interpolation formula takes on value f_i at $x = x_i$, $\quad i = 0, 1, 2, \ldots, n$.

5. The following difference table is pertinent to Everett's six-point interpolation formula:

$$
\begin{array}{cccccc}
x_{-2} & f_{-2} \\
 & & \delta f_{-3/2} \\
x_{-1} & f_{-1} & & \delta^2 f_{-1} \\
 & & \delta f_{-1/2} & & \delta^3 f_{-1/2} \\
x_0 & \boxed{f_0} & & \boxed{\delta^2 f_0} & & \boxed{\delta^4 f_0} \\
 & & \delta f_{1/2} & & \delta^3 f_{1/2} & & \delta^5 f_{1/2} \\
x_1 & \boxed{f_1} & & \boxed{\delta^2 f_1} & & \boxed{\delta^4 f_1} \\
 & & \delta f_{3/2} & & \delta^3 f_{3/2} \\
x_2 & f_2 & & \delta^2 f_2 \\
 & & \delta f_{5/2} \\
x_3 & f_3
\end{array}
$$

For an interpolation between x_0 and x_1 only the circled numbers appear in the formula. Make a similar difference table for each of the formulas listed in Sec. 9.5.

6. Use each of the formulas listed in Sec. 9.5 to calculate approximate value of ln 3.48. Use interpolating polynomials of degree 5 or less with collocation points 2.0, 2.2, 2.4, 2.6, 2.8, 3.0 omitting the last point where necessary.

7. Write polynomials of degree 2 and 5 passing through the points (0, 1), (1, 3), (2, 6), (3, 10), and (4, 15)

8. Suppose sin x known for x at integral multiples of 5°. Calculate sin 38° using each of the interpolation formulas of Sec. 9.5.

9. Suppose sin x known for x at integral multiples of 10°. Calculate sin 46° using each of the interpolation formulas of Sec. 9.5.

10. Make a difference table for the function $g(x)$ defined for discrete values of x:

$$g(x_i) = \begin{cases} 0, & i = \pm 4, \pm 3, \pm 2, \pm 1 \\ \epsilon, & i = 0. \end{cases}$$

Hence show, for example, that a rounding error of 5×10^{-5} in f_0 can cause an error of 10^{-3} in the sixth difference (on same line) of a difference table of the function $f(x)$.

11. Show that if $f^{(n)}(x)$ exists, then there exists at least one number ξ, $x_0 < \xi < x_n$, such that

$$\Delta^n f_0 = h^n f^{(n)}(\xi).$$

HINT: See Sec. 9.2 and Eq. (8.11).

12. If a difference table were to be made for sin x for $1.0 \leq x \leq 2.0$ with $h = 0.1$ radian, in what interval would you expect the fourth difference to lie?

13. Write, in simplest possible form, Everett's cubic formula for interpolation at midpoint of interval (x_0, x_1).

14. Show that the cubic

$$p_3(x_0 + uh) = vf_0 + E_2(v)\,\delta_m^2 f_0 + uf_1 + E_2(u)\,\delta_m^2 f_1$$

where

$$v = 1 - u, \qquad E_2(t) = \tfrac{1}{6}t(t^2 - 1),$$

passes through the points (x_0, f_0) and (x_1, f_1) but need not pass through the points (x_{-1}, f_{-1}) and (x_2, f_2).

15. Find mean value of $E_4(t)/E_2(t)$, $0 \le t \le 1$, in the sense of the integral calculus.

16. (a) Make a difference table of six-place values of sin x for $0 \le x \le 50°$ at intervals of $10°$. (b) Use Everett's formula of fifth degree to calculate sin $26°$. (c) Calculate modified second order differences. (d) Use modified second order differences obtained above to recalculate sin $26°$ using Everett's cubic formula. (e) Compare with table value of sin $26°$.

17. Use Eq. (8.10) to obtain explicit expressions for the remainder R_{n+1} in each of the five formulas of Sec. 9.5. Take into consideration the particular labeling of collocation points used in each.

REFERENCES

1. E. T. Whittaker, and G. Robinson. *The Calculus of Observations*, London: Blackie, 1924.

2. L. M. Milne-Thomson. *The Calculus of Finite Differences*. London: Macmillan, 1933, 1951.

3. H. M. Nautical Almanac Office, *Interpolation and Allied Tables*. London, 1956.

4. L. N. Karmazina, and L. V. Kurockina. *Tables of Interpolation Coefficients*. Moscow: Izdat. Akad. Nauk SSSR, 1956.

5. National Bureau of Standards. *Tables of Bessel Functions of Fractional Order*. New York: Columbia U.P., 1949.

6. L. Fox. *Mathematical Tables, Volume 1*. London: H.M. Stationery Office, 1956.

7. E. Jahnke, Fritz Emde, and F. Lösch. *Tables of Higher Functions*. New York: McGraw-Hill, 1960.

POLYNOMIAL

INTERPOLATION—METHOD

OF LAGRANGE

10.1 DERIVATION I

We have noted in Sec. 8.2 that a divided difference can be expressed as a sum of terms, each of which involves but one ordinate. Thus

$$f(x, x_0, x_1, \ldots, x_n) = \frac{f(x)}{\Pi(x)} + \sum_{i=0}^{n} \frac{f(x_i)}{(x_i - x)\Pi_{(i)}(x_i)},$$

where

$$\Pi(x) = (x - x_0)(x - x_1) \cdots (x - x_n)$$

and

$$\Pi_{(i)}(x) = (x - x_0) \cdots (x - x_{i-1})(x - x_{i+1}) \cdots (x - x_n).$$

Hence

$$f(x) = \sum_{i=0}^{n} \frac{\Pi_{(i)}(x)}{\Pi_{(i)}(x_i)} f(x_i) + \Pi(x) f(x, x_0, \ldots, x_n).$$

The polynomial

$$L_n(x) = \sum_{i=0}^{n} \frac{\Pi_{(i)}(x)}{\Pi_{(i)}(x_i)} f(x_i) \qquad (10.1)$$

of degree $\leq n$, is such that

$$L_n(x_i) = f(x_i), \qquad i = 0, 1, \ldots, n.$$

It is thus but another form of the unique interpolating polynomial of degree $\leq n$ for $f(x)$ with collocation points $x_0, x_1, \ldots, x_n$. This form of the interpolating polynomial is attributed to J. L. Lagrange (1736–1813). A notable feature is that it is a linear combination of $n + 1$ polynomials, each of degree n and each depending only on the abscissae of the given collocation points.

10.2 DERIVATION II

Since a polynomial

$$p(x) = a_0 + a_1 x + a_2 x^2 + \cdots + a_n x^n \qquad (10.2)$$

of degree n has $n + 1$ coefficients it seems reasonable to expect that these coefficients could be determined so that the graph of $y = p(x)$ would pass through $n + 1$ given points having distinct abscissae. Denoting the given points by (x_i, f_i), $i = 0, 1, 2, \ldots, n$, we seek to determine $a_0, a_1, \ldots, a_n$ so that

$$\begin{aligned}
f_0 &= a_0 + a_1 x_0 + a_2 x_0^2 + \cdots + a_n x_0^n \\
f_1 &= a_0 + a_1 x_1 + a_2 x_1^2 + \cdots + a_n x_1^n \\
&\quad \cdot \quad \cdot \quad \cdot \quad \cdots \quad \cdot \\
f_n &= a_0 + a_1 x_n + a_2 x_n^2 + \cdots + a_n x_n^n.
\end{aligned} \qquad (10.3)$$

The determinant of the coefficients of the a_i is

$$\begin{vmatrix}
1 & x_0 & x_0^2 & \cdots & x_0^n \\
1 & x_1 & x_1^2 & \cdots & x_1^n \\
1 & x_2 & x_2^2 & \cdots & x_2^n \\
\cdot & \cdot & \cdot & \cdots & \cdot \\
1 & x_n & x_n^2 & \cdots & x_n^n
\end{vmatrix}$$

This determinant was studied by A. T. Vandermonde (1735–1796) who showed it to be equal to

$$\prod_{0 \leq j < k \leq n} (x_k - x_j),$$

the product of all possible factors $x_k - x_j$ with $0 \leq j < k \leq n$. The determinant is thus not zero since the given x_i were assumed to be distinct. Hence the system of Eq. (10.3) has an unique solution (D.2). However, no simple useful expression has been obtained for the a_i. But it is possible to obtain a useful expression for $p(x)$ of a different form by noting that Eqs. (10.2) and (10.3) together form a system of $n + 2$ equations in the $n + 1$ unknown a_i. We have just noted that these equations are consistent. Hence (D.1.2)

$$\begin{vmatrix} p(x) & 1 & x & x^2 & \cdots & x^n \\ f_0 & 1 & x_0 & x_0^2 & \cdots & x_0^n \\ \cdot & \cdot & \cdot & \cdot & \cdots & \cdot \\ f_n & 1 & x_n & x_n^2 & \cdots & x_n^n \end{vmatrix} = 0. \tag{10.4}$$

The cofactor of each element of the first column is a Vandermonde determinant. Hence the cofactor of f_i is

$$(-1)^{i+1} \prod_{0 \leq j < k \leq n} (x_k - x_j) \prod_{0 \leq k \leq n} (x_k - x)$$

with $j \neq i$ and $k \neq i$. Thus Eq. (10.4) on expanding the determinant by the elements of its first column and after dividing by cofactor of $p(x)$ becomes, upon simplification,

$$p(x) + \sum_{i=0}^{n} (-1)^{i+1} \frac{\prod\limits_{k=i+1}^{n} (x_k - x) \prod\limits_{k=0}^{i-1} (x_k - x)}{\prod\limits_{k=i+1}^{n} (x_k - x_i) \prod\limits_{k=0}^{i-1} (x_i - x_k)} f_i = 0.$$

Hence

$$p(x) = \sum_{i=0}^{n} \frac{\prod\limits_{k=0}^{n} (x_k - x)}{\prod\limits_{k=0}^{n} (x_k - x_i)} f_i,$$

where in each product k is not permitted to be equal to i. As in the preceding section we set

$$\Pi_{(i)}(x) = \prod_{\substack{k=0 \\ k \neq i}}^{n} (x - x_k).$$

Then

$$p(x) = \sum_{i=0}^{n} \frac{\Pi_{(i)}(x)}{\Pi_{(i)}(x_i)} f_i = L_n(x).$$

10.3 EQUALLY SPACED COLLOCATION POINTS

If the collocation points are equally spaced at $x_i = x_0 + ih$, $i = 0$, $1, 2, \ldots, n$, the coefficients of the ordinates in Lagrange's form of the interpolating polynomial can be considerably simplified. Introducing the unitized variable $u = (x - x_0)/h$ and letting

$$\Pi(u) = u(u - 1)(u - 2) \cdots (u - n)$$

and

$$\Pi_{(j)}(u) = \frac{\Pi(u)}{u - i}$$

we note that

$$\frac{\Pi_{(i)}(x)}{\Pi_{(i)}(x_i)} = \frac{\Pi_{(i)}(u)}{\Pi_{(i)}(i)} = \frac{\Pi_{(i)}(u)}{(-1)^{n-i} i! \, (n - i)!}.$$

We designate this polynomial of degree n in u by $\lambda_i(u)$. Then we may write

$$L_n(x_0 + uh) = \sum_{i=0}^{n} \lambda_i(u) f_i. \tag{10.5}$$

We shall see in a later chapter that it is wise, wherever possible, to limit polynomial interpolation to values of x near the middle of a set of values determining the interpolating polynomial. For this reason it is convenient to let X_0 designate the middle or left of middle collocation point. Thus $x = X_0 + Uh$, where

$$X_0 = x_{[n/2]}, \qquad U = u - [n/2],$$

and $[n/2]$ is the largest integer not exceeding $n/2$. The National Bureau of Standards has published extensive tables of Lagrangian interpolation coefficients [1]. In these tables the coefficients are labeled A_i. We give two examples to illustrate the notation:

$n = 2$ (3 points)

$$L_2(X_0 + Uh) = A_{-1}(U) f_{-1} + A_0(U) f_0 + A_1(U) f_1,$$

$n = 3$ (4 points)

$$L_3(X_0 + Uh) = A_{-1}(U) f_{-1} + A_0(U) f_0 + A_1(U) f_1 + A_2(U) f_2.$$

10.4 REMAINDER

Since the formula of Lagrange is but another way of expressing the unique interpolating polynomial of degree $\leq n$ for a function $f(x)$ with collocation points $x_0, x_1, x_2, \ldots, x_n$, Eq. (8.10) for the remainder is valid.

If the collocation points are equally spaced at $x_i = x_0 + ih$, then

$$\Pi(x) = \Pi(u) h^{n+1}$$

and hence

> Remainder in Polynomial Interpolation (Cauchy form)—
> Equally Spaced Collocation Points:
>
> *There exists at least one number ξ such that*
>
> $$R_{n+1}(x_0 + uh) = \binom{u}{n+1} h^{n+1} f^{n+1}(\xi) \qquad (10.6)$$
>
> *where*
>
> $$x_0 < \xi < x_n$$
>
> *if*
>
> $$x_0 < x < x_n.$$

EXAMPLE 10.1. We suppose sin x known for x any integral multiple of 5° and use Lagrange's five-point formula to calculate sin 21°48′.

The nearest known value is sin 20°, so we take $X_0 = 20°$. Then $U = 0.36$ and the needed data and Lagrangian coefficients are:

i	X_i	$\sin X_i$	A_i
-2	10	0.173 648	0.021 411 84
-1	15	0.258 819	-0.148 623 36
0	20	0.342 020	0.842 199 04
1	25	0.422 618	0.315 824 64
2	30	0.500 000	-0.030 812 16

Then

$$\sum_{i=-2}^{2} A_i \sin X_i = 0.371\ 368.$$

The remainder is

$$\binom{2.36}{5} \left(\frac{5\pi}{180}\right)^5 \cos \xi$$

which is in absolute value less than 2×10^{-7}. The error due to rounding of given data cannot exceed 7×10^{-7} (see Exercise 10.3), so that total error is in absolute value $< 9 \times 10^{-7}$. As a matter of fact, the interpolated value is correct to six places of decimals.

10.5 DIVERGENCE

In Chap. 7 we proved the fundamental theorem of Weierstrass to the effect that any continuous function can be approximated on any finite interval by a polynomial with any specified nonzero error. Although the proof we presented consisted of actually constructing a sequence of polynomials converging to the given function, the polynomials used are not well adapted to actual numerical work. The various methods of constructing interpolating polynomials are, on the other hand, of appealing simplicity and they are easily evaluated, especially if the collocation points are equally spaced. Unfortunately, it is not always possible to obtain a desirable agreement between a given function and its interpolating polynomial if equally spaced collocation points are used. The classical example of C. Runge [2,3] is

$$f(x) = \frac{1}{1 + x^2}, \qquad -5 \leq x \leq 5.$$

This function is indeed simple. It possesses derivatives of all orders. However, if $I_n(x)$ denotes the interpolating polynomial of degree $\leq n$ for $f(x)$ having $n + 1$ equally spaced collocation points $-5 = x_0 < x_1 < x_2 < \cdots < x_n = 5$, a simple calculation using tables of Lagrangian coefficients gives the following:

n	$I_n(4.5)$
2	0.2212
4	−0.2891
6	0.9401
8	−0.9596
10	1.5790

But $f(4.5) = 0.0471$. The error appears to increase with n and such is indeed the case. Runge showed that if $|x| > 3.63$, the sequence $\{I_n(x)\}$ is not bounded.

This example is included to emphasize the necessity of examining the remainder term. It is intended as a warning against the indiscriminate use of interpolating formulas.

There is an extensive literature on the subject of convergence of sequences of interpolating polynomials. E. Feldheim [4] has written a beautiful summary of the literature up to 1939. Among the curious theorems discussed are the following:

BERNSTEIN'S THEOREM. Corresponding to any sequence of sets of collocation points there exists a function $f(x)$, continuous for $-1 \leq x \leq 1$, such that the corresponding sequence of interpolating polynomials diverges for at least one number ξ where $-1 \leq \xi \leq 1$.

KRYLOFF'S THEOREM. If the zeros of the Čebyšev polynomials are used as a sequence of sets of collocation points and if $f(x)$ can be expressed in the form

$$f(x) = \int_a^x \phi(u) \, du + C, \qquad -1 \leq x \leq 1,$$

where $\phi(u)$ is integrable Riemann, then the corresponding sequence of interpolating polynomials converges to $f(x)$ for all x in the interval $-1 \leq x \leq 1$.

EXERCISES

1. Using values of sin x for x at integral multiples of $5°$ calculate sin $37°30'$ using Lagrange's three-, four-, and five-point formulas. In each case calculate a bound for the remainder. Compare interpolated values with table value.

2. Show that in any interpolation the sum of the Lagrangian coefficients must (except for rounding) total 1. That is, $\sum_{i=0}^{n} \lambda_i(u) = 1$ for any choice of n and u.

3. Show that the contribution to the error of the interpolated value due to rounding of given ordinates is not greater than $\sum_{i=0}^{n} |\lambda_i(u)|$ times the maximum possible rounding error of the given ordinates.

4. What can you say about the contribution to the error of the interpolated value due to rounding of the Lagrangian coefficients $\lambda_i(u)$?

REFERENCES

1. National Bureau of Standards. *Tables of Lagrangian Interpolation Coefficients.* New York: Columbia U.P., 1944.

2. C. Runge. "Ueber empirische Funktionen und die Interpolation zwischen äquidistanten Ordinaten," *Angew. Math. Phys.* **46:** 224–243 (1901).

3. J. F. Steffenson. *Interpolation.* New York: Chelsea, 1927, 1950.

4. E. Feldheim. *Théorie de la convergence des procédés d'interpolation et de quadrature mécanique.* Paris: Gauthier-Villars, 1939.

11

THE Π-FACTOR

11.1 INTRODUCTION

We have seen (Sec. 8.5) that if $I_n(x)$ is the interpolating polynomial (of degree $\leq n$) for a function $f(x)$ with $n + 1$ distinct collocation points $x_0, x_1, \ldots, x_n$, then the remainder $R_{n+1}(x) = f(x) - I_n(x)$ is such that there exists at least one number ξ for which

$$R_{n+1}(x) = (x - x_0)(x - x_1) \cdots (x - x_n) \frac{f^{(n+1)}(\xi)}{(n + 1)!},$$

where

$$\min(x, x_0, \ldots, x_n) < \xi < \max(x, x_0, \ldots, x_n).$$

We shall refer to the factor $(x - x_0)(x - x_1) \cdots (x - x_n)$ in the remainder as the Π-factor and write

$$\Pi(x) = (x - x_0)(x - x_1) \cdots (x - x_n). \tag{11.1}$$

To study the Π-factor we shall suppose that

$$x_0 < x_1 < x_2 < \cdots < x_n.$$

If the interpolating polynomial is to be used to approximate the function $f(x)$ for $x_0 \leq x \leq x_n$ it is desirable to choose the numbers $x_0, x_1, \ldots, x_n$ so that the

$$\max_{x_0 \leq x \leq x_n} |\Pi(x)|$$

85

is a minimum. The solution to this problem was given by P. L. Čebyšev (1821–1894) and involves the polynomials named after him. These were introduced in Chap. 6. We consider two examples. One of these is a Π-factor of degree 6, the other of degree 7. In each case we show graphs

Figure 11.1

Two graphs of

$$\Pi(x) = (x - x_0)(x - x_1)(x - x_2)(x - x_3)(x - x_4)(x - x_5).$$

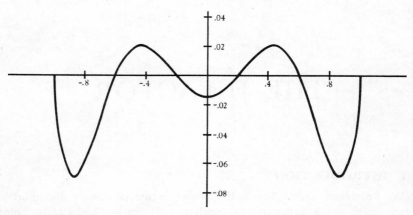

I. Zeros equally spaced:

$$x_i = \pm 0.2, \ \pm 0.6, \ \pm 1.0.$$

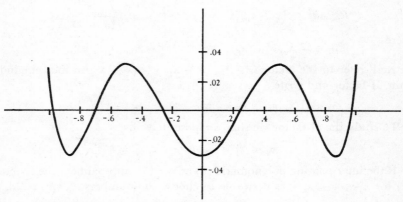

II. Zeros unequally spaced at Čebyšev abscissae:

$$x_i = \cos (2i + 1) \frac{\pi}{12}, \qquad i = 0, 1, \ldots, 5.$$

(Figs. 11.1 and 11.2) for x_i equally spaced in the interval $(-1, 1)$ and those placed at the so-called Čebyšev abscissae. In the latter cases one will observe that the maximum ordinates are the same and in each case less than the biggest maximum ordinate of the Π-factor of the same degree with equally spaced zeros.

Figure 11.2

Two graphs of

$$\Pi(x) = (x - x_0)(x - x_1)(x - x_2)(x - x_3)(x - x_4)(x - x_5)(x - x_6).$$

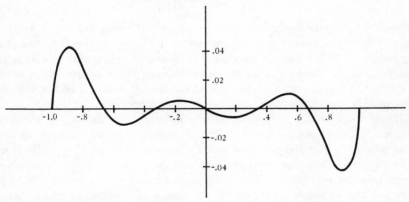

I. Zeros equally spaced:

$$x_i = 0, \pm\tfrac{1}{3}, \pm\tfrac{2}{3}, \pm 1.$$

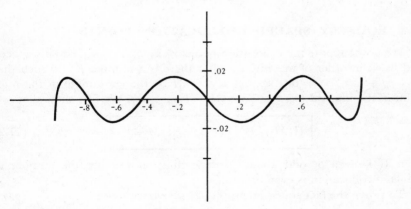

II. Zeros unequally spaced at Čebyšev abscissae:

$$x_i = \cos (2i + 1)\frac{\pi}{12}, \qquad i = 0, 1, 2, \ldots, 6.$$

11.2 THE ČEBYŠEV ABSCISSAE

Recall (Sec. 6.4) that the zeros of $T_{n+1}(x)$, the Čebyšev polynomial of the first kind of degree $n + 1$, are

$$x_i = \cos \frac{2i + 1}{n + 1} \frac{\pi}{2}, \qquad i = 0, 1, 2, \ldots, n$$

with $-1 < x_i < 1$. Since these are all real, $T_{n+1}(x)$ can be written as a product of $n + 1$ real linear factors. Thus

$$T_{n+1}(x) = 2^n \Pi(x).$$

Hence an interpolating polynomial (of degree n) using the $n + 1$ zeros of $T_{n+1}(x)$ for collocation points would have $2^{-n} T_{n+1}(x)$ as the Π-factor of its remainder. Čebyšev has shown that this choice of collocation points is the best possible in the sense that the maximum of the absolute value of the Π-factor is a minimum. This is a restatement of Property 8 of the Čebyšev polynomials (Sec. 6.4).

Thus if one wishes to approximate a function $f(x)$ for $-1 \leq x \leq 1$ by an interpolating polynomial $I_n(x)$ (of degree $\leq n$) it would seem to be a good idea to choose for points of collocation the zeros of $T_{n+1}(x)$. It is not to be supposed, however, that the resulting polynomial $I_n(x)$ is a minimax approximation to $f(x)$ as defined in Sec. 12.4. For the factor $f^{(n+1)}(\xi)/(n + 1)!$ also depends on x and on the choice of collocation points. So, of course, the choice which minimizes the maximum absolute value of the Π-factor may not minimize the maximum absolute value of the remainder.

11.3 EQUALLY SPACED COLLOCATION POINTS

We now suppose the collocation points $x_0, x_1, x_2, \ldots, x_n$, equally spaced and listed in order of magnitude. Thus there is a number $h > 0$ such that $x_i = x_0 + ih$, $i = 0, 1, 2, \ldots, n$. Let M be the coördinate of the midpoint of the interval (x_0, x_n). Thus $M = \frac{1}{2}(x_0 + x_n)$. We first show that

$$\boxed{\Pi(M + t) = (-1)^{n+1} \Pi(M - t)} \tag{11.2}$$

Thus Π is even or odd about M depending on whether the number of points of collocation is even or odd.

To prove the fact stated as Eq. (11.2) above we write

$$\Pi(M + t) = (M + t - x_0)(M + t - x_1) \cdots (M + t - x_n)$$

and

$$\Pi(M - t) = (M - t - x_0)(M - t - x_1) \cdots (M - t - x_n).$$

Note that
$$x_i = x_0 + ih = x_n - (n - i)h = 2M - x_{n-i}.$$
Hence
$$M + t - x_i = -(M - t - x_{n-i}), \qquad i = 0, 1, \ldots, n.$$
Thus the factors of $\Pi(M + t)$ taken in reverse order are those of $\Pi(M - t)$ taken in natural order with each multiplied by -1.

We now show that

$$
\boxed{
\begin{aligned}
|\Pi(x)| &> |\Pi(x + h)| \\
x_{-1} &< x < x + h < M \\
x &\neq x_i, \qquad i = 0, 1, 2, \ldots, n.
\end{aligned}
}
\tag{11.3}
$$

For $x \neq x_i$, let $x = x_{-1} + uh$. Then $0 < u < (n + 1)/2$ and

$$
\left| \frac{\Pi(x + h)}{\Pi(x)} \right| = \left| \frac{u(u - 1)(u - 2) \cdots (u - n)}{(u - 1)(u - 2) \cdots (u - n)(u - n - 1)} \right|
$$

$$
= \left| \frac{u}{u - n - 1} \right| = \left| \frac{u}{n + 1 - u} \right| < 1.
$$

11.4 POLYNOMIAL INTERPOLATION

The properties of the Π-factor discussed in the preceding section show that for equally spaced collocation points the values of $|\Pi(x)|$ are smallest for x near the middle of the smallest interval (a, b) containing all the collocation points. Thus lacking any special information about $f^{(n+1)}(\xi)$ we should arrange, if possible, to use an interpolation formula only for such values. It is for this reason that tables of interpolation coefficients usually presuppose x_0 to be the middle or left of middle collocation point. The central difference interpolation formulas are set up to facilitate interpolation near the middle of the interval (a, b).

EXERCISES

1. Sketch the graphs of $\Pi(x) = (x - x_0)(x - x_1)(x - x_2)$ and $\Pi(x) = (x - x_0)(x - x_1)(x - x_2)(x - x_3)$ for x_i spaced at intervals of h.

2. Remainder in three-point interpolation: Let $I_2(x)$ be the interpolating polynomial for a function $f(x)$ with collocation points $x_0, x_0 \pm h$. Show that

$$|R_3(x)| = |f(x) - I_2(x)| \leq \frac{h^3}{16} M_3,$$

for $|x - x_0| \leq h/2$, where M_3 is an upper bound for $f'''(x)$ on the interval $[x_0 - h, x_0 + h]$. Find corresponding bound for remainder of quadratic Taylor approximation to $f(x)$ on this same interval.

3. Use result of preceding exercise to determine the largest value of h for which $|R_3(x)| \leq 5 \times 10^{-6}$ for $|x - x_0| \leq h/2$ given $f(x) = \ln x$, $x_0 = 3$.

4. Remainder in four-point interpolation: Show that the cubic interpolating polynomial for $f(x)$ with equally spaced collocation points x_{-1}, x_0, x_1, x_2 has a remainder $R_4(x)$ such that

where
$$|R_4(x)|_{x_0 < x < x_1} \leq \tfrac{3}{128} h^4 M_4$$
$$\max_{x_{-1} < \xi < x_2} |f^{(4)}(\xi)| \leq M_4.$$

5. Remainder in five-point interpolation: Show that the quartic interpolating polynomial for $f(x)$ with equally spaced collocation points x_{-2}, x_{-1}, x_0, x_1, x_2 has a remainder $R_5(x)$ for which

where
$$|R_5^{(x)}|_{|x-x| \leq h/2_0} \leq \tfrac{3}{256} h^5 M_5$$
$$\max_{x_{-2} < \xi < x_2} |f^{(5)}(\xi)| \leq M_5$$

6. Show that the following function does not change sign:
$$J_n(x) = \int_{x_\alpha}^x \Pi_n(w)\, dw, \qquad x_\alpha \leq x \leq x_{n-\alpha},$$
$\alpha = -1, 0, 1; n = 2, 4, 6, \ldots;$ where
$$\Pi_n(w) = (w - x_0)(w - x_1) \cdots (w - x_n)$$
and $x_i = x_0 + ih$.

HINT: Use Eqs. (11.2) and (11.3).

It can be shown, but not so easily, that this integral does not change sign for n odd. (See [8] of Chap. 15.)

7. Show that the integrals
$$\int_\alpha^{n-\alpha-1} \Pi_n(u)\, du \qquad \text{and} \qquad \int_{n-\alpha-1}^{n-\alpha} \Pi_n(u)\, du$$
are of the same sign for n any odd integer,
$$\alpha = 0, \pm 1 \quad \text{and} \quad \Pi_n(u) = u(u - 1)(u - 2) \cdots (u - n).$$

HINT: Show by integration by parts that
$$-\int_\alpha^{n-\alpha-1} J_{n-1}(u)\, du = \int_\alpha^{n-\alpha-1} \Pi_n(u)\, du$$
and then determine signs from Eqs. (11.2) and (11.3).

12

EVALUATION OF

FUNCTIONS

12.1 INTRODUCTION

Although the Weierstrass polynomial approximation theorem assures the existence of excellent polynomial approximations for all continuous functions, neither of the proofs considered gave a practical means for producing these approximations. The approximations given by Taylor polynomials and interpolating polynomials can be obtained in routine fashion, but there usually exist polynomial approximations of the same degree which are in some sense better. We shall consider those polynomial approximations that are best in the least-squares sense and those that minimize the maximum absolute deviation. These are related to the polynomials of Legendre and Čebyšev.

The ever-increasing availability of high-speed digital computers has revived interest in polynomial approximations. Inasmuch as table look up on punched cards or tape is a time-consuming process, it is usually preferable to store the coefficients of a polynomial which adequately approximates a given function and then let the machine evaluate that polynomial as needed.

Our discussion is limited to approximation of functions by polynomials. We shall not consider such important alternatives as trigonometric polynomials or rational functions. Nor shall we consider curve-fitting problems— that is, "best-fitting" curves—to *finite* sets of points.

12.2 LEAST-SQUARES POLYNOMIAL APPROXIMATIONS

If $f(x)$ is any function defined on a closed interval $[a, b]$ and $S_n(x)$ an approximating polynomial of degree $\leq n$ then

$$\rho = \int_a^b [f(x) - S_n(x)]^2 \, dx \tag{12.1}$$

is a measure of how well $S_n(x)$ approximates $f(x)$ on $[a, b]$ provided, of course, that this integral exists. For this it is sufficient to suppose that $f(x)$ and $[f(x)]^2$ are integrable on the interval $[a, b]$. For such a given function $f(x)$ there is thus associated with every polynomial $S_n(x)$ of degree $\leq n$ a number ρ. The set of all such numbers will be shown to contain a minimum and the polynomial giving rise to this minimum to be unique. It is called the *least-squares polynomial approximation to* $f(x)$ *on* $[a, b]$. Its coefficients are expressible in terms of integrals involving $f(x)$ and Legendre polynomials.

12.3 LEGENDRE EXPANSIONS

The Legendre polynomials form a basic set and hence any polynomial $f_n(x)$ of degree n can be uniquely expressed as a linear combination of Legendre polynomials of degrees $\leq n$. Thus

$$f_n(x) = \sum_{k=0}^{n} A_k P_k(x) \tag{12.2}$$

where $P_k(x)$ is the Legendre polynomial of degree k. The orthogonality property of the Leg polendreynomials can be used to obtain formulas for the coefficients in this expansion. Thus

$$\int_{-1}^{1} f_n(x) P_j(x) \, dx = \sum_{k=0}^{n} A_k \int_{-1}^{1} P_j(x) P_k(x) \, dx = A_j \frac{2}{2j+1}$$

and hence

$$A_k = \frac{2k+1}{2} \int_{-1}^{1} f_n(x) P_k(x) \, dx. \tag{12.3}$$

This suggests approximating an integrable function $f(x)$ by a polynomial $S_n(x)$ of degree $\leq n$ of the form

$$S_n(x) = \sum_{k=0}^{n} a_k P_k(x)$$

where

$$a_k = \frac{2k+1}{2} \int_{-1}^{1} f(x) P_k(x) \, dx.$$

We now prove that the polynomial $S_n(x)$ so obtained is the least-squares polynomial approximation of degree $\leq n$ to $f(x)$ on the interval $[-1, 1]$. For let

$$t_n(x) = \sum_{k=0}^{n} \alpha_k P_k(x)$$

be an arbitrary polynomial of degree $\leq n$ not identical with $S_n(x)$ and define

$$r_n(x) = f(x) - S_n(x),$$

and

$$\rho_n(x) = t_n(x) - S_n(x).$$

Since

$$\int_{-1}^{1} f(x) P_k(x) \, dx = \frac{2}{2k+1} a_k = \int_{-1}^{1} S_n(x) P_k(x) \, dx,$$

it follows that

$$\int_{-1}^{1} r_n(x) P_k(x) \, dx = 0, \qquad 0 \leq k \leq n.$$

But $\rho_n(x)$ is a linear combination of the $P_k(x)$, $k \leq n$, and hence

$$\int_{-1}^{1} r_n(x) \rho_n(x) \, dx = 0.$$

Since $S_n(x)$ and $t_n(x)$ are not identical polynomials

$$\int_{-1}^{1} [\rho_n(x)]^2 \, dx > 0.$$

From these relations it follows that

$$\int_{-1}^{1} [f(x) - t_n(x)]^2 \, dx = \int_{-1}^{1} [r_n(x) - \rho_n(x)]^2 \, dx$$

$$= \int_{-1}^{1} [r_n(x)]^2 \, dx - 2 \int_{-1}^{1} r_n(x) \rho_n(x) \, dx + \int_{-1}^{1} [\rho_n(x)]^2 \, dx$$

$$= \int_{-1}^{1} [f(x) - S_n(x)]^2 \, dx + \int_{-1}^{1} [\rho_n(x)]^2 \, dx$$

$$> \int_{-1}^{1} [f(x) - S_n(x)]^2 \, dx.$$

We summarize these results in a

THEOREM.   If $f(x)$ and $[f(x)]^2$ are integrable on the interval $[-1, 1]$ and

$$S_n(x) = \sum_{k=0}^{n} a_k P_k(x)$$

where $P_k(x)$ is the Legendre polynomial of degree k and

$$a_k = \frac{2k+1}{2} \int_{-1}^{1} f(x) P_k(x) \, dx$$

then

$$\int_{-1}^{1} [f(x) - S_n(x)]^2 \, dx < \int_{-1}^{1} [f(x) - t_n(x)]^2 \, dx$$

where $t_n(x)$ is an arbitrary polynomial of degree $\leq n$ not identical with $S_n(x)$.

12.4 MINIMAX POLYNOMIAL APPROXIMATIONS

If $f(x)$ is any continuous real function defined on a closed interval $[a, b]$ and $P_n(x)$ an approximating polynomial of degree $\leq n$ with real coefficients, then

$$E_n(x) = f(x) - P_n(x)$$

is the error at x of the approximation. The least upper bound ρ of $|E_n(x)|$, $a \leq x \leq b$, is a measure of how well $P_n(x)$ approximates $f(x)$ on $[a, b]$. Thus with each polynomial of degree $\leq n$ there is associated a number ρ. The set of all such numbers has been shown to contain a minimum and the polynomial giving rise to this minimum to be unique [1]. We shall call it the *minimax* polynomial approximation of degree $\leq n$ to $f(x)$ on $[a, b]$. Briefly it is that polynomial $M_n(x)$ of degree $\leq n$ among the set of all polynomials of degree $\leq n$ such that

$$\max_{a \leq x \leq b} |f(x) - M_n(x)| \qquad (12.4)$$

is a minimum. This minimax approximation is thus a "best" approximation in a certain sense. Čebyšev introduced the idea. Although some minimax polynomial approximations have been obtained [2] the methods used were not routine. The known algorithms for producing such approximations are far from simple [7]. The Čebyšev polynomials are useful in this connection. Usually a compromise must be made between the conflicting desires of obtaining a true minimax approximation and simplicity. In Sec. 11.2 we discussed the desirability of using the Čebyšev abscissae for collocation points for interpolating polynomials. In this chapter we describe a method for obtaining such an interpolating polynomial as well as a method based upon expansions of Taylor polynomials in terms of Čebyšev polynomials. For some functions these provide simple routines for obtaining approximate minimax approximations.

12.5 ČEBYŠEV INTERPOLATION

We saw in Chap. 11 the desirability of using the zeros of $T_{n+1}(x)$ as collocation points for an interpolating polynomial of degree $\leq n$ for a function $f(x)$ defined on the interval $[-1, 1]$. Since any polynomial of degree $\leq n$ can be written as a linear combination of Čebyšev polynomials of degrees $\leq n$, we may write $f(x)$ as the sum of this interpolating polynomial and a remainder term as follows:

$$f(x) = \sum_{r=0}^{n} A_r T_r(x) + \frac{T_{n+1}(x)}{2^n (n+1)!} f^{(n+1)}(\xi), \qquad -1 < \xi < 1. \quad (12.5)$$

While the coefficients A_r could be obtained from the formula of Lagrange it is simpler to make use of the finite orthogonal property of the Čebyšev polynomials (Sec. 6.4).

Let

$$P_n(x) = \sum_{s=0}^{n} A_s T_s(x)$$

be the unique polynomial of degree $\leq n$ such that

$$P_n(x_i) = f(x_i)$$

for

$$x_i = \cos \frac{2i + 1}{n + 1} \frac{\pi}{2}, \qquad i = 0, 1, 2, \ldots, n.$$

Then

$$\sum_{i=0}^{n} P_n(x_i) T_r(x_i) = \sum_{i=0}^{n} \sum_{s=0}^{n} A_s T_r(x_i) T_s(x_i)$$

$$= \sum_{s=0}^{n} A_s \sum_{i=0}^{n} T_r(x_i) T_s(x_i)$$

$$= \begin{cases} (n+1) A_0, & r = 0 \\ \dfrac{n+1}{2} A_r, & 1 \leq r \leq n. \end{cases}$$

Thus

$$A_0 = \frac{1}{n+1} \sum_{i=0}^{n} f(x_i) \qquad\qquad (12.6)$$

$$A_r = \frac{2}{n+1} \sum_{i=0}^{n} f(x_i) T_r(x_i), \qquad 1 \leq r \leq n.$$

Tables of values of the x_i and $T_r(x_i)$ are useful in this connection. We give an example of such a table:

Table 12.1

TABLE OF $T_r(x_i)$ **FOR** $n = 5$

i	$x_i = T_1(x_i)$	$T_2(x_i)$	$T_3(x_i)$	$T_4(x_i)$	$T_5(x_i)$
0	0.965 93	0.866 03	0.707 11	0.5	0.258 82
1	0.707 11	0	−0.707 11	−1	−0.707 11
2	0.258 82	−0.866 03	−0.707 11	0.5	0.965 93
3	−0.258 82	−0.866 03	0.707 11	0.5	−0.965 93
4	−0.707 11	0	0.707 11	−1	0.707 11
5	−0.965 93	0.866 03	−0.707 11	0.5	−0.258 82

12.6   MINIMAX POLYNOMIAL APPROXIMATIONS OF POLYNOMIALS

We have noted (Property 8, Sec. 6.4) that

$$\max_{-1 \le x \le 1} |2^{1-n} T_n(x)| \le \max_{-1 \le x \le 1} |P_n(x)|$$

where $T_n(x)$ is the Čebyšev polynomial of the first kind of degree n and $P_n(x)$ is any polynomial of degree $\le n$ having leading coefficient unity. Suppose now that $M_{n-1}(x)$ is the unique minimax polynomial approximation of degree $\le n - 1$ to x^n on the interval $[-1, 1]$. Then $x^n - M_{n-1}(x)$ is a polynomial of degree n having leading coefficient unity and whose maximum absolute value is as small as possible. It can therefore only be $2^{1-n} T_n(x)$. Thus

$$M_{n-1}(x) = x^n - 2^{1-n} T_n(x)$$

is the minimax polynomial approximation of degree $\le n - 1$ to x^n on the interval $[-1, 1]$. Note that $M_{n-1}(x)$ is actually of degree $n - 2$.

EXAMPLE 12.1. Since

$$x^6 = 2^{-5}(10 T_0 + 15 T_2 + 6 T_4 + T_6)$$

then

$$M_5(x) = 2^{-5}(10 T_0 + 15 T_2 + 6 T_4)$$
$$= 2^{-5}(1 - 18x^2 + 48x^4)$$

is minimax approximation of degree ≤ 5 to x^6 on the interval $[-1, 1]$. Furthermore,

$$\max_{-1 \le x \le 1} |x^6 - M_5(x)| = 2^{-5}$$

By essentially the same argument it can be proven that if $f_n(x)$ is any polynomial of degree n having leading coefficient a_n, then its minimax polynomial approximation of degree $\leq n - 1$ on interval $[-1, 1]$ is

$$f_n(x) - a_n 2^{1-n} T_n(x).$$

The nth degree polynomial $f_n(x)$ has an unique expansion of the form $\sum_{k=0}^{n} A_k T_k(x)$ in terms of Čebyšev polynomials (Chap. 6). Table 6.4 provides a useful means of obtaining such expansions. Since $A_n = a_n 2^{1-n}$ it follows that $\sum_{k=0}^{n-1} A_k T_k(x)$ is the minimax approximation of degree $\leq n - 1$ to $f_n(x)$ on the interval $[-1, 1]$. Furthermore, the sequence of polynomials

$$S_\lambda(x) = \sum_{k=0}^{\lambda} A_k T_k(x), \qquad \lambda = 0, 1, 2, \ldots, n$$

is such that $S_\lambda(x)$ is the minimax polynomial approximation of degree $\leq \lambda$ to $S_{\lambda+1}(x)$. We summarize this in a

THEOREM. *Any polynomial $f_n(x)$ of degree n is uniquely expressible as a linear combination of Čebyšev polynomials of the first kind. Thus*

$$f_n(x) = \sum_{k=0}^{n} A_k T_k(x).$$

Each initial segment

$$S_\lambda(x) = \sum_{k=0}^{\lambda} A_k T_k(x), \qquad \lambda = 0, 1, 2, \ldots, n - 1$$

of this expansion is the minimax approximation of degree $\leq \lambda$ to the "next" segment $S_{\lambda+1}(x)$ on the interval $[-1, 1]$. In particular $S_{n-1}(x)$ is the minimax approximation of degree $\leq n - 1$ to $f_n(x)$.

Thus if we drop the last term of the expansion of a polynomial $f_n(x)$ of degree n in a series of Čebyšev polynomials we obtain the minimax polynomial approximation to $f_n(x)$ of degree $\leq n - 1$. It is known that by dropping the last $\nu \geq 2$ terms of this expansion we do not necessarily obtain the minimax polynomial approximation to $f_n(x)$ of degree $\leq n - \nu$. See Exercise 12.2. However, since $\max_{-1 \leq x \leq 1} |T_k(x)| = 1$, it follows that

$$\max_{-1 \leq x \leq 1} |f_n(x) - S_\lambda(x)| \leq |A_{\lambda+1}| + \cdots + |A_n|.$$

This may be used to determine number of terms to retain to assure an approximation of less than specified maximum error.

12.7 ECONOMIZATION OF POWER SERIES

Although many functions can be represented by power series, the number of terms needed to obtain a specified accuracy is sometimes prohibitive. But if the degree of the Taylor polynomial $t_n(x)$ which adequately represents a function $f(x)$ on the interval $[-1, 1]$ is not excessive, it may be practical to expand $t_n(x)$ in a Čebyšev series and truncate to obtain an adequate approximation of lower degree. Thus if

$$|f(x) - t_n(x)| < \epsilon, \qquad -1 \leq x \leq 1,$$

$$S_\lambda(x) = \sum_{k=0}^{\lambda} A_k T_k(x)$$

and

$$S_n(x) = t_n(x),$$

then

$$|f(x) - S_\lambda(x)| \leq \epsilon + |A_{\lambda+1}| + \cdots + |A_n|, \qquad -1 \leq x \leq 1.$$

This process has been termed "telescoping of power series by rearrangement" and "economization of power series" by Lanczos [3,4].

An example will clarify the method. In order to approximate $\sin \pi x$ on the interval $[-1, 1]$ by a Taylor polynomial with a guarantee of an error of not more than 0.02 we must use the ninth degree polynomial

$$\pi x - \frac{(\pi x)^3}{3!} + \frac{(\pi x)^5}{5!} - \frac{(\pi x)^7}{7!} + \frac{(\pi x)^9}{9!}. \tag{12.7}$$

Table 6.4 may be used to expand this in terms of Čebyšev polynomials of the first kind:

$$0.5724\,T_1(x) - 0.6647\,T_3(x) + 0.1054\,T_5(x)$$
$$- 0.0065\,T_7(x) + 0.0003\,T_9(x). \tag{12.8}$$

The error of (12.7) is actually less than 0.0074 and hence the fifth degree polynomial

$$0.572\,T_1(x) - 0.665\,T_3(x) + 0.105\,T_5(x) \tag{12.9}$$

approximates $\sin \pi x$ on the interval $[-1, 1]$ with a guarantee of an error of less than 0.016. Thus within the stated limits of accuracy we have replaced a ninth degree polynomial by another of the fifth degree.

More dramatic examples of the power of the method have been given by Lanczos [4].

Functions defined as solutions of linear differential equations can be approximated by a method related to the above but which makes use of recurrence relations defining the coefficients of its power series solution [4,5,6].

EXERCISES

1. Let

$$I(\alpha_0, \alpha_1, \ldots, \alpha_n) = \int_{-1}^{1} [f(x) - f_n(x)]^2 \, dx$$

where

$$f_n(x) = \sum_{k=0}^{n} \alpha_k P_k(x)$$

and $P_k(x)$ is the Legendre polynomial of degree k. By forming derivatives of I with respect to the α_k show that $\alpha_k = a_k$, $k = 0, 1, 2, \ldots, n$ (Sec. 12.3), are necessary conditions for a minimum. Do you know enough multivariate calculus to establish their sufficiency?

2. Show that the minimax approximations to $f(x) = 2x^2 + x$ of degrees 1 and 0 are $x + 1$ and $\frac{23}{16}$. Show also that successive truncations of the expansion of $f(x)$ in terms of Čebyšev polynomials yield $x + 1$ (minimax, of course) and 1 (not minimax).

3. Make a table similar to Table 12.1 but for $n = 4$.

4. Obtain the following fifth degree polynomial approximations for $\sin \pi x/2$, $-1 \leq x \leq 1$, with all coefficients rounded to five places of decimals: (*a*) Taylor polynomial; (*b*) interpolating polynomial using equally spaced collocation points including ± 1; (*c*) Čebyšev interpolation (that is, interpolating polynomial using zeros of $T_6(x)$ for collocation points; (*d*) polynomial obtained by economization of power series.

5. Show that there exists a unique linear transformation

$$x = A + Bt$$

which carries a specified interval $a \leq x \leq b$ into a specified interval $c \leq t \leq d$. In particular, note that

$$x = a + (b - a)t$$

carries the interval $a \leq x \leq b$ into $0 \leq t \leq 1$ and

$$x = \frac{a}{2}(1 - t) + \frac{b}{2}(1 + t)$$

carries the interval $a \leq x \leq b$ into $-1 \leq t \leq 1$.

Note that under a linear transformation a polynomial in x is transformed into a polynomial in t of the *same* degree.

REFERENCES

1. C. J. de la Vallée Poussin. *Leçons sur l'approximation des fonctions d'une variable réelle.* Paris: Gauthier-Villars, 1919.

2. C. Hastings. *Approximations for Digital Computers.* Princeton: Princeton U.P. 1955.

3. C. Lanczos. *Applied Analysis.* Englewood Cliffs: Prentice-Hall, 1956.

4. ————. "Trigonometric interpolation of empirical and analytical functions," *J. Math. Phys.* **17:** 123–199 (1938).

5. National Bureau of Standards. *Tables of Chebyshev Polynomials $S_n(x)$ and $C_n(x)$.* Washington D.C.: U.S. Government Printing Office, 1952.

6. Y. L. Luke. "Remarks on The τ-Method For the Solution of Linear Differential Equations with Rational Coefficients," *J. Soc. Indust. Appl. Math.* **3:** 179–191 (1955).

7. F. D. Murnaghan, and J. W. Wrench. "The approximation of differentiable functions by polynomials," U.S. Navy, David Taylor Model Basin, Applied Mathematics Laboratory, *Research and Development Report* 1175 (1958).

$$I3$$

NUMERICAL
DIFFERENTIATION—
METHOD OF LAGRANGE

13.1 DERIVATION

We have seen that if $f(x)$ is a function having a derivative of order $n + 1$ then there exists at least one number ξ for which

$$f(x) = p(x) + \Pi(x) \frac{f^{(n+1)}(\xi)}{(n+1)!},$$

where $p(x)$ is the unique polynomial of degree n or less such that

$$f(x_i) = p(x_i), \qquad i = 0, 1, 2, \ldots, n$$

and

$$\Pi(x) = (x - x_0)(x - x_1) \cdots (x - x_n).$$

Hence

$$f'(x) = p'(x) + \Pi'(x) \frac{f^{(n+1)}(\xi)}{(n+1)!} + \Pi(x) \frac{d}{dx} \frac{f^{(n+1)}(\xi)}{(n+1)!}. \qquad (13.1)$$

Since the nature of the dependence of ξ on x is not known, we can evaluate the third term on the right only in case $x = x_i$.* At any of these collocation points $f'(x)$ equals $p'(x)$ plus a remainder term which can be expressed in terms of $f^{(n+1)}(\xi)$.

We now carry out the details of the calculation of $p'(x)$ and $\Pi'(x)$ in case the x_i are equally spaced with $x_i = x_0 + ih$. To facilitate the calculation we again introduce functions of the unitized variable $u = (x - x_0)/h$. Let

$$\Pi(u) = u(u-1)(u-2)\cdots(u-n),$$

$$\Pi_{(i)}(u) = \frac{\Pi(u)}{u-i}, \qquad \Pi_{(ij)}(u) = \frac{\Pi(u)}{(u-i)(u-j)}, \qquad i \neq j.$$

$$\lambda_i(u) = \frac{\Pi_{(i)}(u)}{\Pi_{(i)}(i)}.$$

Thus

$$\lambda_i(j) = \delta_{ij} = \begin{cases} 0, & i \neq j \\ 1, & i = j \end{cases}$$

and, according to the polynomial interpolation formula of Lagrange,

$$p(x_0 + uh) = \sum_{i=0}^{n} \lambda_i(u) f_i,$$

where $f_i = f(x_i)$.

We now prepare to calculate

$$\frac{d}{dx} p(x) \bigg]_{x=x_k} = p'_k.$$

Throughout, *primes will be used to designate derivatives with respect to x—irrespective of what the argument may be.* Note that

$$\Pi'_{(i)}(u) = \frac{1}{h} \sum_{j=0}^{n} \Pi_{(ij)}(u), \qquad j \neq i.$$

Hence

$$\Pi'_{(i)}(k) = \begin{cases} \dfrac{1}{h} \Pi_{(ik)}(k), & k \neq i \\[2em] \dfrac{1}{h} \displaystyle\sum_{\substack{j=0 \\ j \neq k}}^{n} \Pi_{(kj)}(k), & k = i \end{cases}$$

* We could, of course, avoid this difficulty by using Newton's form of the remainder in polynomial interpolation. See, for example, Exercise 13.2.

and therefore

$$\lambda'_{(i)}(k) = \begin{cases} \dfrac{1}{h} \dfrac{\Pi_{(ik)}(k)}{\Pi_{(i)}(i)}, & k \neq i \\[3mm] \dfrac{1}{h} \displaystyle\sum_{\substack{j=0 \\ j \neq k}}^{n} \dfrac{1}{k-j}, & k = i. \end{cases}$$

Hence

$$p'_k = \frac{1}{h}\left\{ \sum_{\substack{i=0 \\ i \neq k}}^{n} f_i \frac{\Pi_{(ik)}(k)}{\Pi_{(i)}(i)} + f_k \sum_{\substack{j=0 \\ j \neq k}}^{n} \frac{1}{k-j} \right\}. \tag{13.2}$$

13.2 AUXILIARY TABLES

Brief tables of the functions occurring in the coefficients of the f_i are listed below.

Table 13.1
$$\Pi_{(i)}(i)$$

n / i	2	3	4
0	2	−6	24
1	−1	2	−6
2	2	−2	4
3		6	−6
4			24

Table 13.2
$$\Pi_{(ik)}(k)$$
$$i \neq k$$

$n = 2$

k / i	0	1	2
0		−1	1
1	−2		2
2	−1	1	

$n = 3$

k / i	0	1	2	3
0		2	−1	2
1	6		−2	3
2	3	−2		6
3	2	−1	2	

Table 13.2 (*continued*)

$n = 4$	k	0	1	2	3	4
i						
0			−6	2	−2	6
1		−24		4	−3	8
2		−12	6		−6	12
3		−8	3	−4		24
4		−6	2	−2	6	

Table 13.3

$$12 \sum_{\substack{i=0 \\ i \neq k}}^{n} \frac{1}{k - i}$$

n	2	3	4
k			
0	−18	−22	−25
1	0	−6	−10
2	18	6	0
3		22	10
4			25

As an example we list for $n = 3$:

$$p_0' = \frac{1}{h}\left\{-\frac{22}{12}f_0 + \frac{6}{2}f_1 - \frac{3}{2}f_2 + \frac{2}{6}f_3\right\}$$

$$= \frac{1}{6h}\left\{-11f_0 + 18f_1 - 9f_2 + 2f_3\right\}.$$

We shall list other differentiation formulas after we have considered the remainder term.

13.3 REMAINDER

Since

$$\Pi(x) = h^{n+1}\,\Pi(u), \quad \Pi'(x) = h^n\frac{d}{du}\,\Pi(u),$$

and it follows that

$$\Pi'(x_k) = h^n\Pi_{(k)}(k).$$

The remainder term may therefore be written

$$h^n \Pi_{(k)}(k) \frac{f^{(n+1)}(\xi)}{(n+1)!}$$

where $x_0 < \xi < x_n$.

13.4 SUMMARY

There exists at least one number ξ with $x_0 < \xi < x_n$ for which

$$f_k' = \frac{1}{h} \left\{ \sum_{\substack{i=0 \\ i \neq k}}^{n} f_i \frac{\Pi_{(ik)}(k)}{\Pi_{(i)}(i)} + f_k \sum_{\substack{j=0 \\ j \neq k}}^{n} \frac{1}{k-j} \right\} + h^n \Pi_{(k)}(k) \frac{f^{(n+1)}(\xi)}{(n+1)!}. \tag{13.3}$$

13.5 COLLECTION OF LAGRANGIAN DIFFERENTIATION FORMULAS

We list for reference purposes a few special cases of the formula of Sec 13.4

$n = 2$ (Three points)

$$f_0' = \frac{1}{2h}(-3f_0 + 4f_1 - f_2) + \frac{h^2}{3}f'''(\xi)$$

$$f_1' = \frac{1}{2h}(-f_0 + f_2) - \frac{h^2}{6}f'''(\xi)$$

$$f_2' = \frac{1}{2h}(f_0 - 4f_1 + 3f_2) + \frac{h^2}{3}f'''(\xi)$$

$n = 3$ (Four points)

$$f_0' = \frac{1}{6h}(-11f_0 + 18f_1 - 9f_2 + 2f_3) - \frac{h^3}{4}f^{IV}(\xi)$$

$$f_1' = \frac{1}{6h}(-2f_0 - 3f_1 + 6f_2 - f_3) + \frac{h^3}{12}f^{IV}(\xi)$$

$$f_2' = \frac{1}{6h}(f_0 - 6f_1 + 3f_2 + 2f_3) - \frac{h^3}{12}f^{IV}(\xi)$$

$$f_3' = \frac{1}{6h}(-2f_0 + 9f_1 - 18f_2 + 11f_3) + \frac{h^3}{4}f^{IV}(\xi)$$

$n = 4$ (Five points)

$$f_0' = \frac{1}{12h}(-25f_0 + 48f_1 - 36f_2 + 16f_3 - 3f_4) + \frac{h^4}{5}f^{\text{V}}(\xi)$$

$$f_1' = \frac{1}{12h}(-3f_0 - 10f_1 + 18f_2 - 6f_3 + f_4) - \frac{h^4}{20}f^{\text{V}}(\xi)$$

$$f_2' = \frac{1}{12h}(f_0 - 8f_1 + 8f_3 - f_4) + \frac{h^4}{30}f^{\text{V}}(\xi)$$

$$f_3' = \frac{1}{12h}(-f_0 + 6f_1 - 18f_2 + 10f_3 + 3f_4) - \frac{h^4}{20}f^{\text{V}}(\xi)$$

$$f_4' = \frac{1}{12h}(3f_0 - 16f_1 + 36f_2 - 48f_3 + 25f_4) + \frac{h^4}{5}f^{\text{V}}(\xi)$$

In each of the above formulas it is to be understood that there exists at least one number ξ with $x_0 < \xi < x_n$, for which the stated relationship is true, provided, of course, that all ordinates used are exact.

13.6 WARNING

USE NUMERICAL DIFFERENTIATION FORMULAS ONLY WHERE ABSOLUTELY NECESSARY, AND NEVER WITHOUT DUE CONSIDERATION OF THE REMAINDER.

It is intuitively clear that since the graph of $p(x)$ oscillates around the graph of $f(x)$, their derivatives can differ appreciably even if $p(x)$ given excellent approximation to $f(x)$. Furthermore, round-off errors in the is an ordinates can appreciably affect the calculated value of the derivative, especially if these errors alternate in sign. As a simple example consider the formula

$$f_1' = \frac{1}{2h}(-f_0 + f_2) - \frac{h^2}{6}f'''(\xi).$$

Here a round-off error of $-\epsilon$ in f_0 and $+\epsilon$ in f_2 results in a contribution of ϵ/h to the total error of the calculated value of the derivative. This contribution *increases* with *decreasing* h.

Fortunately, in the numerical solution of many differential equations (where one might naturally expect numerical differentiation to be used), it is possible to use higher-accuracy numerical integration methods.

EXERCISES

1. (An academic example which does not follow the advice of Sec. 13.6).
If

$$f(x) = \frac{1}{\sqrt{2\pi}} \int_0^x e^{-v^2/2} \, dv,$$

calculate $f'(0.3)$ using values of x at 0, 0.1, 0.2, 0.3, 0.4.*

2. Obtain the Lagrangian three-point first derivative formula (starting with the Lagrangian interpolation formula for $f(x)$ with collocation points 0, $\pm h$):

$$f'(x) = \frac{2x - h}{2h^2} f_{-1} - \frac{2x}{h^2} f_0 + \frac{2x + h}{2h^2} f_1$$
$$+ \frac{1}{6}(3x^2 - h^2) f'''(\xi_1) + \frac{x}{24}(x^2 - h^2) f^{IV}(\xi_2),$$

where ξ_1, ξ_2, and x all lie in the open interval $(-h, h)$.
HINT: Use Newton's form of the remainder and Eq. (8.11).

3. Derive the following formula for second derivative:

$$f_0'' = \frac{1}{h^2}[f_{-1} - 2f_0 + f_1] - \frac{h^2}{12} f^{(4)}(\xi),$$

where $x_{-1} < \xi < x_1$.
HINT: Use Newton's form of remainder (Sec. 8.3) and Eq. (8.11).

* These [and $f'(0.3)$] may be found in many handbooks of mathematical tables, such as *C.R.C. Standard Mathematical Tables*, Cleveland: Chemical Rubber Publishing Company, 1959.

14

NUMERICAL

INTEGRATION—METHOD OF

LAGRANGE

14.1 INTRODUCTION

We shall use integrals of interpolating polynomials for a given function to approximate the corresponding integrals of that function. Since the graph of an interpolating polynomial for a given function can oscillate around the graph of that function, some cancellation of error might be expected if the integration is over an interval containing more than two collocation points. Thus we think of numerical integration as a *smoothing* process, which may give high accuracy even when the interpolating polynomial upon which it is based only reasonably approximates the function whose integral is desired. Recently a bibliography was published of the extensive literature of this subject [1].

In this chapter we shall consider only numerical integration formulas derived from Lagrangian interpolating polynomials associated with equally spaced collocation points. In a later chapter we shall consider what is known as *Gaussian quadrature*.

14.2 NEED FOR NUMERICAL INTEGRATION

Of the possible applications of numerical integration we cite but three:

(1) The indefinite integral of a relatively simple function can be of a fairly complicated mathematical form. Examples are readily available in tables of integrals [2,3]. For example,

$$\int \frac{dx}{5 - x^3} = \frac{1}{5^{2/3}6} \ln \frac{5^{2/3} + 5^{1/3}x + x^2}{(5^{1/3} - x)^2} + \frac{1}{5^{2/3}\, 3^{1/2}} \tan^{-1} \frac{2x + 5^{1/3}}{5^{1/3}3^{1/2}}.$$

To obtain the numerical value of this integral over a finite interval would probably entail more calculation (not to mention use of numerical tables of the functions involved) than an evaluation by numerical methods.

(2) The indefinite integral

$$\int e^{-x^2}\, dx$$

is one of a large class that cannot be expressed in finite form. Roughly this means that no finite combination of the functions familiar to students of elementary calculus has a derivative equal to e^{-x^2}. A precise formulation would carry us too far afield. [4,5,6].

(3) Many differential equations of practical interest do not have solutions expressible even in terms of the functions for which we have tables. We shall amplify this situation in the chapter on numerical solution of differential equations. Many numerical procedures for producing a particular solution of a given differential equation in tabled form make use of numerical integration formulas. This is, beyond all doubt, one of the applications of numerical methods of primary interest in engineering work.

14.3 CLASSIFICATION OF FORMULAS

Numerical integration formulas based upon polynomials are of the form

$$\int_a^b f(x)\, dx = A_0 f_0 + A_1 f_1 + \cdots + A_n f_n + R$$

where $f_i = f(x_i)$ and the A_i and/or x_i are chosen so that $R = 0$ for polynomials of as high a degree as possible. These formulas may be classified as follows:

I. Newton-Cotes Formulas: x_i specified and equally spaced, A_i are constants depending only on n.

II. Method of Čebyšev: A_i specified and the x_i chosen so that formulas are exact for polynomials of as high a degree as possible. Only the case of all the A_i taken to be equal seems to have been solved [7].

III. Gaussian Quadrature: A_i and x_i chosen so that formula is exact for polynomials of degree $\leq 2n + 1$. We shall briefly describe this method in Chap. 16.

14.4 NEWTON-COTES FORMULAS—METHOD OF LAGRANGE

Let $p(x)$ be the unique interpolating polynomial of degree $\leq n$ for a given function $f(x)$ with the $n + 1$ distinct collocation points $x_0, x_1, x_2, \ldots, x_n$. We suppose these points equally spaced at intervals of h. That is,

$$x_i = x_0 + ih, \qquad i = 0, 1, 2, \ldots, n.$$

Thus

$$p(x_0 + uh) = \sum_{i=0}^{n} \lambda_i(u) f_i$$

where $\lambda_i(u)$ is the ith Lagrangian polynomial of degree n in terms of the unitized variable $u = (x - x_0)/h$. Recall that

$$\lambda_i(u) = \frac{\Pi_{(i)}(u)}{\Pi_{(i)}(i)},$$

where

$$\Pi_{(i)}(u) = u(u - 1)(u - 2) \cdots (u - i + 1)(u - i - 1) \cdots (u - n).$$

Since

$$\int_{x_p}^{x_q} p(x) \, dx = h \sum_{i=0}^{n} \left[\int_{p}^{q} \lambda_i(u) \, du \right] f_i, \tag{14.1}$$

p and q integers with $p < q$, we shall need a table of $\int_{0}^{k} \Pi_{(i)}(u) \, du$. Later we shall present such a table for a few values of the parameters. We shall, of course, also make use of Table 13.1 of $\Pi_{(i)}(i)$.

14.5 CLASSIFICATION OF NEWTON–COTES FORMULAS

Although numerical integration formulas could be obtained for any interval we shall here consider only three types:

1. CLOSED FORMULAS: The interval of integration is (x_0, x_n). These are commonly used for evaluation of definite integrals and in the numerical solution of differential equations.

2. OPEN FORMULAS:* The interval of integration is (x_{-1}, x_{n+1}) where $x_{-1} = x_0 - h$ and $x_{n+1} = x_n + h$. This amounts to an extrapolation. Such formulas are useful in connection with differential equations.

3. PARTIAL-RANGE FORMULAS:* The interval of integration is (x_1, x_{n-1}). These are often of higher accuracy than corresponding closed formulas.

These formulas, particularly those of type 1, are referred to as those of *Newton-Cotes*.

As to specific examples, we shall here limit ourselves to integration formulas derived from interpolating polynomials of degree ≤ 4. For a more extensive collection of numerical integration formulas see Appendix IV of reference [8].

14.6 AUXILIARY TABLES

We define

$$I_0^k(i, n) = \int_0^k \Pi_{(i)}(u) \, du$$

where

$$\Pi_{(i)}(u) = u(u - 1) \cdots (u - i + 1)(u - i - 1) \cdots (u - n).$$

Table 14.1

$$2I_0^k(i, 1)$$

i \ k	−1	1	2
0	3	−1	0
1	1	1	4

Table 14.2

$$6I_0^k(i, 2)$$

i \ k	−1	1	2	3
0	−23	5	4	9
1	−8	−4	−8	0
2	−5	−1	4	27

* The definitions given here are often relaxed somewhat.

Table 14.3

$$12I_0^k(i, 3)$$

i \ k	−1	1	2	3	4
0	165	−27	−24	−27	0
1	59	19	32	27	64
2	37	5	−8	−27	32
3	27	3	0	27	192

Table 14.4

$$60I_0^k(i, 4)$$

i \ k	−1	1	3	4	5
0	−3802	502	486	448	950
1	−1387	−323	−459	−512	125
2	−872	−88	216	128	1000
3	−637	−53	−189	−512	875
4	−502	−38	−54	448	4250

14.7 DERIVATION OF FORMULAS

As an example of the procedure by which numerical integration formulas may be obtained from the preceding tables, we consider the open formula associated with three points. Thus

$$\int_{x_{-1}}^{x_3} f(x) \, dx = \int_{x_{-1}}^{x_3} p(x) \, dx + R$$

where $p(x)$ is the unique interpolating polynomial of degree ≤ 2 associated with the three collocation points x_0, x_1, x_2. The remainder R will be discussed in Chap. 15. Integrating $p(x)$ we obtain:

$$\int_{x_{-1}}^{x_3} p(x) \, dx = h \int_{-1}^{3} \left[\sum_{i=0}^{2} \frac{\Pi_{(i)}(u)}{\Pi_{(i)}(i)} f_i \right] du$$

$$= h \left\{ \frac{f_0}{2} \int_{-1}^{3} \Pi_{(0)}(u) \, du - f_1 \int_{-1}^{3} \Pi_{(i)}(u) \, du \right.$$

$$\left. + \frac{f_2}{2} \int_{-1}^{3} \Pi_{(2)}(u) \, du \right\}$$

$$= \frac{4h}{3} \left\{ 2f_0 - f_1 + 2f_2 \right\}.$$

The Milne method [9] for solving initial value problems in ordinary differential equations uses Simpson's rule and this formula. Since this method has been widely used the above integration formula is sometimes referred to as *Milne's formula*.

14.8 SHORT COLLECTION OF INTEGRATION FORMULAS

We make a systematic list of formulas that can be obtained from the brief tables of Sec. 14.6. For reference purposes we include the remainder terms; the derivation of these will be discussed in Chap. 15. In each case it is to be understood that ξ lies in the interval between the leftmost and rightmost points involved in the formula and in the integral which it approximates.

14.81   *CLOSED FORMULAS*

$n = 1$ (2 points)   TRAPEZOIDAL RULE

$$\int_{x_0}^{x_1} f(x)\,dx = \frac{h}{2}\,(f_0 + f_1) - \frac{h^3}{12}\,f''(\xi)$$

$n = 2$ (3 points)   SIMPSON'S RULE

$$\int_{x_0}^{x_2} f(x)\,dx = \frac{h}{3}\,(f_0 + 4f_1 + f_2) - \frac{h^5}{90}\,f^{IV}(\xi)$$

$n = 3$ (4 points)   THREE-EIGHTHS RULE

$$\int_{x_0}^{x_3} f(x)\,dx = \frac{3h}{8}\,(f_0 + 3f_1 + 3f_2 + f_3) - \frac{3}{80}\,h^5 f^{IV}(\xi)$$

$n = 4$ (5 points)   BOOLE'S RULE

$$\int_{x_0}^{x_4} f(x)\,dx = \frac{2h}{45}\,(7f_0 + 32f_1 + 12f_2 + 32f_3 + 7f_4) - \frac{8}{945}\,h^7 f^{VI}(\xi)$$

14.82   *OPEN FORMULAS*

$n = 0$ (1 point)

$$\int_{x_{-1}}^{x_1} f(x)\,dx = 2hf_0 + \frac{h^3}{3}\,f''(\xi)$$

$n = 1$ (2 points)

$$\int_{x_{-1}}^{x_2} f(x)\,dx = \frac{3h}{2}\,(f_0 + f_1) + \frac{3}{4}\,h^3 f''(\xi)$$

$n = 2$ (3 points)   MILNE'S FORMULA

$$\int_{x_{-1}}^{x_3} f(x)\, dx = \frac{4h}{3}\left(2f_0 - f_1 + 2f_2\right) + \frac{14}{45} h^5 f^{IV}(\xi)$$

$n = 3$ (4 points)

$$\int_{x_{-1}}^{x_4} f(x)\, dx = \frac{5h}{24}\left(11f_0 + f_1 + f_2 + 11f_3\right) + \frac{95}{144} h^5 f^{IV}(\xi)$$

$n = 4$ (5 points)

$$\int_{x_{-1}}^{x_5} f(x)\, dx = \frac{3h}{10}\left(11f_0 - 14f_1 + 26f_2 - 14f_3 + 11f_4\right) + \frac{41}{140} h^7 f^{VI}(\xi)$$

14.83   PARTIAL-RANGE FORMULAS

$n = 3$ (4 points)

$$\int_{x_1}^{x_2} f(x)\, dx = \frac{h}{24}\left[-f_0 + 13f_1 + 13f_2 - f_3\right] + \frac{11}{720} h^5 f^{IV}(\xi)$$

$n = 4$ (5 points)

$$\int_{x_1}^{x_3} f(x)\, dx = \frac{h}{180}\left[-2f_0 + 68f_1 + 228f_2 + 68f_3 - 2f_4\right] + \frac{1}{42{,}336} h^7 f^{(6)}(\xi)$$

EXAMPLE 14.1.   The solution of the initial value problem

$$y' = 1 - 2xy$$

$$y(0) = 0$$

is

$$y(x) = e^{-x^2} \int_0^x e^{u^2}\, du.$$

We shall use Simpson's rule to calculate values of $y(x)$ at $x = 0, 0.1, 0.2, \ldots$.

x	u	u^2	e^{u^2}	$\int_0^x e^{u^2}\, du$	e^{-x^2}	y
0	0	0	1	0	1	0
	0.05	0.0025	1.00250			
0.1	0.1	0.01	1.01005	0.10033	0.99005	0.0993
	0.15	0.0225	1.02276			
0.2	0.2	0.04	1.04081	0.20269	0.96079	0.1947
	0.25	0.0625	1.06449			

x	u	u^2	e^{u^2}	$\int_0^x e^{u^2}\,du$	e^{-x^2}	y
0.3	0.3	0.09	1.09417	0.30923	0.91393	0.2826
	0.35	0.1225	1.13032			
0.4	0.4	0.16	1.17351	0.42237	0.85214	0.3599
	0.45	0.2025	1.22446			
0.5	0.5	0.25	1.28403	0.54495	0.77880	0.4244
	0.55	0.3025	1.35324			
0.6	0.6	0.36	1.43333	0.68045	0.69768	0.4747
	0.65	0.4225	1.52577			
0.7	0.7	0.49	1.63232	0.83326	0.61263	0.5105
	0.75	0.5625	1.75505			
0.8	0.8	0.64	1.89648	1.00907	0.52729	0.5321

14.9 REPETITION OF INTEGRATION FORMULAS

It is often more convenient to use a simple formula over several consecutive intervals than to use a more complicated formula based on an interpolating polynomial of higher degree. We illustrate using Simpson's rule:

$$\int_{x_0}^{x_2} f(x)\,dx = \frac{h}{3}\left[f_0 + 4f_1 + f_2\right] - \frac{h^5}{90} f^{IV}(\xi_1), \qquad x_0 < \xi_1 < x_2.$$

$$\int_{x_2}^{x_4} f(x)\,dx = \frac{h}{3}\left[f_2 + 4f_3 + f_4\right] - \frac{h^5}{90} f^{IV}(\xi_2), \qquad x_2 < \xi_2 < x_4.$$

Hence, applying Theorem 7 of Appendix A, we find:

$$\int_{x_0}^{x_4} f(x)\,dx = \frac{h}{3}\left[f_0 + 4f_1 + 2f_2 + 4f_3 + f_4\right] - \frac{2}{90} h^5 f^{IV}(\xi), \quad x_0 < \xi < x_4.$$

It is convenient to speak of this as an integration over four panels. Using $2k$ panels we obtain:

$$\int_{x_0}^{x_{2k}} f(x)\,dx = \frac{h}{3}\left[f_0 + 4f_1 + 2f_2 + 4f_3 + \cdots + 4f_{2k-1} + f_{2k}\right] - \frac{k}{90} h^5 f^{IV}(\xi).$$

EXERCISES

1. Derive Simpson's rule and the three-eighths rule.

2. Evaluate

$$\int_2^{10} (x^3 - 3x^2 + x)\,dx$$

using: (a) Simpson's rule with two panels; (b) Simpson's rule with four panels; (c) An antiderivative.

3. By repeated application of the trapezoidal rule over k consecutive panels show that

$$\int_{x_0}^{x_k} f(x) \, dx = h[\tfrac{1}{2}f_0 + f_1 + f_2 + \cdots + f_{k-1} + \tfrac{1}{2}f_k] - \tfrac{1}{12}kh^3f''(\xi).$$

4. By repeated application of the first partial-range formula of Sec. 14.83 over k consecutive panels show that

$$\int_{x_0}^{x_k} f(x) \, dx = h\left[\frac{1}{2}f_0 + f_1 + f_2 + \cdots + f_{k-1} + \frac{1}{2}f_k\right]$$
$$+ \frac{h}{24}[-f_{-1} + f_1 + f_{k-1} - f_{k+1}] + \frac{11}{720}kh^5f^{IV}(\xi).$$

This amounts to applying the trapezoidal rule over k panels and adding a correction term. Unless f^{IV} is appreciably larger than f'', the remainder here will be considerably smaller than the remainder using only the trapezoidal rule.

5. Use Simpson's rule over two, four, then ten panels to calculate

$$\int_1^2 \frac{dx}{x}.$$

Compare your answers with the tabled value of ln 2.

6. Find approximate value of

$$\int_0^1 \frac{dx}{1 + x^2}$$

using the trapezoidal rule over ten panels with and without the correction term of Exercise 14.4. Compare with known value of $\pi/4$.

7. Use the appropriate auxiliary tables to obtain the integration formula

$$\int_{x_1}^{x_2} f(x) \, dx = \frac{h}{12}(-f_0 + 8f_1 + 5f_2) + R.$$

It is known [10] that

$$R = -h^4 \frac{f'''(\xi)}{4!}.$$

See Exercise 15.3.

8. Use appropriate auxiliary tables to obtain the integration formula:

$$\int_{x_2}^{x_3} f(x) \, dx = \frac{h}{12}[5f_0 - 16f_1 + 23f_2] + R.$$

It can be shown (Exercise 15.4) that

$$R = \tfrac{3}{8}h^4f'''(\xi).$$

9. By integrating the formula given in Exercise 8.5 obtain the following formula for numerical integration:

$$\int_{x_0}^{x_1} f(x)\,dx = \frac{h}{2}\left[f_0 + f_1\right] + \frac{h^2}{12}\left[f_0' - f_1'\right] + \frac{h^5 f^{\mathrm{IV}}(\xi)}{720}\,, \qquad x_0 < \xi < x_1.$$

10. Find approximate value of $\int_0^{0.6} \dfrac{dx}{1+x}$ using one application only of (a) Simpson's rule; (b) three-eighths rule. Compare your answers with ln 1.6.

11. The trapezoidal rule (Exercise 14.3) is to be used to calculate $\int_1^2 \dfrac{dx}{x}$. How should we choose the number k of panels to guarantee $|R| < 0.5 \times 10^{-6}$? How for Simpson's rule?

12. Approximate by Simpson's rule the length of arc of the curve $3y = x^3$ from $(0, 0)$ to $(1, \tfrac{1}{3})$. Use two panels, then four panels.

REFERENCES

1. A. H. Stroud. "A Bibliography on Approximate Integration," *Math. Comput.* **15:** 52–80 (1961).

2. B. O. Peirce. *A Short Table of Integrals.* Boston: Ginn, 1929.

3. H. B. Dwight. *Tables of Integrals and Other Mathematical Data.* New York: Macmillan, 1961.

4. G. H. Hardy. *The Integration of Functions of a Single Variable.* Cambridge U.P., 1905.

5. J. F. Ritt. *Integration in Finite Terms; Liouville's Theory of Elementary Methods.* New York: Columbia U.P., 1948.

6. D. G. Mead, "Integration," *Am. Math. Monthly* **68:** 152–156 (1961).

7. L. M. Milne-Thomson. *The Calculus of Finite Differences.* London: Macmillan, 1933, 1951.

8. Z. Kopal. *Numerical Analysis.* New York: Wiley, 1962.

9. W. E. Milne. "Numerical Integration of Ordinary Differential Equations," *Am. Math. Monthly* **33:** 455–460 (1926).

10. T. H. Southard, and E. C. Yowell. "An Alternative 'Predictor-Corrector' Process," *Math. Tables Aids Comput.* **6:** 253–4 (1952).

11. V. I. Krylov. *Approximate Calculations of Integrals.* New York: Macmillan, 1962, translated from Russian edition of 1959.

15

REMAINDER IN NUMERICAL

INTEGRATION

15.1 INTRODUCTION

The remainder terms listed in Chap. 14 are all of the form

$$Ch^{k+2}\frac{f^{(k+1)}(\xi)}{(k+1)!},\tag{15.1}$$

where C is a constant [independent of h and $f(x)$]. Such a formula is exact (has zero remainder) only if $f(x)$ is a polynomial of degree $\leq k$. A numerical integration formula whose remainder is of the form (15.1) is said to be *simplex* [1]. If it is known that a given formula is simplex, then k could be determined by trial and error as the largest integer for which $R = 0$ for $f(x)$ a convenient polynomial of degree k. Then C could be determined by using for $f(x)$ any convenient polynomial of degree $k + 1$. However, there does not seem to exist at present any convenient general method for determining in advance whether or not any given formula is simplex.

118

EXAMPLE 15.1.   For the three-eighths rule

$$R = \int_{x_0}^{x_3} f(x) \, dx - \frac{3h}{8} [f_0 + 3f_1 + 3f_2 + f_3].$$

Using the convenient polynomial $f(x) = (x - x_0)^p$ we find by direct calculation that $R = 0$ for $p = 0, 1, 2, 3$ and that $R = -0.9h^5$ for $p = 4$. Hence $k = 3$ and if the rule is simplex, then $-0.9h^5 = Ch^5$. Whence $C = -0.9$ and

$$R = -\tfrac{3}{80} h^5 f^{IV}(\xi).$$

There are available several unified treatments of the remainder which we shall not discuss [2, 3, . . . , 6]. We shall limit our consideration to the method of Steffensen [7]. This method is sufficiently general to take care of all the Newton-Cotes formulas.

15.2   ONE-PANEL FORMULAS

If the numerical integration formula is for a single panel, that is, the limits of integration are consecutive collocation points, then the second theorem of the mean for integrals (A.5) can be applied to yield the remainder term. We illustrate with the first partial-range formula of Sec. 14.83:

Let

$$f(x) = I_3(x) + R_4(x)$$

where $I_3(x)$ is the unique interpolating polynomial (of degree ≤ 3) for $f(x)$ with the equally spaced collocation points x_0, x_1, x_2, x_3. Then the remainder of the integration formula under consideration is

$$\int_{x_1}^{x_2} R_4(x) \, dx = \int_{x_1}^{x_2} \frac{(x - x_0)(x - x_1)(x - x_2)(x - x_3)}{4!} f^{IV}(\xi) \, dx.$$

Since the Π-factor does not change sign in the interval (x_1, x_2) we may apply (A.5) and obtain

$$\frac{f^{IV}(\xi(\zeta))}{4!} \int_{x_1}^{x_2} \Pi_3(x) \, dx,$$

where $x_1 < \zeta < x_2$ and hence $x_0 < \xi(\zeta) < x_3$. Letting $\xi(\zeta) = \xi^\star$ and introducing the unitized variable $u = \dfrac{1}{h}(x - x_0)$ we may write

$$\int_{x_1}^{x_2} R_4(x) \, dx = \frac{h^5 f^{IV}(\xi^\star)}{4!} \int_1^2 \Pi_3(u) \, du$$

$$= \frac{11}{720} h^5 f^{IV}(\xi^\star), \qquad x_0 < \xi^\star < x_3.$$

Generally, if a numerical integration formula has been obtained by integrating from x_i to x_{i+1} the unique interpolating polynomial of degree $\leq n$ with collocation points $x_0 < x_1 < \cdots < x_n$, then the remainder in the integration formula is

$$\frac{h^{n+2} f^{(n+1)}(\xi)}{(n+1)!} \int_i^{i+1} \Pi_n(u) \, du,$$

where $\min(x_0, x_i) < \xi < \max(x_n, x_{i+1})$ and $\Pi_n(u) = u(u-1)(u-2) \cdots (u-n)$. In this connection the following table of definite integrals will be found useful.

Table 15.1

$$\int_0^k u(u-1) \cdots (u-n) \, du = \frac{N_k(n)}{D(n)}$$

$N_k(n)$

k \ n	−1	1	2	3	4	5	D(n)
1	−5	−1	4	27	80	175	6
2	9	1	0	9	64	225	4
3	−251	−19	−8	−27	224	2125	30
4	475	27	16	27	0	475	12
5	−19087	−863	−592	−783	−512	−1375	84

From this table we find, for example,

$$\int_1^2 \Pi_3(u) \, du = -\tfrac{8}{30} - \left(-\tfrac{19}{30}\right) = \tfrac{11}{30}.$$

15.3 SIMPSON'S RULE

Let

$$f(x) = I_2(x) + R_3(x)$$

where $I_2(x)$ is the unique interpolating polynomial for $f(x)$ with the equally spaced collocation points x_0, x_1, x_2. Since the Π-factor changes sign in the interval (x_0, x_2) the second theorem of the mean for integrals is not immediately applicable to the integral of $R_3(x)$. We may, however, proceed as follows.

We define

$$J_2(x) = \int_{x_0}^x \Pi_2(\omega) \, d\omega$$

where

$$\Pi_2(\omega) = (\omega - x_0)(\omega - x_1)(\omega - x_2)$$

and observe that $J_2(x)$ has the following properties:

1. $J_2(x) > 0$ for $x_0 < x < x_2$,

2. $J_2(x_0) = J_2(x_2) = 0$,

3. $\dfrac{d}{dx} J_2(x) = \Pi_2(x)$.

Then from Newton's form of the remainder in polynomial interpolatio we obtain

$$\int_{x_0}^{x_2} R_3(x)\, dx = \int_{x_0}^{x_2} \Pi_2(x)\, f(x, x_0, x_1, x_2)\, dx$$

$$= \int_{x_0}^{x_2} f(x, x_0, x_1, x_2)\, \frac{d}{dx} J_2(x)\, dx.$$

An integration by parts reduces this to

$$-\int_{x_0}^{x_2} J_2(x)\, \frac{d}{dx}\, f(x, x_0, x_1, x_2)\, dx$$

which, according to Eq. (8.15) may be written

$$-\int_{x_0}^{x_2} J_2(x)\, \frac{f^{\mathrm{IV}}(\xi(x))}{4!}\, dx$$

where $x_0 < \xi(x) < x_2$. Since $J_2(x)$ does not change sign in the interval (x_0, x_2) we may apply (A.5) to obtain

$$-\frac{f^{\mathrm{IV}}(\xi^\star)}{4!} \int_{x_0}^{x_2} J_2(x)\, dx.$$

Again using integration by parts, we find

$$\int_{x_0}^{x_2} J_2(x)\, dx = x J_2(x) \Big]_{x_0}^{x_2} - \int_{x_0}^{x_2} x \Pi_2(x)\, dx$$

$$= -\int_{x_0}^{x_2} x \Pi_2(x)\, dx = -h^5 \int_0^2 u \Pi_2(u)\, du$$

$$= -h^5 \int_0^2 \Pi_3(u)\, du,$$

where $\Pi_3(u) = u(u - 1)(u - 2)(u - 3)$. From Table 15.3 we find

$$\int_0^2 \Pi_3(u)\, du = -\tfrac{4}{15}.$$

Hence

$$\int_{x_0}^{x_2} R_3(x) \, dx = - \frac{h^5}{90} f^{IV}(\xi^\star), \quad x_0 < \xi^\star < x_2.$$

15.4 FOUR-POINT OPEN FORMULA

Let

$$f(x) = I_3(x) + R_4(x)$$

where $I_3(x)$ is the unique interpolating polynomial (of degree ≤ 3) for $f(x)$ with equally spaced collocation points x_0, x_1, x_2, x_3. The remainder in the associated open integration formula (Sec. 14.82) is

$$
\begin{aligned}
R_4 &= \int_{x_{-1}}^{x_4} R_4(x) \, dx = \int_{x_{-1}}^{x_4} f(x, x_0, x_1, x_2, x_3) \Pi_3(x) \, dx \\
&= \int_{x_{-1}}^{x_3} \frac{f(x_0, x_1, x_2, x_3) - f(x, x_0, x_1, x_2)}{x_3 - x} \Pi_3(x) \, dx \\
&\quad + \int_{x_3}^{x_4} f(x, x_0, x_1, x_2, x_3) \Pi_3(x) \, dx \\
&= -f(x_0, x_1, x_2, x_3) \int_{x_{-1}}^{x_3} \Pi_2(x) \, dx \\
&\quad + \int_{x_{-1}}^{x_3} f(x, x_0, x_1, x_2) \Pi_2(x) \, dx \\
&\quad + \int_{x_3}^{x_4} f(x, x_0, x_1, x_2, x_3) \Pi_3(x) \, dx.
\end{aligned}
$$

The first of these integrals is 0. The second can be treated precisely as in the preceding section, except that now we let

$$J_2(x) = \int_{x_{-1}}^{x} \Pi_2(\omega) \, d\omega, \qquad x_{-1} \leq x \leq x_3.$$

To the third integral we may apply the second theorem of the mean for integrals and then use Eq. (8.11). We find

$$R_4 = \frac{f^{IV}(\xi_1) \, h^5}{4!} \int_{-1}^{3} \Pi_3(u) \, du + \frac{f^{IV}(\xi_2)}{4!} h^5 \int_{3}^{4} \Pi_3(u) \, du.$$

We note from Table 15.1 that the two integrals of this last equation are of the same sign. Hence we may apply (A.7) to obtain

$$R_4 = \frac{f^{IV}(\xi)}{4!} h^5 \int_{-1}^{4} \Pi_3(u) \, du.$$

According to Table 15.2 this last integral has the value $\frac{475}{30}$. Hence

$$R_4 = \tfrac{95}{144} h^5 f^{IV}(\xi), \qquad x_{-1} < \xi < x_4.$$

15.5 NEWTON-COTES FORMULAS (GENERAL CASE)

The method of Steffensen used in the preceding sections can be generalized to cover all the Newton-Cotes formulas as defined in Sec. 14.5.

Let

$$f(x) = I_n(x) + R_{n+1}(x)$$

where $I_n(x)$ is the unique interpolating polynomial for $f(x)$ with collocation points $x_0, x_1, \ldots, x_n$. The Newton-Cotes formulas were obtained by integrating $I_n(x)$ over intervals (x_0, x_n), (x_1, x_{n-1}) and (x_{-1}, x_{n+1}), or more briefly, over the intervals $(x_\alpha, x_{n-\alpha})$, $\alpha = -1, 0, 1$. Then according to Newton's form of the remainder in polynomial interpolation (Sec. 8.3),

$$R_{n+1} = \int_{x_\alpha}^{x_{n-\alpha}} R_{n+1}(x) \, dx = \int_{x_\alpha}^{x_{n-\alpha}} f(x, x_0, x_1, \ldots, x_n) \Pi_n(x) \, dx \quad (15.2)$$

where

$$\Pi_n(x) = (x - x_0)(x - x_1) \cdots (x - x_n).$$

As in the illustrative examples of the preceding sections the method of simplifying the above integral depends on whether n is odd or even. We therefore consider these two cases separately.

CASE I. n EVEN

We define

$$J_n(x) = \int_{x_\alpha}^{x} \Pi_n(\omega) \, d\omega, \qquad x_\alpha \leq x \leq x_{n-\alpha},$$

where

$$\Pi_n(\omega) = (\omega - x_0)(\omega - x_1) \cdots (\omega - x_n).$$

Observe that $J_n(x)$ has the following properties:

1. $J_n(x)$ does not change sign (Exercise 11.6).

2. $J_n(x_\alpha) = J_n(x_{n-\alpha}) = 0, \qquad \alpha = -1, 0, 1.$

3. $\dfrac{d}{dx} J_n(x) = \Pi_n(x).$

We now integrate Eq. (15.2) by parts and obtain, using Eq. (8.15),

$$R_{n+1} = f(x, x_0, x_1, \ldots, x_n) J_n(x) \Big]_{x_\alpha}^{x_{n-\alpha}}$$

$$- \int_{x_\alpha}^{x_{n-\alpha}} J_n(x) \frac{f^{(n+2)}(\xi)}{(n+2)!} \, dx,$$

$$\min(x_0, x_\alpha) < \xi < \max(x_n, x_{n-\alpha}).$$

Since $J_n(x)$ does not change sign in the interval $(x_\alpha, x_{n-\alpha})$ we may apply the second theorem of the mean for integrals (A.5) to obtain

$$
\begin{aligned}
R_{n+1} &= -\frac{f^{(n+2)}(\xi\star)}{(n+2)!} \int_{x_\alpha}^{x_{n-\alpha}} J_n(x)\, dx \\
&= -\frac{f^{(n+2)}(\xi\star)}{(n+2)!} \left\{ x\, J_n(x) \Big]_{x_\alpha}^{x_{n-\alpha}} - \int_{x_\alpha}^{x_{n-\alpha}} x\Pi_n(x)\, dx \right\} \\
&= \frac{f^{(n+2)}(\xi\star)}{(n+2)!} h^{n+3} \int_\alpha^{n-\alpha} u\Pi_n(u)\, du \\
&= \frac{f^{(n+2)}(\xi\star)}{(n+2)!} h^{n+3} \int_\alpha^{n-\alpha} \Pi_{n+1}(u)\, du,
\end{aligned}
$$

$$
\min (x_0, x_\alpha) < \xi\star < \max (x_n, x_{n-\alpha}),
$$

where $\Pi_{n+1}(u) = u(u-1)\cdots(u-n)(u-n-1)$. Table 15.3 gives values of integrals of $\Pi_{n+1}(u)$.

CASE II. n ODD

From the definition of a divided difference we may write

$$
\begin{aligned}
R_{n+1} &= \int_{x_\alpha}^{x_{n-\alpha-1}} \frac{f(x_0, x_1, \ldots, x_n) - f(x, x_0, \ldots, x_{n-1})}{x_n - x} \Pi_n(x)\, dx \\
&\quad + \int_{x_{n-\alpha-1}}^{x_{n-\alpha}} f(x, x_0, \ldots, x_n)\Pi_n(x)\, dx \\
&= -f(x_0, x_1, \ldots, x_n) \int_{x_\alpha}^{x_{n-\alpha-1}} \Pi_{n-1}(x)\, dx \\
&\quad + \int_{x_\alpha}^{x_{n-\alpha-1}} f(x, x_0, \ldots, x_{n-1})\Pi_{n-1}(x)\, dx \\
&\quad + \int_{x_{n-\alpha-1}}^{x_{n-\alpha}} f(x, x_0, \ldots, x_n)\Pi_n(x)\, dx.
\end{aligned}
$$

Since $n - 1$ is an even integer the first of these integrals is 0 and the second falls under Case I. The third integral may be simplified by using the second theorem of the mean for integrals and Eq. (8.11). Thus

$$
R_{n+1} = \frac{f^{(n+1)}(\xi_1)}{(n+1)!} h^{n+2} \int_\alpha^{n-\alpha-1} \Pi_n(u)\, du + \frac{f^{(n+1)}(\xi_2)}{(n+1)!} h^{n+2} \int_{n-\alpha-1}^{n-\alpha} \Pi_n(u)\, du.
$$

These last two integrals are of the same sign. This can be observed from Table 15.1 for all cases listed. For proof in general we refer to Exercise 11.7.

Hence we may apply (A.7) to obtain

$$R_{n+1} = \frac{f^{(n+1)}(\xi)}{(n+1)!} h^{n+2} \int_{\alpha}^{n-\alpha} \Pi_n(u) \, du,$$

where

$$\min(x_0, x_\alpha) < \xi < \max(x_n, x_{n-\alpha})$$

and

$$\Pi_n(u) = u(u-1) \cdots (u-n).$$

Values of integrals of $\Pi_n(u)$ may be found in Table 15.2.

15.6 SUMMARY

We have called numerical integration formulas of the form

$$\int_{x_\alpha}^{x_{n-\alpha}} f(x) \, dx = \sum_{k=0}^{n} A_k f_k + R_{n+1}$$

those of Newton-Cotes. They were further classified as open, closed, and partial range for $\alpha = -1, 0, 1$, respectively. In the preceding section we have shown that

$$R_{n+1} = \begin{cases} \dfrac{f^{(n+2)}(\xi) h^{n+3}}{(n+2)!} \displaystyle\int_{\alpha}^{n-\alpha} \Pi_{n+1}(u) \, du, & n \text{ even} \\[3mm] \dfrac{f^{(n+1)}(\xi) h^{n+2}}{(n+1)!} \displaystyle\int_{\alpha}^{n-\alpha} \Pi_n(u) \, du, & n \text{ odd} \end{cases}$$

where $\Pi_k(u) = u(u-1) \cdots (u-k)$. Brief tables of the integrals involved follow.

Table 15.2

$$30 \int_{\alpha}^{n-\alpha} \Pi_n(u) \, du$$

$\alpha \backslash n$	1	3
1	45	475
0	−5	−27
1		11

Table 15.3

$$105 \int_{\alpha}^{n-\alpha} \Pi_{n+1}(u) \, du$$

$\alpha \backslash n$	2	4
−1	784	22140
0	−28	−640
1		100

It should be noted that each of the Newton-Cotes formulas is based on $n + 1$ points. If $n + 1$ is odd the formula is exact for all polynomials of degree $n + 1$ or less. But if $n + 1$ is even, the formula is exact only for polynomials of degree n or less. Thus where a choice is available, the formulas based on an odd number of points are to be preferred. See Exercise 15.9.

We offer a simple explanation. All of the Newton-Cotes formulas are symmetrical. In particular, those based on an odd number $n + 1$ of points are of the form

$$\int_{x_{-(n/2)-\alpha}}^{x_{(n/2)+\alpha}} f(x) \, dx = A_0 f_0 + \sum_{i=1}^{(n/2)+\alpha} A_i (f_i + f_{-i}) + R_{n+1}.$$

These integration formulas are linear, and if a formula is exact ($R_{n+1} = 0$) for $f(x)$ and $g(x)$ it is necessarily exact for any linear combination of $f(x)$ and $g(x)$. Note that $R_{n+1} = 0$ for $f(x) = (x - x_0)^{n+1}$, where $n + 1$ is any odd integer. Any polynomial of degree $n + 1$ can be written in the form $\sum_{i=0}^{n+1} a_i (x - x_0)^i$. Hence, if a formula is exact for all polynomials of degree n or less, it is necessarily exact for all polynomials of degree $n + 1$ or less. Note that this is not true for $n + 1$ an even integer.

EXERCISES

1. Calculate the remainder in Simpson's rule under the assumption that the rule is simplex.

2. Obtain formula for remainder in the trapezoidal rule without assuming rule to be simplex.

3. Obtain remainder for integration formula of Exercise 14.7.

4. Obtain remainder for integration formula given in Exercise 14.8.

5. Use properties of the Π-factor to show that

$$\int_0^{2k} \lambda_{2k+1}(u) \, du = 0,$$

where $\lambda_{2k+1}(u)$ is the Lagrangian coefficient of f_{2k+1} and is a polynomial of degree $2k + 1$. Thus no quadrature formula obtained by integrating from x_0 to x_{2k} a Lagrangian interpolation formula of degree $2k + 1$ with collocation points $x_0, x_1, \ldots, x_{2k+1}$ will involve the ordinate f_{2k+1}. For an example see Exercise 15.7 below.

6. Use properties of the Π-factor to show that

$$\int_{-1}^{2k+1} \lambda_{2k+1}(u) \, du = 0.$$

7. Let $f(x) = I_3(x) + R_4(x)$ where $I_3(x)$ is the unique interpolating polynomial of degree ≤ 3 for $f(x)$ with collocation points x_0, x_1, x_2, x_3. Use the auxiliary tables of Secs. 13.2 and 14.6 to show that

$$\int_{x_0}^{x_2} I_3(x)\, dx = \frac{h}{3}\, [f_0 + 4f_1 + f_2].$$

This is, of course, Simpson's rule. We have seen (Sec. 15.3) that the remainder is $-(h^5/90)\, f^{(4)}(\xi\star)$. Hence

$$\int_{x_0}^{x_2} R_4(x)\, dx = \int_{x_0}^{x_2} \Pi_3(x)\, \frac{f^{(4)}(\xi(x))}{4!}\, dx = -\frac{h^5}{90}\, f^4(\xi\star), \qquad x_0 < \xi\star < x_2.$$

From Table 15.3 we find that

$$\int_{x_0}^{x_2} \Pi_3(x)\, dx = -\tfrac{4}{15}\, h^5.$$

Hence

$$\int_{x_0}^{x_2} \Pi_3(x)\, \frac{f^{(4)}(\xi(x))}{4!}\, dx = \frac{f^{(4)}(\xi\star)}{4!} \int_{x_0}^{x_2} \Pi_3(x)\, dx.$$

Thus the conclusion of the second theorem of the mean for integrals is valid though the hypothesis is not satisfied. There does not seem to be a simple general theorem of the mean for integrals which would readily permit this to be anticipated. Show, however, that

$$\int_{x_0}^{x_2} \Pi_2(x)\, \frac{f^{(3)}(\xi(x))}{3!}\, dx \neq \frac{f^{(3)}(\xi\star)}{3!} \int_{x_0}^{x_2} \Pi_2(x)\, dx.$$

8. The remainder in Simpson's rule can be written

$$R(f) = f_2 - f_0 - (h/3)[f_0' + 4f_1' + f_2'].$$

Show that

(a) $R(af + bg) = aR(f) + bR(g)$.

Thus R is a linear operator.

(b) $R[(x - x_0)^n] = 0, \qquad n = 0, 1, 2, 3, 4.$

(c) $R[(x - x_0)^5] = -\tfrac{4}{3}h^5$

(d) If $f(x)$ is any differentiable function then there exists a polynomial $p(x) = a_0 x^5 + a_1 x^4 + \cdots$ such that

$$p(x_i) = f(x_i)$$
$$p'(x_i) = f'(x_i), \qquad i = 0, 1, 2.$$

(e) If $g(x) = f(x) - p(x)$, then $g'(x)$ has at least five distinct zeros in closed interval $[x_0, x_2]$. Hence $g^{(5)}(x)$ has at least one zero in this interval.

(f) Hence show that

$$R(f) = R(p) = -\tfrac{4}{3}a_0 h^5 = -\tfrac{1}{90}h^5 f^{(5)}(\xi), \qquad x_0 < \xi < x_2.$$

9. Suppose $\int_a^b f(x) \, dx$ were to be approximated by Simpson's rule (two panels) and by the three-eighths rule (three panels). Write each remainder in terms of $b - a$. The answers have apparently been overlooked by those writers who have observed that since the remainders in the two rules (with same panel width h) have numerical coefficients in the ratio $\tfrac{8}{27}$, the three-eighths rule should be avoided. (See Exercise 14.10.) But as a counter argument, compare remainders when both integrations are over the same interval and use same number of panels, namely, $6k$, where k is any positive integer.

REFERENCES

1. P. J. Daniel. "Remainders in Interpolation and Quadrature Formulae," *Math. Gaz.* **24**: 238–244 (1940).

2. G. D. Birkoff. "General Mean Value and Remainder Theorems with Applications to Mechanical Differentiation and Quadrature," *Trans. Am. Math. Soc.* **7**: 107–136 (1906).

3. D. V. Widder. "Some Mean-Value Theorems Connected with Cote's Method of Mechanical Quadrature," *Bull. Am. Math. Soc.* **31**: 56–62 (1925).

4. E. B. Leach. "The Remainder Term in Numerical Integration Formulas," *Am. Math. Monthly* **68**: 273–275 (1961).

5. A. Sard. "Integral Representation of Remainders," *Duke Math. J.* **15**: 333–345 (1948).

6. W. E. Milne. "The Remainders in Linear Methods of Approximation," *J. Res. Nat. Bur. Standards* **43**: 501–511 (1949).

7. J. F. Steffensen. *Interpolation.* New York: Chelsea, 1927, 1950; Copenhagen, 1925.

8. R. J. Lambert. "Error Terms of Numerical Integration Formulas," *Proc. Iowa Acad. Sc.* **67**: 369–381 (1960).

16

GAUSSIAN QUADRATURE

16.1 INTRODUCTION

Our summary (Sec. 14.3) of various types of formulas for numerical integration included the so-called Gaussian quadrature formula. By a special selection of the collocation points for the interpolating polynomial upon which his quadrature formula is based, Gauss was able approximately to double the degree of the polynomials for which his formula is exact. We shall show that in the formula

$$\int_a^b f(x)\, dx = \sum_{i=0}^n A_i f_i + R$$

it is possible so to choose the A_i and x_i that $R = 0$ for $f(x)$ any polynomial of degree $\leq 2n + 1$. Brief tables of A_i and x_i are included to expedite the use of the formula.

16.2 DERIVATION

It is convenient to transform the interval $a \leq x \leq b$ into the interval $-1 \leq t \leq 1$ by letting

$$t = \frac{2x - (a + b)}{b - a}.$$

Then

$$\int_a^b f(x)\ dx = \frac{b-a}{2} \int_{-1}^1 F(t)\ dt$$

where

$$F(t) = f\left(\frac{b-a}{2}\ t + \frac{b+a}{2}\right).$$

We seek an integration formula of the form

$$\int_{-1}^1 F(t)\ dt = \sum_{i=0}^n W_i F_i + R^\star \tag{16.1}$$

where

$$F_i = f\left(\frac{b-a}{2}\ t_i + \frac{b+a}{2}\right) = f_i$$

and the W_i and t_i are independent of $F(t)$. Then

$$\int_a^b f(x)\ dx = \frac{b-a}{2} \sum_{i=0}^n W_i f_i + R$$

where $R = \dfrac{b-a}{2}\ R^\star$.

Let $L_n(t)$ be the Lagrangian form of the unique interpolating polynomial of degree $\leq n$ for $F(t)$ with collocation points $t_0, t_1, \ldots, t_n$ (yet to be determined). If $F(t)$ is itself a polynomial of degree $\leq 2n + 1$, then $F(t)$ must be of the form

$$F(t) = L_n(t) + \phi_n(t)\Pi(t) \tag{16.2}$$

where $\phi_n(t)$ is a polynomial of degree $\leq n$ and

$$\Pi(t) = (t - t_0)(t - t_1) \cdots (t - t_n).$$

Integrating both sides of Eq. (16.2) we obtain

$$\int_{-1}^1 F(t)\ dt = \int_{-1}^1 L_n(t)\ dt + \int_{-1}^1 \phi_n(t)\Pi(t)\ dt. \tag{16.3}$$

By integrating the Lagrangian coefficients in $L_n(t)$ we can write

$$\int_{-1}^1 L_n(t)\ dt = \sum_{i=0}^n W_i L_n(t_i) = \sum_{i=0}^n W_i F_i. \tag{16.4}$$

Combining Eqs. (16.3) and (16.4) we obtain

$$\int_{-1}^1 F(t)\ dt = \sum_{i=0}^n W_i F_i + \int_{-1}^1 \phi_n(t)\Pi(t)\ dt. \tag{16.5}$$

Then if we are to have $R^\star = 0$ for $F(t)$ any polynomial of degree $\leq 2n + 1$ we must have

$$\int_{-1}^1 \phi_n(t)\Pi(t)\ dt = 0 \tag{16.6}$$

for $\phi_n(t)$ any polynomial of degree $\leq n$. That is, $\Pi(t)$, a polynomial of degree $n + 1$, must be orthogonal on the interval $(-1, 1)$ to all polynomials of degree $\leq n$. Hence according to Property 6 (Sec. 6.3) $\Pi(t) = CP_{n+1}(t)$, where C is a constant and $P_{n+1}(t)$ the Legendre polynomial of degree $n + 1$. Thus the t_i are the zeros of $P_{n+1}(t)$. For this reason the quadrature formulas under discussion are sometimes referred to as those of Legendre-Gauss.

According to the formula of Lagrange

$$L_n(t) = \sum_{i=0}^{n} \frac{\Pi_{(i)}(t)}{\Pi_{(i)}(t_i)} F_i \tag{16.7}$$

and hence from Eq. (16.4)

$$W_i = \int_{-1}^{1} \frac{\Pi_{(i)}(t)}{\Pi_{(i)}(t_i)} \, dt \, . \tag{16.8}$$

According to Property 7 (Sec. 6.3) the t_i are all real, distinct and lie in the interval $(-1, 1)$.

It is known [1] that if $f(x)$ has a continuous derivative of order $2n + 2$ in the interval (a, b) then there exists in that interval a number ξ for which

$$R = (b - a)^{2n+3} \left[\frac{(n + 1)!}{(n + 2)(n + 3) \cdots (2n + 2)} \right]^2 \frac{f^{(2n+2)}(\xi)}{(2n + 3)!} \, .$$

16.3 SUMMARY AND TABLES

The quadrature formulas of Gauss are of the form

$$\int_a^b f(x) \, dx = \frac{b - a}{2} \sum_{i=0}^{n} W_i f_i + R$$

where

$$f_i = f\left(\frac{b - a}{2} t_i + \frac{b + a}{2} \right)$$

and

$$R = K_n (b - a)^{2n+3} f^{(2n+2)}(\xi), \qquad a < \xi < b.$$

Brief tables of values of W_i, t_i and K_n are given below.

The Legendre polynomials of even degree contain only even powers of t while those of odd degree contain only odd powers. Hence the zeros of these polynomials are symmetrically placed with respect to the origin. If the zeros of $P_{n+1}(t)$ are $t_0 < t_1 < \cdots < t_n$ then $t_i = -t_{n-i}$ and consequently $W_i = W_{n-i}$ (Exercise 16.2). Thus only the positive t_i and corresponding W_i need be tabulated.

The following table with values rounded to eight decimals is from a more extensive table to fifteen places of decimals [2].

Table 16.1

n	$\pm t$	W
1	0.577 350 27	1.000 000 00
2	0.000 000 00	0.888 888 89
	0.774 596 67	0.555 555 56
3	0.339 981 04	0.652 145 15
	0.861 136 31	0.347 854 85
4	0.000 000 00	0.568 888 89
	0.538 469 31	0.478 628 67
	0.906 179 85	0.236 926 89

Table 16.2

n	K_n
1	2.31×10^{-4}
2	4.96×10^{-7}
3	5.62×10^{-10}
4	3.94×10^{-13}

EXAMPLE 16.1

$$\int_0^1 \frac{dx}{1 + x^2} = \frac{1}{2} \sum_{i=0}^4 W_i f_i + R$$

$$f_i = \left[1 + \left(\frac{t_i + 1}{2} \right)^2 \right]^{-1}.$$

i	t_i	W_i	f_i
0	$-0.906\ 179\ 85$	0.236 926 89	0.997 804 27
1	$-0.538\ 469\ 31$	0.478 628 67	0.949 439 82
2	0.000 000 00	0.568 888 89	0.800 000 00
3	0.538 469 31	0.478 628 67	0.628 250 04
4	0.906 179 85	0.236 926 89	0.524 004 54

$$\frac{1}{2} \sum_{i=0}^4 W_i f_i = 0.785\ 398\ 07 \,.$$

The exact answer is

$$\pi/4 \doteq 0.785\ 398\ 16.$$

For purposes of comparison we note that Boole's rule (based on five equally spaced ordinates) gives 0.785 529 41.

Table 16.3 summarizes some examples of the reduction in error effected by use of Legendre-Gauss formulas.

Table 16.3

EXAMPLES OF ERRORS IN NUMERICAL INTEGRATION

		$\displaystyle\int_0^1 \frac{dx}{1+x}$	$\displaystyle\int_0^1 \frac{dx}{1+x^2}$
Three points	Newton-Cotes	−12972	20649
	Legendre-Gauss	255	1312
Five points	Newton-Cotes	−274	−1312
	Legendre-Gauss	2	2

(All numbers in the table are to be multiplied by 10^{-7}.)

EXERCISES

1. If $t_0 < t_1 < t_2 < \cdots < t_n$ are the zeros of the Legendre polynomial of degree $n + 1$ and if $f_n(t)$ and $f_{2n+1}(t)$ are any two polynomials of degree n and $2n + 1$, respectively, such that $f_n(t_i) = f_{2n+1}(t_i)$, $\quad i = 0, 1, 2, \ldots, n$, then

$$\int_{-1}^1 f_n(t)\ dt = \int_{-1}^1 f_{2n+1}(t)\ dt.$$

HINT: $f_{2n+1}(t) = f_n(t) + g_n(t)P_{n+1}(t).$

2. Show that $W_i = W_{n-i}$.

3. Approximate

$$\int_1^2 \frac{dx}{x}$$

using the Legendre-Gauss formula with $n = 2$ and eight decimals. Find an upper bound for absolute value of remainder. Compare with Exercise 14.5.

REFERENCES

1. F. B. Hildebrand. *Introduction to Numerical Analysis.* New York: McGraw-Hill, 1956.

2. A. N. Lowan, N. Davids, and A. Levinson. "Tables of the Zeros of the Legendre Polynomials of Order 1–16 and the Weight Coefficients for Gauss's Mechanical Quadrature Formulas," *Bull. Am. Math. Soc.* **48**: 739–742 (1942); **49**: 939 (1943).

17

METHOD OF

UNDETERMINED

COEFFICIENTS

17.1 INTRODUCTION

In the preceding chapters we have shown how formulas for numerical differentiation and integration can be obtained by differentiating and integrating interpolating polynomials. These results can also be obtained by the so-called *method of undetermined coefficients*. This method is such that it can also be used to produce a larger class of formulas, some of which are especially useful in connection with the numerical solution of differential equations. Briefly the method is simply to anticipate the form of the desired formula with certain undetermined coefficients entering linearly. Conditions upon the formula (for example, that it be exact for polynomials of degree $\leq n$) lead to linear equations in these coefficients. The formula is obtained by solving this system of linear equations.

17.2　EXAMPLES

We illustrate the method with three examples.

EXAMPLE 17.1.　SIMPSON'S RULE.　We suppose

$$\int_{x_0}^{x_2} f(x)\,dx = A_0 f_0 + A_1 f_1 + A_2 f_2 + R$$

where $x_i = x_0 + ih,$　$i = 0, 1, 2$. We wish to determine A_0, A_1, A_2, independent of $f(x)$ and such that $R = 0$ if $f(x)$ is any polynomial of degree ≤ 2. The calculation is simplified by writing the polynomial

$$p(x) = a_0 x^2 + a_1 x + a_2$$

in the form

$$b_0(x - x_0)^2 + b_1(x - x_0) + b_2$$

and observing that if we choose the A_i so that $R = 0$ for $f(x) = 1$, $x - x_0$ and $(x - x_0)^2$ then $R = 0$ for $f(x) = p(x)$. Using these three special polynomials we obtain three equations in the three unknown A_i:

$$A_0 + A_1 + A_2 = 2h$$

$$A_1 + 2A_2 = 2h$$

$$A_1 + 4A_2 = \frac{8}{3}h$$

whence

$$A_0 = \frac{h}{3}, \qquad A_1 = \frac{4}{3}h, \qquad A_2 = \frac{h}{3}$$

and

$$\int_{x_0}^{x_2} f(x)\,dx = \frac{h}{3}\,[f_0 + 4f_1 + f_2] + R$$

where $R = 0$ if $f(x)$ is any polynomial of degree ≤ 2. Actually in this case $R = 0$ for any polynomial of degree ≤ 3.

EXAMPLE 17.2.　TWO-POINT OSCULATORY INTERPOLATION FORMULA.　We seek a polynomial of the form

$$p(x_0 + uh) \doteq A_0(u) f_0 + A_1(u) f_1 + h[B_0(u) f_0' + B_1(u) f_1'],$$

where

$$f_i = f(x_i), \qquad f_i' = \frac{d}{dx} f(x)\bigg]_{x_i}$$

and

$$u = (x - x_0)/h.$$

Here

$$f(x) = p(x) + R(x)$$

and we determine the A_i and B_i so that $R = 0$ if $f(x)$ is any polynomial of degree ≤ 3. Using in turn, as in Example 17.1, the polynomials $1, x - x_0$, $(x - x_0)^2$, and $(x - x_0)^3$ we obtain the equations:

$$A_0 + A_1 \qquad\qquad = 1$$

$$A_1 + B_0 + B_1 = u$$

$$A_1 \qquad + 2B_1 = u^2$$

$$A_1 \qquad + 3B_1 = u^3.$$

Hence

$$A_0 = 1 - u^2(3 - 2u)$$

$$A_1 = u^2(3 - 2u)$$

$$B_0 = u(u - 1)^2$$

$$B_1 = u^2(u - 1)$$

and

$$p(x_0 + uh) = [1 - u^2(3 - 2u)]f_0 + u^2(3 - 2u)f_1$$
$$+ h\{u(u - 1)^2 f_0' + u^2(u - 1)f_1'\}.$$

Note that

$$p(x_i) = f(x_i)$$

$$p'(x_i) = f'(x_i), \qquad i = 0, 1.$$

This is an example of a class of interpolating polynomials first studied by Charles Hermite (1822–1901). (See Exercise 8.5.)

The proof given in Sec. 8.5 can be adapted to show that

$$R(x) = (x - x_0)^2(x - x_1)^2\frac{f^{IV}(\xi)}{4!},$$

$$\min{(x, x_0, x_1)} < \xi < \max{(x, x_0, x_1)}.$$

Tables are available for the coefficients in this two-point formula as well as those for three-, four- and five-point formulas [1].

EXAMPLE 17.3. HAMMING'S CORRECTOR FORMULA. The Hamming method for solving initial value problems in ordinary differential equations (to be discussed in Chap. 18) makes use of a formula of the form

$$f_3 = A_2 f_2 + A_0 f_0 + h[B_3 f_3' + B_2 f_2' + B_1 f_1'] + R.$$

Taking $f(x)$ to be 1, $x - x_0$, $(x - x_0)^2$, $(x - x_0)^3$ and $(x - x_0)^4$ we obtain the equations:

$$A_2 + A_0 = 1$$
$$B_3 + B_2 + B_1 + 2A_2 = 3$$
$$6B_3 + 4B_2 + 2B_1 + 4A_2 = 9$$
$$27B_3 + 12B_2 + 3B_1 + 8A_2 = 27$$
$$108B_3 + 32B_2 + 4B_1 + 16A_2 = 81$$

whence

$$A_0 = -\tfrac{1}{8} \qquad B_1 = -\tfrac{3}{8}$$
$$A_2 = \tfrac{9}{8} \qquad B_2 = \tfrac{6}{8}$$
$$B_3 = \tfrac{3}{8}$$

and

$$f_3 = \tfrac{1}{8}[9f_2 - f_0 + 3h(f_3' + 2f_2' - f_1')].$$

It is known [2] that $R = -\tfrac{1}{40}h^5 f^{\text{V}}(\xi)$.

EXERCISES

1. Use method of undetermined coefficients to establish the following formula for interpolation at the midpoint of an interval of length $2h$:

$$f_0 = \frac{1}{2}[f_1 + f_{-1}] - \frac{h^2}{4}[f_1'' + f_{-1}''] + R.$$

It is known [3] that

$$R = -\tfrac{5}{24}h^4 f^{\text{IV}}(\xi), \qquad x_{-1} < \xi < x_1.$$

2. Use the method of undetermined coefficients to obtain a numerical integration formula of form

$$\int_{x_1}^{x_2} f(x)\, dx = A_0 f_0 + A_1 f_1 + A_2 f_2 + R$$

where $R = 0$ if $f(x)$ is any polynomial of degree ≤ 2. (See Exercise 14.7.)

3. Use the method of undetermined coefficients to determine a polynomial interpolation formula of the form:

$$f(x_0 + uh) = A_{-1}(u)f_{-1} + A_0(u)f_0 + A_1(u)f_1 + B_0(u)f_0' + R.$$

4. The formula of Exercise 17.3 above can be written

$$f'(x_0 + uh) = A_{-1}(u)f_{-1}' + A_0(u)f_0' + A_1(u)f_1' + B_0(u)f_0'' + R.$$

Integrate this formula over appropriate intervals to obtain the so-called Milne starter formulas for numerical solution of initial value problems in ordinary differential equations:

$$f_1 = f_0 + \frac{h}{24}\left[7f_1' + 16f_0' + f_{-1}'\right] + \frac{h^2}{4}f_0'' + R_1$$

$$f_{-1} = f_0 - \frac{h}{24}\left[f_1' + 16f_0' + 7f_{-1}'\right] + \frac{h^2}{4}f_0'' + R_{-1}$$

$$f_2 = f_0 + \frac{2h}{3}\left[5f_1' - f_0' - f_{-1}'\right] - 2h^2 f_0'' + R_2.$$

It is known [4] that

$$R_1 = -\tfrac{1}{180}h^5 f^{\mathrm{V}}(\xi), \qquad R_{-1} = \tfrac{1}{180}h^5 f^{\mathrm{V}}(\xi), \qquad R_2 = \tfrac{7}{45}h^5 f^{(5)}(\xi).$$

5. Use method of undetermined coefficients to derive the formula

$$f_{j+1} = 5f_{j-1} - 4f_j + 2h[f_{j-1}' + 2f_j'] + R.$$

It is known [5] that $R = \tfrac{1}{6}h^4 f^{\mathrm{IV}}(\xi)$.

6. Use method of undetermined coefficients to derive Milne's stabilizer formula [6]:

$$f_{j+1} = f_j + \frac{h}{24}\left[9f_{j+1}' + 19f_j' - 5f_{j-1}' + f_{j-2}'\right] + R$$

Milne found that $R = -\tfrac{19}{720}h^5 f^{\mathrm{V}}(\xi)$. Derive above formula using integral tables of Chap. 14.

REFERENCES

1. H .E. Salzer. *Tables of Osculatory Interpolation Coefficients*. Washington D.C.: National Bureau of Standards, U.S. Government Printing Office, 1959.

2. R. W. Hamming. "Stable Predictor-Corrector Methods for Ordinary Differential Equations," *J. Assoc. Comput. Mach.* **6:** 37–47 (1959).

3. D. A. Pope. "A Method of 'Alternating Corrections' for the Numerical Solution of Two-Point Boundary Value Problems," *Math Comput.* **14:** 354–361 (1960).

4. W. E. Milne. "Note on The Numerical Integration of Differential Equations," *Am. Math. Monthly* **48:** 52–53 (1941).

5. T. H. Southard, and E. C. Yowell. "An Alternative 'predictor-Corrector' Process," *Math. Tables Aids Comput.* **6:** 253–254 (1952).

6. W. E. Milne, and R. R. Reynolds, "Fifth-Order Methods for the Numerical Solution of Ordinary Differential Equations," *J. Assoc. Comput. Mach.* **9:** 64–70 (1962).

18

INITIAL VALUE PROBLEMS

IN ORDINARY

DIFFERENTIAL EQUATIONS

18.1 INTRODUCTION

Numerical methods in differential equations produce particular solutions in tabular form. A wide variety of methods are available which produce discrete sets of points on or near the solution curve. Such methods are required when explicit expressions for the solution are either not available or are too complicated to be of computational interest.

The solution of the initial value problem

$$y' = 1 - 2xy$$

$$y = 0 \quad \text{at} \quad x = 0$$

is

$$y = e^{-x^2} \int_0^x e^{u^2} \, du.$$

139

It is known that the integral on the right cannot be evaluated in terms of elementary functions. Although this integral could be evaluated by the methods of Chap. 14 (see Example 14.1), it is just about as easy to obtain the solution directly by one of the methods to be described. It happens in this particular case that the solution has been tabulated [1,2]. The existence of tabulations of functions can be discovered by consulting indices of mathematical tables to be found in the world mathematical literature [3,4,5]. On the other hand, the solution [6] of the initial value problem

$$\frac{dy}{dx} = x + \frac{2y}{1 - x^4}$$

$$y = 1 \quad \text{at} \quad x = 0$$

is

$$y = \left(\frac{1 + x}{1 - x}\right)^{1/2} e^{\tan^{-1} x} \left\{ \int_0^x u \left(\frac{1 - u}{1 + u}\right)^{1/2} e^{-\tan^{-1} u} \, du + 1 \right\}.$$

It does not seem to be known whether or not the integral on the right can be expressed in terms of functions for which we have tables. But there seems little chance that such an expression, if it exists, would be simple. The numerical work involved in evaluating the expression given above is far greater than that involved in obtaining the solution directly in tabular form by the methods to be discussed.

Actually the class of problems that can be solved in terms of elementary functions is quite limited. Furthermore, few problems have series solutions that are sufficiently simple and rapidly enough convergent over a wide interval to be of computational interest. But Taylor series can be used locally to good advantage and also form the basis of the popular Runge-Kutta methods to be discussed.

In practice, the differential equation may involve functions which are known only in tabular form and for which no simple analytical expressions are available. Ballistic problems involving an air resistance function are usually of this type. Here numerical methods are mandatory.

Most of the present chapter will be devoted to the initial value problem

$$y' = f(x, y)$$

$$y = y_0 \quad \text{at} \quad x = x_0. \tag{18.1}$$

It is known [7] that for mildly restricted functions $f(x, y)$ the problem has a solution and it is unique. That is, there exists an unique function $\phi(x)$ such that

$$\phi'(x) \equiv f(x, \phi(x))$$

and

$$\phi(x_0) = y_0.$$

The methods to be discussed in this chapter have, however, been extended to equations of higher order and to systems of differential equations. We shall briefly describe some of these extensions.

18.2 POLYGON OR EULER'S METHOD

The simplest of all numerical methods for solving initial value problems is that attributed to Euler. It is a naïve method of very limited accuracy and not recommended in practice. It furnishes, however, a very convenient starting point for the discussion of methods of practical interest.

In Euler's method, points (x_i, y_i) "near" the solution curve of the initial value problem, Eq. (18.1), are calculated successively by the formula

$$y_{i+1} = y_i + hf(x_i, y_i), \qquad i = 1, 2, 3, \ldots \qquad (18.2)$$

starting with the point (x_0, y_0). Here $h = x_{i+1} - x_i$ and is usually kept fixed. The successive points (x_i, y_i) are vertices of a polygon each segment of which has a slope equal to that of the solution curve through its left end point.

EXAMPLE 18.1.   The solution of the initial value problem

$$\frac{dy}{dx} = y - \frac{2x}{y}$$

$$y = 1 \quad \text{at} \quad x = 0$$

is

$$y = \sqrt{2x + 1},$$

so we can directly assess the accuracy of the Euler method. In cases of practical interest, the accuracy must, of course, be estimated by some indirect means. Here, taking $h = 0.2$, we find

$$y_0 = 1,$$

$$y_{i+1} = y_i + 0.2\left(y_i - \frac{2x_i}{y_i}\right)$$

$$= 1.2y_i - \frac{0.08i}{y_i}.$$

Thus

$$y_1 = 1.200$$

$$y_2 = 1.2 \times 1.2 - \frac{0.08}{1.2} = 1.373.$$

Continuing in this way, we obtain the following table of points (x_i, y_i). Points on the exact solution $y = \sqrt{2x + 1}$ are included for comparison.

x_i	y_i	$\sqrt{2x_i + 1}$
0	1	1
0.2	1.200	1.183
0.4	1.373	1.342
0.6	1.532	1.483
0.8	1.681	1.612
1.0	1.827	1.732

The values in the middle column were originally computed using five places of decimals and then rounded to 3, so as not to confuse the considerable truncation error (error of the method) with the cumulation of error due to rounding.

Among the various geometrical and analytical interpretations of the Euler method are the following two, which suggest generalizations producing methods of practical interest to be described later.

(a) The linear Taylor polynomial

$$y(x_i + h) = y(x_i) + hy'(x_i) \tag{18.3}$$

approximates the solution in the neighborhood of the point (x_i, y_i). It is, of course, only another way of writing the recursion formula, Eq. (18.2) of Euler's method. But writing it in form of Eq. (18.3) suggests using Taylor polynomials of higher degree. This is an effective method, except that the evaluation of the higher-order derivatives can be very tedious. The Runge-Kutta methods make use of Taylor approximations indirectly in such a way as to eliminate this problem.

(b) Integrating the identity

$$y'(x) = f(x, y(x))$$

between the limits x_i and x_{i+1} gives

$$y(x_{i+1}) - y(x_i) = \int_{x_i}^{x_{i+1}} f(x, y(x)) \, dx. \tag{18.4}$$

Using the crude approximation $hf(x_i, y(x_i))$ for the integral we identify Eq. (18.4) with Eq. (18.2). The use of more accurate formulas to approximate this integral is one of the ideas involved in the popular predict-correct methods to be discussed in a later section.

18.3 RUNGE-KUTTA METHODS FOR FIRST-ORDER DIFFERENTIAL EQUATIONS

The Runge-Kutta methods are the most popular of the *single-step methods*, that is, of the methods in which y_{i+1} can be obtained from y_i alone and the differential equation. The methods are thus self-starting and are not difficult to program for high-speed digital computers. In this section we shall limit our attention to the initial value problem, Eqs. (18.1). While Taylor series can be used directly to proceed from point to point, the differentiations required are tedious. Runge [8] pointed out a way of using Taylor series indirectly so as to avoid the evaluation of derivatives. His method required only the computation of several values of f itself for each step. Kutta [9] simplified and extended the method.

According to the theorem of the mean for derivatives (A.1), there exists at least one number α_i, $0 < \alpha_i < 1$, for which

$$y_{i+1} = y_i + hy'(x_i + \alpha_i h).$$

But

$$y'(x_i + \alpha_i h) = f(x_i + \alpha_i h, y(x_i + \alpha_i h))$$

and

$$y(x_i + \alpha_i h) = y_0 + \beta_i h.$$

Thus there exists a pair of numbers (α_i, β_i) such that

$$\Delta y_i = y_{i+1} - y_i = f(x_i + \alpha_i h, y_i + \beta_i h)h. \tag{18.5}$$

This suggests the possibility of approximating Δy_i in terms of values of f at certain predetermined values of its arguments.

The Runge-Kutta methods used in practice are based on quartic Taylor approximations. Although these methods are simple and accurate, their derivations entail somewhat complicated calculations. So we shall derive only the Runge-Kutta methods based on quadratic Taylor approximations. While these are of little computational interest, they are completely adequate to describe the idea of all Runge-Kutta methods.

18.31 *RUNGE-KUTTA QUADRATIC METHODS.* For the sake of simplicity of notation we shall describe the method of going from the initial point (x_0, y_0) to the point (x_1, y_1). It is to be understood, however, that the identical procedure is to be used in going from the point (x_i, y_i) to the point (x_{i+1}, y_{i+1}). We have noted, Eq. (18.5), that numbers α_0, β_0 exist for which

$$y_1 = y_0 + f(x_0 + \alpha_0 h, y_0 + \beta_0 h)h$$

where $h = x_1 - x_0$. We shall see that it is possible to approximate $f(x_0 + \alpha_0 h,$ $y_0 + \beta_0 h)h$ by a linear combination k of two values of fh at specified points near (x_0, y_0) in such a way that the quadratic Taylor approximation to $Y_1 = y_0 + k$ (as a function of h) is precisely equal to the quadratic Taylor approximation to $y_1(h)$, the solution curve through the point (x_0, y_0).

The quadratic Taylor approximation to y_1 is

$$y_1^\star = y_0 + f(x_0, y_0)h + \tfrac{1}{2}[f_x(x_0, y_0) + f(x_0, y_0)f_y(x_0, y_0)]h^2.$$

We let

$$Y_1 = y_0 + k$$

where

$$
\begin{aligned}
k &= a_1 k_1 + a_2 k_2 \\
k_1 &= f(x_0, y_0)h \\
k_2 &= f(x_0 + \alpha h, y_0 + \beta k_1)h.
\end{aligned}
\tag{18.6}
$$

The quadratic Taylor approximations to k_1 and k_2 are

$$
\begin{aligned}
k_1^\star &= k_1 = f(x_0, y_0)h \\
k_2^\star &= f(x_0, y_0)h + [f_x(x_0, y_0)\alpha + f(x_0, y_0)f_y(x_0, y_0)\beta]h^2.
\end{aligned}
$$

Then the quadratic Taylor approximation to Y_1 is

$$Y_1^\star = y_0 + a_1 k_1^\star + a_2 k_2^\star$$

and $Y_1^\star = y_1^\star$ if and only if

$$
\begin{aligned}
a_1 + a_2 &= 1 \\
a_2 \alpha &= \tfrac{1}{2} \\
a_2 \beta &= \tfrac{1}{2}.
\end{aligned}
$$

Thus Y_1 and y_1 (as functions of h) have the same quadratic Taylor approximations if we take

$$a_1 = 1 - \lambda, \quad a_2 = \lambda, \quad \alpha = \beta = \frac{1}{2\lambda},$$

where λ is arbitrary but $\neq 0$. It is thus reasonable to use Y_1 to approximate y_1. Therefore, by using a weighted average of values of f at two points, we obtain an approximation for y_1 whose quadratic Taylor approximation is precisely the quadratic Taylor approximation to y_1 itself *without* evaluation of partial derivatives of f.

Two methods of special interest, obtained by taking $\lambda = \tfrac{1}{2}$ and $\lambda = 1$, are discussed in two following sections.

18.311 *IMPROVED EULER-CAUCHY METHOD.* Taking $\lambda = \tfrac{1}{2}$ in (18.6) we obtain

$$Y_1 = y_0 + k$$

where

$$k = \tfrac{1}{2}(k_1 + k_2)$$
$$k_1 = f(x_0, y_0)h$$
$$k_2 = f(x_0 + h, y_0 + k_1)h.$$

These may be combined to give the following formula for passing from the point (x_i, y_i) to the point (x_{i+1}, y_{i+1}):

$$y_{i+1} = y_i + (h/2)[f(x_i, y_i) + f(x_i + h, y_i + f(x_i, y_i)h)]. \qquad (18.7)$$

This method is sometimes also referred to as the *Heun method*. It admits of a simple geometric interpretation. (See Exercise 18.1.)

18.312   *IMPROVED POLYGON METHOD.*   Taking $\lambda = 1$ in Eq. (18.6) we obtain

$$Y_1 = y_0 + k$$

where

$$k = k_2$$
$$k_1 = f(x_0, y_0)h$$
$$k_2 = f(x_0 + \tfrac{1}{2}h, y_0 + \tfrac{1}{2}k_1)h.$$

These may be combined to give the following formula:

$$y_{i+1} = y_i + hf\left(x_i + \frac{1}{2}h, y_i + \frac{h}{2}f(x_i, y_i)\right). \qquad (18.8)$$

Here we are using the slope at an intermediate point and obtain somewhat more accurate results than in the polygon method wherein

$$y_{i+1} = y_i + hf(x_i, y_i).$$

18.32   *RUNGE-KUTTA QUARTIC METHODS.*   The discussion of the preceding sections has been extended to obtain linear combinations of four values of fh having precisely the same quartic Taylor approximations as the solution curve of the differential equation through the point (x_i, y_i). We let

$$k_1 = f(x_0, y_0)h$$
$$k_2 = f(x_0 + \alpha h, y_0 + \beta k_1)h$$
$$k_3 = f(x_0 + \alpha_1 h, y_0 + \beta_1 k_1 + \gamma_1 k_2)h$$
$$k_4 = f(x_0 + \alpha_2 h, y_0 + \beta_2 k_1 + \gamma_2 k_2 + \delta_2 k_3)h$$

and

$$k = a_1 k_1 + a_2 k_2 + a_3 k_3 + a_4 k_4.$$

By equating the quartic Taylor approximations to $Y_1 = y_0 + k$ and the solution y_1 (as functions of h) we obtain, after a somewhat laborious calculation, the following eleven equations in the thirteen parameters α, β, α_1, β_1, γ_1, α_2, β_2, γ_2, δ_2, a_1, a_2, a_3, a_4:

$$
\begin{aligned}
a_1 + \quad a_2 + \quad a_3 + \qquad\qquad\quad a_4 &= 1 \\
\alpha a_2 + \quad \alpha_1 a_3 + \qquad\qquad \alpha_2 a_4 &= \tfrac{1}{2} \\
\alpha^2 a_2 + \quad \alpha_1^2 a_3 + \qquad\qquad \alpha_2^2 a_4 &= \tfrac{1}{3} \\
\alpha^3 a_2 + \quad \alpha_1^3 a_3 + \qquad\qquad \alpha_2^3 a_4 &= \tfrac{1}{4} \\
\alpha \gamma_1 a_3 + (\alpha \gamma_2 + \alpha_1 \delta_2) a_4 &= \tfrac{1}{6} \\
\alpha^2 \gamma_1 a_3 + (\alpha^2 \gamma_2 + \alpha_1^2 \delta_2) a_4 &= \tfrac{1}{12} \\
\alpha \alpha_1 \gamma_1 a_3 + (\alpha \gamma_2 + \alpha_1 \delta_2) a_4 &= \tfrac{1}{8} \\
\alpha \gamma_1 \delta_2 a_4 &= \tfrac{1}{24}
\end{aligned}
\tag{18.9}
$$

$$
\begin{aligned}
\alpha &= \beta \\
\alpha_1 &= \beta_1 + \gamma_1 \\
\alpha_2 &= \beta_2 + \gamma_2 + \delta_2.
\end{aligned}
$$

Since there are fewer equations than unknowns, the system has many solutions [10]. The solution favored by Runge [11] and Collatz [12] leads to the following:

$$
\begin{aligned}
k_1 &= f(x_0, y_0)h \\
k_2 &= f(x_0 + \tfrac{1}{2}h, y_0 + \tfrac{1}{2}k_1)h \\
k_3 &= f(x_0 + \tfrac{1}{2}h, y_0 + \tfrac{1}{2}k_2)h \\
k_4 &= f(x_0 + h, y_0 + k_3)h \\
k &= \tfrac{1}{6}(k_1 + 2k_2 + 2k_3 + k_4).
\end{aligned}
\tag{18.10}
$$

This may be summarized in the following table:

x	y	$k_\nu = f(x,y)h$	k
x_0	y_0	k_1	
$x_0 + \tfrac{1}{2}h$	$y_0 + \tfrac{1}{2}k_1$	k_2	
$x_0 + \tfrac{1}{2}h$	$y_0 + \tfrac{1}{2}k_2$	k_3	
$x_0 + h$	$y_0 + k_3$	k_4	$\tfrac{1}{6}(k_1 + 2k_2 + 2k_3 + k_4)$
$x_1 = x_0 + h$	$y_1 = y_0 + k$		

Another solution of the system of Eqs. (18.9) has been recommended by Gill [13,14] which has the advantage for automatic computation on machines with small memories of requiring minimum storage as well as relatively few program instructions.

EXAMPLE 18.2.   We use the Runge-Kutta quartic method to calculate three additional points on the solution curve of the initial value problem

$$\frac{dy}{dx} = 1 - 2xy$$

$$y = 0 \quad \text{at} \quad x = 0.$$

x	y	k_v	k
0	0	0.1	
0.05	0.05	0.099 5	
0.05	0.049 75	0.099 502	
0.1	0.099 502	0.098 010	0.099 336
0.1	0.099 336	0.098 013	
0.15	0.148 343	0.095 550	
0.15	0.147 111	0.095 587	
0.2	0.194 923	0.092 203	0.095 415
0.2	0.194 751	0.092 210	
0.25	0.240 856	0.087 957	
0.25	0.238 730	0.088 064	
0.3	0.282 815	0.083 031	0.087 881
0.3	0.282 632	0.083 042	

The underscored numbers in the above table are coördinates of points on solution curve of our initial value problem. The calculated ordinates differ by at most 1 in the last place from those given in the table of Miller and Gordon [2]. (See also Example 14.1.)

Error estimates of this method have been given by Bieberbach [7,12] and by Carr [15].

18.33   *RUNGE-KUTTA METHODS FOR SECOND ORDER DIF-FERENTIAL EQUATIONS.*   The initial value problem

$$y'' = f(x, y, y')$$

$$y = y_0, \qquad y' = y_0' \quad \text{at} \quad x = x_0 \tag{18.11}$$

can be solved by a natural generalization of the methods of the preceding sections. Again many possibilities arise. Nyström [16] found the following simple procedure. Starting with x_0, y_0 and $v_0 = hy_0'$ the following quantities are calculated in the order listed:

$$k_1 = \frac{1}{2} h^2 f\left(x_0, y_0, \frac{v_0}{h}\right)$$

$$k_2 = \frac{1}{2} h^2 f\left(x_0 + \frac{1}{2} h, y_0 + \frac{1}{2} v_0 + \frac{1}{4} k_1, \frac{v_0 + k_1}{h}\right)$$

$$k_3 = \frac{1}{2} h^2 f\left(x_0 + \frac{1}{2} h, y_0 + \frac{1}{2} v_0 + \frac{1}{4} k_1, \frac{v_0 + k_2}{h}\right)$$

$$k_4 = \frac{1}{2} h^2 f\left(x_0 + h, y_0 + v_0 + k_3, \frac{v_0 + 2k_3}{h}\right) \qquad (18.12)$$

$$k = \tfrac{1}{3}(k_1 + k_2 + k_3)$$

$$k' = \tfrac{1}{3}(k_1 + 2k_2 + 2k_3 + k_4)$$

$$x_1 = x_0 + h$$

$$y_1 = y_0 + v_0 + k$$

$$v_1 = v_0 + k'.$$

Again we have a procedure which can be very briefly summarized in a table:

x	y	$hy' = v$	$k_v = \dfrac{h^2}{2} f\left(x, y, \dfrac{v}{h}\right)$	Corrections
x_0	y_0	v_0	k_1	
$x_0 + \tfrac{1}{2}h$	$y_0 + \tfrac{1}{2}v_0 + \tfrac{1}{4}k_1$	$v_0 + k_1$	k_2	
$x_0 + \tfrac{1}{2}h$	$y_0 + \tfrac{1}{2}v_0 + \tfrac{1}{4}k_1$	$v_0 + k_2$	k_3	k
$x_0 + h$	$y_0 + v_0 + k_3$	$v_0 + 2k_3$	k_4	k'
$x_1 = x_0 + h$	$y_1 = y_0 + v_0 + k$	$v_1 = v_0 + k'$		

where $k = \tfrac{1}{3}(k_1 + k_2 + k_3)$ and $k' = \tfrac{1}{3}(k_1 + 2k_2 + 2k_3 + k_4)$.

Similar extensions to equations of third and fourth orders are summarized in Collatz [12].

18.34   *RUNGE-KUTTA METHODS FOR A SYSTEM OF DIFFER-ENTIAL EQUATIONS.*   The initial value problem

$$\frac{dy}{dx} = f(x, y, z)$$

$$\frac{dz}{dx} = g(x, y, z)$$

(8.13)

$$y = y_0, \qquad z = z_0 \quad \text{at} \quad x = x_0$$

can be solved by the following procedure. Starting with x_0, y_0, z_0 the following quantities are calculated in the order given:

$$
\begin{aligned}
k_1 &= f(x_0, y_0, z_0)h \\
l_1 &= g(x_0, y_0, z_0)h \\
k_2 &= f(x_0 + \tfrac{1}{2}h, y_0 + \tfrac{1}{2}k_1, z_0 + \tfrac{1}{2}l_1)h \\
l_2 &= g(x_0 + \tfrac{1}{2}h, y_0 + \tfrac{1}{2}k_1, z_0 + \tfrac{1}{2}l_1)h \\
k_3 &= f(x_0 + \tfrac{1}{2}h, y_0 + \tfrac{1}{2}k_2, z_0 + \tfrac{1}{2}l_2)h \\
l_3 &= g(x_0 + \tfrac{1}{2}h, y_0 + \tfrac{1}{2}k_2, z_0 + \tfrac{1}{2}l_2)h \\
k_4 &= f(x_0 + h, y_0 + k_3, z_0 + l_3)h \\
l_4 &= g(x_0 + h, y_0 + k_3, z_0 + l_3)h \\
k &= \tfrac{1}{6}(k_1 + 2k_2 + 2k_3 + k_4) \\
l &= \tfrac{1}{6}(l_1 + 2l_2 + 2l_3 + l_4) \\
y_1 &= y_0 + k \\
z_1 &= z_0 + l.
\end{aligned}
$$

(8.14)

Again we have a procedure that can be summarized in the form of a table:

x	y	z	k_ν	l_ν	Corrections
x_0	y_0	z_0	k_1	l_1	
$x_0 + \tfrac{1}{2}h$	$y_0 + \tfrac{1}{2}k_1$	$z_0 + \tfrac{1}{2}l_1$	k_2	l_2	
$x_0 + \tfrac{1}{2}h$	$y_0 + \tfrac{1}{2}k_2$	$z_0 + \tfrac{1}{2}l_2$	k_3	l_3	k
$x_0 + h$	$y_0 + k_3$	$z_0 + l_3$	k_4	l_4	l
$x_1 = x_0 + h$	$y_1 = y_0 + k$	$z_1 = z_0 + l$			

where

$$k_\nu = f(x, y, z)h, \qquad l_\nu = g(x, y, z)h$$

and

$$k = \tfrac{1}{6}(k_1 + 2k_2 + 2k_3 + k_4), \qquad l = \tfrac{1}{6}(l_1 + 2l_2 + 2l_3 + l_4).$$

18.4 PREDICT-CORRECT METHODS

If $\phi(x)$ is the solution of the initial value problem

$$\frac{dy}{dx} = f(x, y)$$

$$y = y_0 \quad \text{at} \quad x = x_0,$$

then

$$\phi(x_{j+1}) = \phi(x_i) + \int_{x_i}^{x_{j+1}} f(x, \phi(x)) \, dx$$
$$= \phi(x_i) + \int_{x_i}^{x_{j+1}} \phi'(x) \, dx. \tag{18.15}$$

Many numerical integration formulas are available for approximating the integral involved, each leading to an approximation for $\phi(x_{j+1})$. If the formula does not require a prior estimate of $\phi'(x_{j+1})$ we shall call it a *predictor*, otherwise a *corrector*. Any of the open integration formulas of Chap. 14 may be used for predictors and the closed formulas for correctors but there are other possibilities. The choice of integration formula is usually a compromise between simplicity and accuracy, although there are other considerations which will not be entered into here. Naturally a reasonably accurate approximation of the integral involved requires several "previous" values of ϕ'. Thus if four previous values are known, we may approximate the integral

$$\int_{x_i}^{x_{j+1}} \phi'(x) \, dx$$

by formulas of the form:

$$a_0 \phi'_j + a_1 \phi'_{j-1} + a_2 \phi'_{j-2} + a_3 \phi'_{j-3},$$
$$b_0 \phi'_{j+1} + b_1 \phi'_j + b_2 \phi'_{j-1} + b_3 \phi'_{j-2} + b_4 \phi'_{j-3}$$

thus obtaining predictors and correctors, respectively. In each case x_i is some one of the four preceding values of x.

Milne's method uses Milne's formula (Sec. 14.82) as predictor and Simpson's rule as corrector. In the notation of this chapter they would be written:

$$\phi_{j+1} = \phi_{j-3} + \frac{4h}{3} [2\phi'_j - \phi'_{j-1} + 2\phi'_{j-2}]$$
$$+ \frac{28}{90} h^5 \phi^{V}(\xi_1), \qquad x_{j-3} < \xi_1 < x_{j+1},$$

$$\phi_{j+1} = \phi_{j-1} + \frac{h}{3} [\phi'_{j+1} + 4\phi'_j + \phi'_{j-1}]$$
$$- \frac{1}{90} h^5 \phi^{V}(\xi_2), \qquad x_{j-1} < \xi_2 < x_{j+1}.$$

The advantage of following up a predictor with a corrector is, of course, that the latter type formula can have a much smaller remainder. The remainders in the example just quoted are in the approximate ratio $1:28$.

Once we write the predictor and corrector formulas furnished by numerical integration formulas, it is natural to investigate formulas for ϕ_{j+1} involving several previous values of ϕ as well as of ϕ'. Hamming's corrector formula (Example 17.3) is one such:

$$\phi_{j+1} = \tfrac{1}{8}[9\phi_j - \phi_{j-2} + 3h(\phi'_{j+1} + 2\phi'_j - \phi'_{j-1})] - \tfrac{1}{40} h^5 \phi^{\mathrm{V}}(\xi).$$

Predict-correct methods are step-by-step procedures for obtaining from a set of points on the solution curve a "next" point. The Runge-Kutta methods are, of course, examples of step-by-step procedures with each step depending on only the one preceding. Our initial value problem has been very aptly described as a "marching" problem.

18.5   THE HAMMING METHOD [17]

Once four "consecutive" points on the solution curve of the initial value problem have been found, a fifth point is found by the following sequence of calculations:

Predict: $p_{j+1} = y_{j-3} + \dfrac{4h}{3} (2y'_j - y'_{j-1} + 2y'_{j-2})$

Modify: $m_{j+1} = p_{j+1} + \tfrac{112}{121}(c_j - p_j)$ (18.18)

Correct: $c_{j+1} = \tfrac{1}{8}[9y_j - y_{j-2} + 3h(m'_{j+1} + 2y'_j - y'_{j-1})]$

Final Value: $y_{j+1} = c_{j+1} - \tfrac{9}{121}(c_{j+1} - p_{j+1}).$

This is essentially a predict-correct method based on the following two formulas:

$$y_{j+1} = y_{j-3} + \frac{4h}{3} (2y'_j - y'_{j-1} + 2y'_{j-2})$$
$$+ \frac{28}{90} h^5 y^{(5)}(\xi_1), \qquad x_{j-3} < \xi_1 < x_{j+1},$$

$$y_{j+1} = \tfrac{1}{8}[9y_j - y_{j-2} + 3h(y'_{j+1} + 2y'_j - y'_{j-1})]$$
$$- \tfrac{1}{40}h^5 y^{(5)}(\xi_2), \qquad x_{j-2} < \xi_2 < x_{j+1}.$$

(18.19)

It has the added feature that estimates of the errors of the predictor and corrector are used to "mop up" their errors.

The corrector formula used here is preferable to Simpson's rule in spite of the fact that the numerical coefficient in its remainder is $-1/40$, while for Simpson's rule it is $-1/90$. It is known that if Simpson's rule were to be used for the corrector the method would be *unstable*. Roughly speaking, this means that an error at step j (due to truncation and/or round-off) tends to propagate with increasing magnitude in succeeding steps [14]. Thus Milne's method is unstable, whereas Hamming's method can be shown to be stable. Although other choices are available for the corrector, none have the appealing simplicity of the one used here.

The basic assumption in the derivation of the method is that the fifth derivative of the solution is essentially constant over the interval involved in any one step of the calculation. The method is exact if the solution is a polynomial of degree ≤ 6. Note that

$$y_{j+1} = p_{j+1} + \tfrac{28}{90} h^5 y^{(5)}(\xi_1), \qquad x_{j-3} < \xi_1 < x_{j+1},$$

and

$$y_{j+1} = c_{j+1} - \tfrac{1}{40} h^5 y^{(5)}(\xi_2), \qquad x_{j-2} < \xi_2 < x_{j+1}. \tag{18.20}$$

Then (A.7)

$$0 = p_{j+1} - c_{j+1} + \tfrac{121}{360} h^5 y^{(5)}(\xi), \qquad x_{j-3} < \xi < x_{j+1}.$$

Hence

$$h^5 y^{(5)}(\xi) = \tfrac{360}{121} (c_{j+1} - p_{j+1})$$

and under our basic assumption

$$\begin{aligned}
y_{j+1} &\doteq p_{j+1} + \tfrac{112}{121} (c_{j+1} - p_{j+1}) \\
&\doteq p_{j+1} + \tfrac{112}{121} (c_j - p_j) = m_{j+1}
\end{aligned} \tag{18.21}$$

and

$$y_{j+1} \doteq c_{j+1} - \tfrac{9}{121} (c_{j+1} - p_{j+1}).$$

The fifth line of the solution (the first line using the Hamming method) requires the value of $c_3 - p_3$ which is, of course, not available. The best procedure seems to be to set $c_3 - p_3 = 0$.

EXAMPLE 18.3. We use the Hamming method to continue the solution of the initial value problem started in Example 18.2:

x	y	y'	$c - p$
0	0	1	
0.1	0.099 336	0.980 133	
0.2	0.194 751	0.922 100	
0.3	0.282 632	0.830 421	
0.4	0.359 945	0.712 044	0.000 084
0.5	0.424 435	0.575 565	55
0.6	0.474 759	0.430 289	19
0.7	0.510 497	0.285 304	−0.000 016

18.6 REMARKS

The Runge-Kutta quartic method requires four evaluations of $f(x, y)$ to obtain a single point on the solution curve of the initial value problem. This may be impractical if $f(x, y)$ is complicated in form. Another disadvantage of the method is that the calculation procedure furnishes no direct estimate of the error. On the positive side of the ledger, the method is "self-starting," that is, only one point on the solution curve is required to find a "next." For the above reasons we recommend using the Runge-Kutta quartic method to obtain three points on the solution curve in addition to the initial point and then proceeding with the Hamming method. This seems to be a popular method for use with digital computers.

Of all the predict-correct methods available in the literature, we have emphasized the Hamming method because of its appealing simplicity and because it can be shown to be stable. The problem of assessing the relative merits of various methods is, of course, an important one for the numerical analyst. Its study involves, among other things, a knowledge of difference equations, which we consider more appropriate for a second course [18].

EXERCISES

1. Make sketches showing various points and slopes involved in the improved Euler-Cauchy and improved polygon methods.

2. Apply the improved Euler-Cauchy and improved polygon methods to the initial value problem of Example 18.1. Compare results with exact solution.

3. Verify [show that the parameters satisfy Eqs. (18.9)] that another Runge-Kutta quartic method is that summarized in the following table:

x	y	$k_\nu = f(x, y)h$	k
x_0	y_0	k_1	
$x_0 + \frac{1}{4}h$	$y_0 + k_1$	k_2	
$x_0 + \frac{1}{2}h$	$y_0 + \frac{1}{2}k_2$	k_3	
$x_0 + h$	$y_0 + k_1 - 2k_2 + 2k_3$	k_4	$\frac{1}{6}(k_1 + 4k_3 + k_4)$
$x_1 = x_0 + h$	$y_1 = y_0 + k$		

4. Show that the Runge-Kutta methods given in Sec. 18.32 and in Exercise 18.3 above both reduce to Simpson's rule in case f is a function of x alone.

5. The unique solution of the initial value problem

$$\frac{dy}{dx} = -xy, \qquad y(0) = 1$$

is $y(x) = e^{-x^2/2}$. Find approximate value of $y(0.2)$ using one application of the Runge-Kutta quartic method. Find value of Taylor quartic approximation to $e^{-x^2/2}$ at $x = 0.2$.

6. Use Runge-Kutta quartic method together with the Hamming method to solve the initial value problem

$$\frac{dy}{dx} = 0.1y^2 - xy, \qquad y(0) = 1, \qquad 0 \le x \le 1.$$

Take $h = 0.2$. Compare with analytical solution

$$y = e^{-x^2/2}\left[1 - \frac{1}{10}\int_0^x e^{-u^2/2}\,du\right]^{-1},$$

using a table of the normal probability integral.

7. Develop a Hamming-type (predictor-modifier-corrector-final value) method based on the formulas:

$$y_{j+1} = y_{j-3} + \frac{4h}{3}\left(2y_j' - y_{j-1}' + 2y_{j-2}'\right) + \frac{28}{90}h^5 y^{(5)}(\xi_1)$$

$$y_{j+1} = y_{j-1} + \frac{h}{3}(y_{j+1}' + 4y_j' + y_{j-1}') - \frac{1}{90}h^5 y^{(5)}(\xi_2).$$

8. Develop Hamming-type method [20] based on the formulas:

$$y_{j+1} = \frac{1}{3}\left(2y_{j-1} + y_{j-2}\right) + \frac{h}{72}\left(191y_j' - 107y_{j-1}'\right.$$

$$\left. + 109y_{j-2}' - 25y_{j-3}'\right) + \frac{707}{2160}\,h^5 y^{(5)}(\xi_1),$$

$$y_{j+1} = \frac{1}{3}\left(2y_{j-1} + y_{j-2}\right) + \frac{h}{72}\left(25m_{j+1}' + 91y_j'\right.$$

$$\left. + 43y_{j-1}' + 9y_{j-2}'\right) - \frac{43}{2160}\,h^5 y^{(5)}(\xi_2).$$

9. The fourth of the five five-point numerical differentiation formulas of Sec. 13.5 can be written so as to express y_{j+1} in terms of preceding values of y and y'. Do so, thus obtaining a low accuracy predictor.

10. Rewrite the numerical integration formulas in Exercises 14.7 and 14.8 in form suitable for use as corrector and predictor, respectively.

11. The Hamming method can be applied to the second-order initial value problem

$$y'' = f(x, y, y')$$

$$y = y_0, \qquad y' = y'_0 \quad \text{at} \quad x = x_0.$$

One possibility is to calculate the following sequence:

$$p'_{j+1} = y'_{j-3} + \frac{4h}{3}(2y''_j - y''_{j-1} + 2y''_{j-2})$$

$$m'_{j+1} = p'_{j+1} + \tfrac{112}{121}(c'_j - p'_j)$$

$$p_{j+1} = \tfrac{1}{8}[9y_j - y_{j-2} + 3h(m'_{j+1} + 2y'_j - y'_{j-1})]$$

$$c'_{j+1} = \tfrac{1}{8}[9y'_j - y'_{j-2} + 3h(p''_{j+1} + 2y''_j - y''_{j-1})]$$

$$y'_{j+1} = c'_{j+1} - \tfrac{9}{121}(c'_{j+1} - p'_{j+1})$$

$$y_{j+1} = p_{j+1} + \frac{3h}{8}(y'_{j+1} - m'_{j+1}).$$

Continue the following solution of the initial value problem

$$y'' = -2yy'$$

$$y = 0, \qquad y' = 1, \qquad \text{at } x = 0$$

for at least two lines:

x	y	y'	y''
0	0	1	0
0.1	0.099 669	0.990 07	−0.197 36
0.2	0.197 377	0.961 04	−0.379 37
0.3	0.291 315	0.915 14	−0.533 19

Compare calculated values with tabled values of the solution, tanh x.

REFERENCES

1. H. M. Terrill, and L. Sweeny. "An Extension of Damson's Table of the Integral of e^{x^2}," *J. Franklin Inst.* **237**: 495–497 (1944) and **238**: 220–222 (1944).

2. W. L. Miller, and A. R. Gordon. "Numerical Evaluation of Infinite Series and Integrals which Arise in Certain Problems of Linear Heat Flow, Electrochemical Diffusion, etc.," *J. Phys. Chem.* **35**: 2878–2882 (1931).

3. A. V. Lebedev, and A. R. Fedorova. *Spravochnik po Matematicheskim Tablitsam* (*An Index of Mathematical Tables*). Moscow: Izdatel'stvo Akademii Nauk SSSR, 1956; also available in English, New York: Pergamon, 1960.

4. N. M. Burunova. *Spravochnik po Matematicheskim Tablitsam. Dopolenenie No. 1* (*An Index of Mathematical Tables. Supplement No.* 1) Moscow: Izdatel'stvo Akademii Nauk SSSR, 1959; Also available in English, New York: Pergamon, 1960.

5. A. Fletcher, J. C. P. Miller, L. Rosenhead, and L. J. Comrie. *Index of Mathematical Tables*. 2nd ed., two vols., Reading: Addison-Wesley, 1962.

6. National Physical Laboratory. *Modern Computing Methods*. London: H.M. Stationery Office, 1957, revised and enlarged 1961.

7. L. Bieberbach. *Theorie der Differentialgleichungen*. Berlin: Springer, 1930, reprinted by Dover, New York 1944.

8. C. Runge. Ueber die Numerische Auflösung von Differentialgleichungen, *Math. Ann.* **46**: 167–178 (1895).

9. W. Kutta. Beitrag zur Näherungsweisen Integration Totaler Differential Gleichungen, *Z. Angew. Math. Phys.* **46**: 435–453 (1901).

10. Z. Kopal. *Numerical Analysis*. New York: Wiley, 1961.

11. C. Runge, and H. König. *Vorlesungen über Numerisches Rechnen*. Berlin: Springer, 1924.

12. L. Collatz. *The Numerical Treatment of Differential Equations*. Berlin: Springer, 1960.

13. S. Gill. "A Process for the Step-by-Step Integration of Differential Equations in an Automatic Computer," *Proc. Cambridge Philos. Soc.* **47**: 96–108 (1951).

14. A. Ralston, and S. Wilf (eds.). *Numerical Methods for Digital Computers*. New York: Wiley, 1960.

15. J. W. Carr III. "Error Bounds for the Runge-Kutta Single-Step Integration Process," *J. Assoc. Comput. Mach.* **5**: 39–44 (1958).

16. E. J. Nyström. "Über die Numerische Integration von Differentialgleichungen," *Acta Soc. Sci. Fenn.* **50**: 1–55 (1925).

17. R. W. Hamming. "Stable Predictor-Corrector Methods for Ordinary Differential Equations," *J. Assoc. Comput. Mach.* **6**: 37–47 (1959).

18. P. Henrici. *Discrete Variable Methods in Ordinary Differential Equations*. New York: Wiley, 1962.

19. A. Ralston. "Runge-Kutta Methods with Minimum Error Bounds," *Math. of Comput.* **16**: 431–437 (1962).

20. R. W. Hamming. *Numerical Methods for Scientists and Engineers*. New York: McGraw-Hill, 1962.

21. L. Fox. *Numerical Solution of Ordinary and Partial Differential Equations*. Reading, Mass: Addison-Wesley, 1962.

BOUNDARY VALUE

PROBLEMS IN ORDINARY

DIFFERENTIAL EQUATIONS

19.1 INTRODUCTION

The solution of a differential equation which must satisfy certain conditions for two or more values of the independent variable is called a boundary value problem.

We shall limit our discussion to the second-order boundary value problem

$$\frac{d^2y}{dx^2} = f(x, y, y')$$

$$y(a) = \alpha, \qquad y(b) = \beta.$$

For even very well-behaved functions $f(x, y, y')$ this boundary value problem may have 0, 1, n or infinitely many solutions. For example, the problem

$$y'' + y = 0, \qquad y(0) = y(\pi) = 1$$

has no solution, while the problem

$$y'' + y = 0, \qquad y(0) = 1, \qquad y(\pi) = -1$$

has infinitely many solutions. We shall suppose our problem to be such that there exists an unique solution.

One procedure that has been used for obtaining the solution to the boundary value problem is to solve a succession of initial value problems

$$\frac{d^2y}{dx^2} = f(x, y, y')$$

$$(a) = \alpha, \qquad y'(a) = \gamma,$$

varying γ until a solution is obtained which passes through the point (b, β). (See Exercise 19.5.)

It is possible, however, by finite-difference methods to reduce the problem to one of solving a system of algebraic equations.

19.2 FINITE-DIFFERENCE METHOD

To solve the two-point boundary value problem

$$\frac{d^2y}{dx^2} = f(x, y, y')$$

$$y(a) = \alpha, \qquad y(b) = \beta$$

we may divide the interval (a, b) in n equal parts by the points

$$x_i = x_0 + ih, \qquad i = 0, 1, 2, \ldots, n,$$

where

$$a = x_0, \qquad b = x_n \quad \text{and} \quad h = \frac{b - a}{n}.$$

and require the ordinate y_i of the solution at these points. If then in the differential equation we replace $y'(x_i)$ by

$$\frac{1}{2h}(y_{i+1} - y_{i-1})$$

and $y''(x_i)$ by

$$\frac{1}{h^2}(y_{i+1} - 2y_i + y_{i-1})$$

(see Sec. 13.5 and Exercise 13.3) we obtain what is known as a *difference equation*, whose solutions may approximate solutions of the differential equation. By writing this difference equation for $i = 1, 2, 3, \ldots, n - 1$ and using the two boundary values we obtain $n - 1$ equations in the $n - 1$ ordinates $y_1, y_2, \ldots, y_{n-1}$. Formulas of higher accuracy than those suggested above can be used [1].

EXAMPLE 19.1. We solve the boundary value problem

$$y'' = x + y$$

$$y(0) = 0, \qquad y(1) = 1$$

using $h = 0.2$. The differential equation may be approximated by the difference equation

$$(1/0.04)(y_{i+1} - 2y_i + y_{i-1}) = x_i + y_i.$$

This and the two boundary values give the following system of four linear equations in the four unknown ordinates:

$$
\begin{aligned}
-2.04y_1 + \quad y_2 \qquad\qquad\qquad &= \quad 0.008 \\
y_1 - 2.04y_2 + \quad y_3 \qquad\qquad &= \quad 0.016 \\
y_2 - 2.04y_3 + \quad y_4 &= \quad 0.024 \\
y_3 - 2.04y_4 &= -0.968.
\end{aligned}
$$

In Chap. 20 we shall discuss methods for solving linear systems of algebraic equations. The solution of the above system is:

$$y_1 = 0.1428, \qquad y_2 = 0.2993, \qquad y_3 = 0.4838, \qquad y_4 = 0.7117.$$

Our boundary-value problem happens to have a simple analytical expression for its solution, namely,

$$2\,\frac{\sinh x}{\sinh 1} - x.$$

For purposes of comparison we table our solutions:

x	$y^\star$	y
0	0.0000	0.0000
0.2	0.1428	0.1426
0.4	0.2993	0.2990
0.6	0.4838	0.4835
0.8	0.7117	0.7114
1.0	1.0000	1.0000

where $y^\star$ is solution obtained by finite difference method and y that obtained from analytic form of solution.

EXERCISES

1. Given the two-point boundary value problem

$$y'' + xy' + y = 2x$$
$$y(0) = 1, \qquad y(1) = 0.$$

Use $h = 0.5$ to obtain a single equation in the unknown ordinate $y_1 = y(0.5)$.

2. Solve the boundary value problem

$$y'' = -(1 + x^2)y - 1$$
$$y(-1) = y(1) = 0.$$

Take $h = 0.5$.

3. Solve the boundary value problem

$$y'' = 2x^2$$
$$y(0) = 0, \qquad y(1) = 1.$$

Take $h = 0.2$. Compare results with analytic solution.

4. Solve the boundary value problem given in Example 19.1 using the higher-accuracy formula

$$y_{i+1} = 2y_i - y_{i-1} + \frac{h^2}{12} (y''_{i+1} + 10y''_i + y''_{i-1}) - \frac{1}{240} h^6 y^{(6)}(\xi).$$

5. The linear boundary value problem

$$y'' + f(x)y' + g(x)y = h(x)$$
$$y(a) = \alpha, \qquad y(b) = \beta,$$

may be conveniently written

$$L[y] = h(x), \qquad y(a) = \alpha, \qquad y(b) = \beta.$$

Let y_1 and y_2 be solutions of the related initial value problems:

$$L[y_1] = h(x), \qquad y_1(a) = \alpha, \qquad y_1'(a) = 0.$$
$$L[y_2] = 0, \qquad y_2(a) = 0, \qquad y_2'(a) = 1.$$

Show that

$$y(x) = y_1(x) + \gamma y_2(x),$$

where

$$\gamma = \frac{\beta - y_1(b)}{y_2(b)},$$

is solution of our boundary value problem.

REFERENCES

1. L. Collatz. *The Numerical Treatment of Differential Equations.* Berlin: Springer, 1960.

2. L. Fox. *The Numerical Solution of Two-Point Boundary Value Problems in Ordinary Differential Equations.* London: Oxford, 1957.

3. D. A. Pope. "A Method of 'Alternating Corrections' for the Numerical Solution of Two-Point Boundary Value Problems," *Math. of Comput.* **14:** 354–361 (1960).

4. W. E. Milne. "On the Numerical Integration of Certain Differential Equations of the Second Order," *Am. Math. Monthly* **40:** 322–327 (1933).

20

SYSTEMS OF LINEAR

ALGEBRAIC EQUATIONS

20.1 INTRODUCTION

We have already had several occasions to solve relatively simple systems of linear algebraic equations, particularly in connection with the method of undetermined coefficients and boundary value problems. As a matter of fact, one of the principal sources of large systems of linear algebraic equations is boundary value problems, both in ordinary and partial differential equations. Another important source is curve-fitting to experimental data by least-squares procedures.

An outline of the classic theory is to be found in Appendix D. We shall be concerned here with efficient numerical procedures for solving a system of n linear equations in n unknowns. This is the basic problem. All others can be reduced to this one. We shall describe modern variations of two methods due to Gauss: iteration and elimination.

Systems arising from differential equations are likely to be *sparse* (coefficient matrix having many zero elements) but of high order. Those arising from statistical problems are more likely to be *dense* (coefficient matrix having few zero elements) but of low order. Usually iterative methods are to be preferred for sparse systems and elimination methods for dense systems.

Since most facts about linear systems can be simply and elegantly stated in terms of matrices we first show how a linear system can be represented in matrix notation.

20.2 LINEAR SYSTEMS IN MATRIX NOTATION

The system of n linear algebraic equations in n unknowns

$$
\begin{aligned}
a_{11}x_1 + a_{12}x_2 + \cdots + a_{1n}x_n &= k_1 \\
a_{21}x_2 + a_{22}x_2 + \cdots + a_{2n}x_n &= k_2 \\
\cdot \quad \cdot \quad \cdot \quad \cdot \quad \cdot \quad \cdot \quad \cdot \quad \cdot \quad \cdot & \\
a_{n1}x_1 + a_{n2}x_2 + \cdots + a_{nn}x_n &= k_n
\end{aligned}
\tag{20.1}
$$

can be written as the single matrix equation

$$
\begin{bmatrix}
a_{11} & a_{12} & \cdots & a_{1n} \\
a_{21} & a_{22} & \cdots & a_{2n} \\
\cdot & \cdot & \cdots & \cdot \\
a_{n1} & a_{n2} & \cdots & a_{nn}
\end{bmatrix}
\begin{bmatrix}
x_1 \\
x_2 \\
\cdots \\
x_n
\end{bmatrix}
=
\begin{bmatrix}
k_1 \\
k_2 \\
\cdots \\
k_n
\end{bmatrix}.
\tag{20.2}
$$

For if we compute the product of the two matrices on the left, this equation becomes

$$
\begin{bmatrix}
a_{11}x_1 + a_{12}x_2 + \cdots + a_{1n}x_n \\
a_{21}x_1 + a_{22}x_2 + \cdots + a_{2n}x_n \\
\cdot \quad \cdot \quad \cdot \quad \cdot \quad \cdot \quad \cdot \quad \cdot \\
a_{n1}x_1 + a_{n2}x_2 + \cdots + a_{nn}x_n
\end{bmatrix}
=
\begin{bmatrix}
k_1 \\
k_2 \\
\cdots \\
k_n
\end{bmatrix}.
$$

But two matrices are equal if and only if their corresponding elements are equal. Hence the single matrix Eq. (20.2) is equivalent to the system in Eq. (20.1). If we define

$$
\mathbf{A} =
\begin{bmatrix}
a_{11} & a_{12} & \cdots & a_{1n} \\
a_{21} & a_{22} & \cdots & a_{2n} \\
\cdot & \cdot & \cdots & \cdot \\
a_{n1} & a_{n2} & \cdots & a_{nn}
\end{bmatrix},
\qquad
\mathbf{x} =
\begin{bmatrix}
x_1 \\
x_2 \\
\cdots \\
x_n
\end{bmatrix},
\qquad
\mathbf{k} =
\begin{bmatrix}
k_1 \\
k_2 \\
\cdots \\
k_n
\end{bmatrix},
$$

then Eqs. (20.2) can be written very compactly as

$$\mathbf{Ax} = \mathbf{k}. \tag{20.3}$$

The column matrices $\mathbf{x}$ and $\mathbf{k}$ are called *vectors*.

20.3 PRINCIPLE OF SUPERPOSITION OF SOLUTIONS AND MATRIX INVERSION

We shall show that by solving certain n systems, all having the same coefficient matrix $\mathbf{A}$ of order n, we can readily obtain the solution of any system having the same coefficient matrix $\mathbf{A}$ and obtain in the process the inverse of $\mathbf{A}$. We assume, of course, $d(\mathbf{A}) \neq 0$, where $d(\mathbf{A})$ means the determinant of the matrix $\mathbf{A}$.

We let $\mathbf{x}^{(i)}$ be the solution vector of the system

$$\mathbf{Ax}^{(i)} = \mathbf{k}^{(i)}, \qquad i = 1, 2, \ldots, n, \tag{20.4}$$

where the vector $\mathbf{k}^{(i)}$ has 1 in its ith row and 0 elsewhere. Then

$$k_1\mathbf{k}^{(1)} + k_2\mathbf{k}^{(2)} + \cdots + k_n\mathbf{k}^{(n)} = \mathbf{k}$$

and

$$k_1\mathbf{x}^{(1)} + k_2\mathbf{x}^{(2)} + \cdots + k_n\mathbf{x}^{(n)}$$

is the solution of Eq. (20.3). Thus the unique solution of Eq. (20.3) can be written as a linear combination of the solution vectors of n related systems all having the same coefficient matrix. This is referred to as the *principle of superposition of solutions*.

The matrix whose ith column is the vector $\mathbf{k}^{(i)}$ is the identity matrix $\mathbf{I}$. The matrix $\mathbf{E}$ whose ith column is the solution vector $\mathbf{x}^{(i)}$ is the inverse of the matrix $\mathbf{A}$. For

$$\mathbf{AE} = \mathbf{I}$$

and by multiplying both members of this equation on the left by $\mathbf{A}^{-1}$ (known to exist since $d(\mathbf{A}) \neq 0$) we find

$$\mathbf{E} = \mathbf{A}^{-1}.$$

Thus by solving n systems of n equations in n unknowns, all having the same coefficient matrix $\mathbf{A}$, we obtain $\mathbf{A}^{-1}$, the inverse of $\mathbf{A}$. Conversely, if $\mathbf{A}^{-1}$ is known then the solution of the system

$$\mathbf{Ax} = \mathbf{k}$$

is readily obtained by a simple matrix multiplication:

$$\mathbf{x} = \mathbf{A}^{-1}\mathbf{k}.$$

Thus the problems of solving square systems of linear equations is closely identified with the problem of matrix inversion.

The classic rule of Cramer (D.2) expresses the solution in terms of the determinants of the matrix of coefficients and certain related matrices. This rule is never used in numerical work (except possibly for $n = 2$) due to the large number of arithmetic operations required. We shall develop several procedures requiring appreciably fewer operations.

20.4 GAUSS'S METHOD OF ELIMINATION

For simplicity we describe the Gauss process of elimination of the unknowns for a system of four equations in four unknowns:

$$
\begin{aligned}
a_{11}x_1 + a_{12}x_2 + a_{13}x_3 + a_{14}x_4 &= a_{15} \\
a_{21}x_1 + a_{22}x_2 + a_{23}x_3 + a_{24}x_4 &= a_{25} \\
a_{31}x_1 + a_{32}x_2 + a_{33}x_3 + a_{34}x_4 &= a_{35} \\
a_{41}x_1 + a_{42}x_2 + a_{43}x_3 + a_{44}x_4 &= a_{45}.
\end{aligned}
\tag{20.5}
$$

By dividing the first of Eqs. (20.5) by a_{11} we obtain a ne wuation eq

$$
x_1 + b_{12}x_2 + b_{13}x_3 + b_{14}x_4 = b_{15} \tag{20.6}
$$

where
$$
b_{1j} = a_{1j}/a_{11}, \qquad j \geq 2.
$$

We suppose, of course, that an equation in which the coefficient of x_1 is not zero has been placed first. By multiplying Eq. (20.6) successively by a_{21}, a_{31}, a_{41} and subtracting each result from corresponding equation of (20.5) we obtain a system of three equations in three unknowns:

$$
\begin{aligned}
a_{22}^{(1)}x_2 + a_{23}^{(1)}x_3 + a_{24}^{(1)}x_4 &= a_{25}^{(1)} \\
a_{32}^{(1)}x_2 + a_{33}^{(1)}x_3 + a_{34}^{(1)}x_4 &= a_{35}^{(1)} \\
a_{42}^{(1)}x_2 + a_{43}^{(1)}x_3 + a_{44}^{(1)}x_4 &= a_{45}^{(1)}
\end{aligned}
\tag{20.7}
$$

where
$$
a_{ij}^{(1)} = a_{ij} - a_{i1}b_{1j}, \qquad i, j \geq 2.
$$

Applying above process to the system of Eqs. (20.7) we obtain first

$$
x_2 + b_{23}x_3 + b_{24}x_4 = b_{25}
$$

where
$$
b_{2j} = a_{2j}^{(1)}/a_{22}^{(1)},
$$

then
$$
\begin{aligned}
a_{33}^{(2)}x_3 + a_{34}^{(2)}x_4 &= a_{35}^{(2)} \\
a_{43}^{(2)}x_3 + a_{44}^{(2)}x_4 &= a_{45}^{(2)}
\end{aligned}
\tag{20.8}
$$

where
$$
a_{ij}^{(2)} = a_{ij}^{(1)} - a_{i2}^{(1)}b_{2j}, \qquad i, j \geq 3.
$$

EXAMPLE 20.1. GAUSS ELIMINATION

x_1	x_2	x_3	x_4		$\sum$	x_1	x_2	x_3	x_4		$\sum$
a_{11}	a_{12}	a_{13}	a_{14}	a_{15}	a_{16}	2	8	4	10	7.6	31.6
a_{21}	a_{22}	a_{23}	a_{24}	a_{25}	a_{26}	-3	-9	15	0	-8.1	-5.1
a_{31}	a_{32}	a_{33}	a_{34}	a_{35}	a_{36}	-1	-2	17	35	9.4	58.4
a_{41}	a_{42}	a_{43}	a_{44}	a_{45}	a_{46}	2	5	-14	21	14.1	28.1
1	b_{12}	b_{13}	b_{14}	b_{15}	b_{16}	1	4	2	5	3.8	15.8
	$a_{22}^{(1)}$	$a_{23}^{(1)}$	$a_{24}^{(1)}$	$a_{25}^{(1)}$	$a_{26}^{(1)}$		3	21	15	3.3	42.3
	$a_{32}^{(1)}$	$a_{33}^{(1)}$	$a_{34}^{(1)}$	$a_{35}^{(1)}$	$a_{36}^{(1)}$		2	19	40	13.2	74.2
	$a_{42}^{(1)}$	$a_{43}^{(1)}$	$a_{44}^{(1)}$	$a_{45}^{(1)}$	$a_{46}^{(1)}$		-3	-18	11	6.5	-3.5
	1	b_{23}	b_{24}	b_{25}	b_{26}		1	7	5	1.1	14.1
		$a_{33}^{(2)}$	$a_{34}^{(2)}$	$a_{35}^{(2)}$	$a_{36}^{(2)}$			5	30	11	46
		$a_{43}^{(2)}$	$a_{44}^{(2)}$	$a_{45}^{(2)}$	$a_{46}^{(2)}$			3	26	9.8	38.8
		1	b_{34}	b_{35}	b_{36}			1	6	2.2	9.2
			$a_{44}^{(3)}$	$a_{45}^{(3)}$	$a_{46}^{(3)}$				8	3.2	11.2
			1	b_{45}	b_{46}				1	0.4	1.4
x_1	x_2	x_3	x_4			0.2	0.5	-0.2	0.4		
$\bar{x}_1$	$\bar{x}_2$	$\bar{x}_3$	$\bar{x}_4$			1.2	1.5	0.8	1.4		

EXAMPLE 20.2. COMPACT ELIMINATION METHOD

x_1	x_2	x_3	x_4		$\sum$	x_1	x_2	x_3	x_4		$\sum$
a_{11}	a_{12}	a_{13}	a_{14}	a_{15}	a_{16}	2	8	4	10	7.6	31.6
a_{21}	a_{22}	a_{23}	a_{24}	a_{25}	a_{26}	-3	-9	15	0	-8.1	-5.1
a_{31}	a_{32}	a_{33}	a_{34}	a_{35}	a_{36}	-1	-2	17	35	9.4	58.4
a_{41}	a_{42}	a_{43}	a_{44}	a_{45}	a_{46}	2	5	-14	21	14.1	28.1
a_{11}	b_{12}	b_{13}	b_{14}	b_{15}	b_{16}	2	4	2	5	3.8	15.8
a_{21}	$a_{22}^{(1)}$	b_{23}	b_{24}	b_{25}	b_{26}	-3	3	7	5	1.1	14.1
a_{31}	$a_{32}^{(1)}$	$a_{33}^{(2)}$	b_{34}	b_{35}	b_{36}	-1	2	5	6	2.2	9.2
a_{41}	$a_{42}^{(1)}$	$a_{43}^{(2)}$	$a_{44}^{(3)}$	b_{45}	b_{46}	2	-3	3	8	0.4	1.4
x_1	x_2	x_3	x_4			0.2	0.5	-0.2	0.4		
$\bar{x}_1$	$\bar{x}_2$	$\bar{x}_3$	$\bar{x}_4$			1.2	1.5	0.8	1.4		

The same elimination process applied to the system of Eqs. (20.8) gives

$$x_3 + b_{34}x_4 = b_{35}$$

where

$$b_{3j} = a_{3j}^{(2)}/a_{33}^{(2)}, \qquad j \geq 4.$$

Then

$$a_{44}^{(3)}x_4 = a_{45}^{(3)}$$

where

$$a_{4j}^{(3)} = a_{4j}^{(2)} - a_{43}^{(2)}b_{3j}, \qquad j \geq 4.$$

Finally

$$x_4 = b_{45}$$

where

$$b_{45} = a_{45}^{(3)}/a_{44}^{(3)}.$$

The equations whose coefficients are b's form a triangular system:

$$\begin{aligned}
x_1 + b_{12}x_2 + b_{13}x_3 + b_{14}x_4 &= b_{15} \\
x_2 + b_{23}x_3 + b_{24}x_4 &= b_{25} \\
x_3 + b_{34}x_4 &= b_{35} \\
x_5 &= b_{45}.
\end{aligned} \qquad (20.9)$$

This triangular system is readily solved by a "back" substitution.

In a numerical example we need write only the coefficients of the successive systems (see Example 20.1). Our example is atypical: it was carefully chosen so that no rounding errors would be introduced.

20.41   CHECK COLUMN. If we make the substitution $x_i = \bar{x}_i - 1$ in Eqs. (20.5) we obtain a new system whose coefficient matrix is the same. The constants on the right are, however, replaced by

$$\sum_{j=1}^{5} a_{ij}, \qquad i = 1, 2, 3, 4.$$

To solve for the $\bar{x}_i$ we have but to add a column in which each element is the sum of the elements to its left (the Σ column in the examples). We then operate on it in precisely the same way as on the original column of constants. In the absence of computational blunders its elements will always be (except for rounding errors) the sum of the elements to the left. We are this provided with a systematic check against blunders in "hand computatuns." This column would, of course, be omitted in programming this method for a digital computer.

20.42   PIVOTS. The first elimination was effected by dividing the first equation of system (20.5) by a_{11}. The element a_{11} is then called a *pivot* for the elimination. In succeeding steps $a_{22}^{(1)}$ and $a_{33}^{(2)}$ were used as pivots.

The effect of the almost inevitable rounding error can be reduced by using at each stage of the elimination the largest element of the current coefficient matrix as pivot. This is especially helpful if the elements of the coefficient matrix vary appreciably in magnitude.

20.43 *VARIATIONS.* Back substitution can be avoided by retaining the same number of rows throughout and using pivot to eliminate corresponding unknown from each of the remaining equations. It is, of course, necessary to choose one pivot from each and every row and from each and every column. This process is attributed to Jordan. Other variations are possible. A recent bibliography by G. Forsythe [1] lists approximately 450 titles of books and research papers concerned with methods for solving systems of linear equations.

20.5 COMPACT ELIMINATION*

The extensive recording required by the Gauss elimination procedure can be appreciably reduced if equipment is available for forming inner products followed by a division. Even desk calculators, for example, can evaluate $(\Sigma a_i b_i)/c$ without the need for recording intermediate results. Again, for simplicity, we consider a system of four nonhomogeneous equations in four unknowns. The augmented matrix of our system, together with check column, is

$$\mathbf{A}^\star = \begin{bmatrix} a_{11} & a_{12} & a_{13} & a_{14} & a_{15} & a_{16} \\ a_{21} & a_{22} & a_{23} & a_{24} & a_{25} & a_{26} \\ a_{31} & a_{32} & a_{33} & a_{34} & a_{35} & a_{36} \\ a_{41} & a_{42} & a_{43} & a_{44} & a_{45} & a_{46} \end{bmatrix}.$$

The elements of the following matrix are calculated in the order indicated by the integers in parentheses:

$$\mathbf{B}^\star = \begin{bmatrix} a_{11}(1) & b_{12}(5) & b_{13}(6) & b_{14}(7) & b_{15}(8) & b_{16}(9) \\ a_{21}(2) & a_{22}^{(1)}(10) & b_{23}(13) & b_{24}(14) & b_{25}(15) & b_{26}(16) \\ a_{31}(3) & a_{32}^{(1)}(11) & a_{33}^{(2)}(17) & b_{34}(19) & b_{35}(20) & b_{36}(21) \\ a_{41}(4) & a_{42}^{(1)}(12) & a_{43}^{(2)}(18) & a_{44}^{(3)}(22) & b_{45}(23) & b_{46}(24) \end{bmatrix}.$$

Each element of the matrix $\mathbf{B}^\star$ occurs at some stage of the Gauss method of elimination. The notation is same as used previously. Each element of

* Variations of the scheme described here are attributed to Crout, Cholesky, Banachiewicz, and Zurmühl.

the matrix $\mathbf{B}^\star$ is expressible in terms of corresponding element of the matrix $\mathbf{A}^\star$ and the elements of $\mathbf{B}^\star$ previously calculated. For example,

$$a_{32}^{(1)} = a_{32} - a_{31}b_{12}$$

and

$$b_{34} = (a_{34}^{(1)} - a_{32}^{(1)}b_{24})/a_{33}^{(2)}$$
$$= (a_{34} - a_{31}b_{14} - a_{32}^{(1)}b_{24})/a_{33}^{(2)}.$$

Similarly,

$$a_{ij}^{(j-1)} = a_{ij} - \sum_{k=1}^{j-1} a_{ik}^{(k-1)}b_{kj}, \qquad i \geq j, \tag{20.10}$$

where

$$a_{i1}^{(0)} = a_{i1},$$

and

$$b_{ij} = \left(a_{ij} - \sum_{k=1}^{i-1} a_{ik}^{(k-1)} b_{kj}\right)/a_{ii}^{(i-1)}, \qquad i < j. \tag{20.11}$$

It is, of course, the triangular matrix of the b's that is needed for the back solution. The compactness is due to the fact that all intermediate calculations which must be temporarily stored can be placed in the positions which would otherwise be occupied by ones and zeros. The back solution is identical with that in the Gauss process, namely:

$$x_i = b_{i5} - \sum_{j=i+1}^{4} b_{ij}x_j, \qquad i = 4, 3, 2, 1;$$

and

$$\bar{x}_i = b_{i6} - \sum_{j=i+1}^{4} b_{ij}\bar{x}_j, \qquad i = 4, 3, 2, 1.$$

The elements of the last or check column of the $\mathbf{B}^\star$ matrix are calculated by the formula for b_{ij}. Except for rounding, and in the absence of blunders, each element of this check column will exceed by 1 the sum of the b_{ij} to its left.

If the inverse of the coefficient matrix $\mathbf{A}$ is desired, it can be calculated by extending the matrix $\mathbf{A}^\star$ to include all columns of the identity matrix. From these additional columns in the $\mathbf{A}^\star$ matrix we obtain additional columns in the $\mathbf{B}^\star$ matrix by precisely the same computational procedure as for the original column of constants of our equations. The inverse matrix is then obtained precisely as in Sec. 20.3.

Example 20.2 is of the compact elimination method applied to the system of Example 20.1. As noted before this example is atypical. The coefficients were chosen so that at no stage of the calculation would rounding be required. This was done to clarify the relation between the two elimination methods discussed. Note that every number in Example 20.2 occurs in Example 20.1.

Example 20.3, on the other hand, does involve the usually inevitable rounding. The **B**★ matrix was calculated twice, once with three decimals and once with five decimals. In both cases the answers obtained depart appreciably from the true solution.

EXAMPLE 20.3. COMPACT ELIMINATION METHOD

	x_1	x_2	x_3	
	10	1	7	33
A★	1	10	8	45
	7	8	10	53
	10	0.1	0.7	3.3
B★	1	9.9	0.737	4.212
	7	7.3	−0.280	3.027
	0.983	1.981	3.027	
	10	0.1	0.7	3.3
B★	1	9.9	0.73737	4.21212
	7	7.3	−0.28280	3.00027
	0.99983	1.99981	3.00027	
Solution:	1	2	3	

The accumulation of rounding errors in lengthy calculations is a very serious problem indeed. It has been extensively studied but will not be explored here [13,14].

20.6 MATRIX FACTORIZATION

One of the bonus features of the compact elimination scheme is that it factors the nonsingular coefficient matrix

$$
\mathbf{A} = \begin{bmatrix}
a_{11} & a_{12} & a_{13} & \cdots & a_{1n} \\
a_{21} & a_{22} & a_{23} & \cdots & a_{2n} \\
a_{31} & a_{32} & a_{33} & \cdots & a_{3n} \\
\cdot & \cdot & \cdot & \cdot & \cdot \\
a_{n1} & a_{n2} & a_{n3} & \cdots & a_{nn}
\end{bmatrix} \cdot
$$

One factor is the lower triangular matrix

$$\mathbf{A}_\Delta = \begin{bmatrix} a_{11} & 0 & 0 & \cdots & 0 \\ a_{21} & a_{22}^{(1)} & 0 & \cdots & 0 \\ a_{31} & a_{32}^{(1)} & a_{33}^{(2)} & \cdots & 0 \\ \cdot & \cdot & \cdot & & \cdot \\ a_{n1} & a_{n2}^{(1)} & a_{n3}^{(2)} & \cdots & a_{nn}^{(n-1)} \end{bmatrix}$$

and the other factor is the upper triangular matrix

$$\mathbf{B}^\Delta = \begin{bmatrix} 1 & b_{12} & b_{13} & \cdots & b_{1n} \\ 0 & 1 & b_{23} & \cdots & b_{2n} \\ 0 & 0 & 1 & \cdots & b_{3n} \\ \cdot & \cdot & \cdot & & \cdot \\ 0 & 0 & 0 & \cdots & 1 \end{bmatrix}.$$

We now show that

$$\mathbf{A} = \mathbf{A}_\Delta \mathbf{B}^\Delta. \tag{20.12}$$

Equations (20.10) and (20.11), while written with $n = 4$ in mind, hold for arbitrary n. Thus

$$a_{ij}^{(j-i)} = a_{ij} - \sum_{k=1}^{j-1} a_{ik}^{(k-1)} b_{kj}, \qquad i \geq j.$$

Since

$$b_{jj} = 1$$

and

$$b_{kj} = 0, \qquad k > j,$$

then for $i \geq j$,

$$a_{ij} = \sum_{k=1}^{j} a_{ik}^{(k-1)} b_{kj}$$

$$= \sum_{k=1}^{n} a_{ik}^{(k-1)} b_{kj}. \tag{20.13}$$

Similarly we can establish that Eq. (20.13) holds for all $i < j$. Thus Eq. (20.13) holds for all integers i, j between 1 and n inclusive. But this is simply the rule for forming the product $\mathbf{A}_\Delta \mathbf{B}^\Delta$.

20.7 EVALUATION OF DETERMINANTS

Since the determinant of a triangular matrix is the product of its diagonal elements and the determinant of a product of two matrices is the product of their determinants, we see that

$$d(\mathbf{A}) = a_{11} a_{22}^{(1)} a_{33}^{(2)} \cdots a_{nn}^{n-1}. \tag{20.14}$$

As far as the actual calculation of $d(\mathbf{A})$ is concerned the above procedure is identical with the familiar procedure of introducing zeros by adding to the elements of a given row an appropriate multiple of the corresponding elements of another row. However, the numbers recorded make it possible to solve a system of nonhomogeneous equations having $\mathbf{A}$ for coefficient matrix with relatively little additional work.

The procedure described requires $\frac{1}{3}(n - 1)(n^2 + n + 3)$ multiplications and divisions to evaluate the determinant of a matrix of order n. A comparison of this with either the $n!\,(n - 1)$ multiplications required by direct application of definition of a determinant or the $n! \sum\limits_{p=2}^{n} (1/(p - 1)!)$ multiplications required by an expansion by cofactors puts the elimination method in extremely favorable light. In this connection the following table is of interest:

Table 20.1

NUMBER OF MULTIPLICATIONS AND/OR DIVISIONS REQUIRED TO EVALUATE DETERMINANT OF ORDER n

$Method \backslash n$	4	6	8	10
Elimination	23	75	175	3,729
Cofactors	40	1236	69,280	5,625,460
Definition	72	3600	282,240	32,659,200

20.8 ITERATIVE METHODS

These methods give the solution vector of the system as the limit of a sequence of vectors constructed by a process which is repeated or *iterated*.

We suppose that our system of n equations

$$\sum_{j=1}^{n} a_{ij}x_j = k_i, \qquad i = 1, 2, \ldots, n, \tag{20.15}$$

has been so ordered that $a_{ii} \neq 0$, $i = 1, 2, \ldots, n$. We may then solve the ith equation for x_i and rewrite our system in the following form:

$$x_i = \frac{1}{a_{ii}} \left(k_i - \sum_{j \neq i} a_{ij}x_j \right), \qquad i = 1, 2, \ldots, n. \tag{20.16}$$

This equation is the basis for two iterative procedures which are known as the Gauss-Jacobi iterative method and the Gauss-Seidel iterative method.

A number of other iterative methods have been developed, primarily with the aim of finding a more rapidly convergent one [1].

20.81 *GAUSS-JACOBI ITERATIVE METHOD* (1823). This iteration is given by

$$x_i^{(\nu+1)} = \frac{1}{a_{ii}}\left(k_i - \sum_{j \neq i} a_{ij} x_j^{(\nu)}\right), \qquad i = 1, 2, \ldots, n. \qquad (20.17)$$

We may take

$$x_i^{(0)} = 0, \qquad i = 1, 2, \ldots, n,$$

if no better approximate solution is available.

20.82 *GAUSS-SEIDEL ITERATIVE METHOD* (1874). This iteration is given by

$$x_i^{(\nu+1)} = \frac{1}{a_{ii}}\left(k_i - \sum_{j=1}^{i-1} a_{ij} x_j^{(\nu+1)} - \sum_{j=i+1}^{n} a_{ij} x_j^{(\nu)}\right), \quad i = 1, 2, \ldots, n. \quad (20.18)$$

Again, in the absence of a better approximation, we take

$$x_i^{(0)} = 0, \qquad i = 1, 2, \ldots, n.$$

20.83 *CONVERGENCE.* One might suppose that the Gauss-Seidel process would be more likely to converge than would the Gauss-Jacobi process and that if both converged that the Gauss-Seidel process would converge more rapidly. Such, however, is not necessarily the case. Examples can be given for which either of the methods converges while the other diverges [4].

An ordering of the equations and unknowns in which each diagonal coefficient is large in comparison to all the other coefficients in its equation will favor convergence of either method.

A sufficient condition [4] for the convergence of the Gauss-Jacobi iterative method is that

$$\max_i \left(\frac{1}{|a_{ii}|} \sum_{j \neq i} |a_{ij}|\right) < 1.$$

In the special case where $a_{ii} > 0$ and $a_{ij} = a_{ji}$ (symmetric coefficient matrix) the Gauss-Seidel iteration converges if and only if each of the n quantities

$$a_{11}, \quad \begin{vmatrix} a_{11} & a_{12} \\ a_{21} & a_{22} \end{vmatrix}, \quad \begin{vmatrix} a_{11} & a_{12} & a_{13} \\ a_{21} & a_{22} & a_{23} \\ a_{31} & a_{32} & a_{33} \end{vmatrix}, \ldots$$

is positive (positive definite coefficient matrix) [6]. These conditions, both necessary and sufficient for convergence, do not involve the initial approximation to the solution vector. Thus the convergence of the Gauss-Seidel iteration is not dependent on the choice of the initial approximation to the solution vector. Lacking any prior knowledge of the solution vector, one may use the zero vector for an initial approximation. The same is true for the Gauss-Jacobi iteration [4].

But even in such special cases, necessary and/or sufficient conditions may be difficult to apply. However, the situation is not as hopeless as it may at first seem. For if either iteration is *internally convergent*, that is, if

$$x_j^{(\nu+1)} - x_j^{(\nu)} = \xi_j^{(\nu+1)}$$

converges to zero for $j = 1, 2, \ldots, n$, the iteration converges to a solution. This is, for example, in the Gauss-Seidel iteration an immediate consequence of the fact that

$$\sum_{j=1}^{n} a_{ij} x_j^{(\nu+1)} - k_i = \sum_{j=i+1}^{n} a_{ij} \xi_j^{(\nu+1)}, \qquad i = 1, 2, \ldots, n-1.$$

But the convergence may be very slow. However, the simple nature of the iteration makes for easy programming on high-speed digital computers and is much used.

EXAMPLE 20.4. The compact elimination method applied to the system

$$10x_1 + x_2 + 7x_3 = 33$$
$$x_1 + 10x_2 + 6x_3 = 39$$
$$7x_1 + 6x_2 + 10x_3 = 49$$

gives

$$x_1 = 1.000\ 02$$
$$x_2 = 2.000\ 03$$
$$x_3 = 2.999\ 97.$$

We write Gauss-Seidel iteration equations as follows:

$$x_1^{(\nu+1)} = 3.3 - 0.1x_2^{(\nu)} - 0.7x_3^{(\nu)}$$
$$x_2^{(\nu+1)} = 3.9 - 0.1x_1^{(\nu+1)} - 0.6x_3^{(\nu)}$$
$$x_3^{(\nu+1)} = 4.9 - 0.7x_1^{(\nu+1)} - 0.6x_2^{(\nu+1)}.$$

From these equations we obtain

ν	$x_1^{(\nu)}$	$x_2^{(\nu)}$	$x_3^{(\nu)}$
0	1.000 02	2.000 03	2.999 97
1	1.000 018	2.000 016 2	2.999 977 7
2	1.000 014 0	2.000 012 0	2.999 983 0
3	1.000 010 7	2.000 009 7	2.999 987 1
. . . .			
16	1.000 000 0	2.000 000 0	3.000 000 0

If we had no prior information about the solution vector the iteration would give the following:

ν	$x_1^{(\nu)}$	$x_2^{(\nu)}$	$x_3^{(\nu)}$
0	0.000 000	0.000 000	0.000 000
1	3.300 000	3.570 000	4.480 000
2	2.629 400	3.368 260	1.038 464
10	1.185 948	2.158 608	2.774 671
20	1.012 427	2.010 600	2.984 941
30	1.000 830	2.000 708	2.998 994
40	1.000 056	2.000 047	2.999 933
50	1.000 004	2.000 003	2.999 996
60	1.000 000	2.000 000	3.000 000

(Machine time: 0 minutes, 13 seconds.)

Note that the exact solution is

$$x_1 = 1, \qquad x_2 = 2, \qquad x_3 = 3.$$

EXAMPLE 20.5. In Example 20.3 we applied the compact elimination method applied to the system

$$10x_1 + \quad x_2 + 7x_3 = 33$$
$$x_1 + 10x_2 + 8x_3 = 45$$
$$7x_1 + \quad 8x_2 + 10x_3 = 53$$

and obtained

$$x_1 = 0.999\ 83$$
$$x_2 = 1.999\ 81$$
$$x_3 = 3.000\ 27.$$

We write Gauss-Seidel iteration equations as follows:

$$x_1^{(\nu+1)} = 3.3 - 0.1x_2^{(\nu)} \qquad - 0.7x_3^{(\nu)}$$
$$x_2^{(\nu+1)} = 4.5 - 0.1x_1^{(\nu+1)} - 0.8x_3^{(\nu)}$$
$$x_3^{(\nu+1)} = 5.3 - 0.7x_1^{(\nu+1)} - 0.8x_2^{(\nu+1)}.$$

From these equations we obtain:

ν	$x_1^{(\nu)}$	$x_2^{(\nu)}$	$x_3^{(\nu)}$
0	0.999 830 00	1.999 810 0	3.000 270 0
1	0.999 830 00	1.999 801 0	3.000 278 2
2	0.999 825 16	1.999 794 9	3.000 286 4
10	0.999 779 20	1.999 741 0	3.000 361 8
20	0.999 704 38	1.999 653 2	3.000 484 4
30	0.999 604 22	1.999 535 7	3.000 648 5
40	0.999 470 11	1.999 378 4	3.000 868 2
50	0.999 290 56	1.999 167 8	3.001 162 4
60	0.999 050 17	1.998 885 8	3.001 556 3
70	0.998 728 33	1.998 508 2	3.002 083 6
80	0.998 297 43	1.998 002 8	3.002 789 6
90	0.997 720 53	1.997 326 0	3.003 734 8
100	0.996 948 14	1.996 420 0	3.005 000 3

(Machine time: 0 minutes, 13 seconds)

Note that the exact solution is

$$x_1 = 1, \qquad x_2 = 2, \qquad x_3 = 3.$$

The iteration is diverging.

20.84 *GAUSS-SEIDEL-HOTELLING ITERATIVE METHOD.* Hotelling [9] has devised a simple procedure for accelerating the convergence of the Gauss-Seidel method. We describe it in terms of a system of four nonhomogeneous equations in four unknowns. Such a system can be written as the homogeneous system

$$k_i x_0 - \sum_{j=1}^{4} a_{ij} x_j = 0, \qquad i = 1, 2, 3, 4,$$

by introducing the symbol $x_0 = 1$.

The first step, consisting of replacing the initial trial value $x_1^{(0)}$ by $x_1^{(1)}$ and leaving $x_2^{(0)}$, $x_3^{(0)}$, $x_4^{(0)}$ unchanged, amounts to subjecting the five variables $x_0^{(0)}, \ldots, x_4^{(0)}$ to a homogeneous transformation

$$x_0^{(1)} = x_0^{(0)}$$
$$x_1^{(1)} = (k_1 x_0^{(0)} - a_{12} x_2^{(0)} - a_{13} x_3^{(0)} - a_{14} x_4^{(0)})/a_{11}$$
$$x_2^{(1)} = \qquad\qquad x_2^{(0)}$$
$$x_3^{(1)} = \qquad\qquad\qquad\qquad x_3^{(0)}$$
$$x_4^{(1)} = \qquad\qquad\qquad\qquad\qquad\qquad x_4^{(0)}$$

which can be written in matrix notation as

$$\mathbf{x}^{(1)} = \mathbf{T}_1 \mathbf{x}^{(0)},$$

where

$$\mathbf{T}_1 = \begin{bmatrix} 1 & 0 & 0 & 0 & 0 \\ k_1/a_{11} & 0 & -a_{12}/a_{11} & -a_{13}/a_{11} & -a_{14}/a_{11} \\ 0 & 0 & 1 & 0 & 0 \\ 0 & 0 & 0 & 1 & 0 \\ 0 & 0 & 0 & 0 & 1 \end{bmatrix}$$

and

$$\mathbf{x}^{(k)} = (x_0^{(k)}, x_1^{(k)}, x_2^{(k)}, x_3^{(k)}, x_4^{(k)}).$$

The second step can be written as

$$\mathbf{x}^{(2)} = \mathbf{T}_2 \mathbf{x}^{(1)}$$

where

$$\mathbf{T}_2 = \begin{bmatrix} 1 & 0 & 0 & 0 & 0 \\ 0 & 1 & 0 & 0 & 0 \\ k_2/a_{22} & -a_{21}/a_{22} & 0 & -a_{23}/a_{22} & -a_{24}/a_{22} \\ 0 & 0 & 0 & 1 & 0 \\ 0 & 0 & 0 & 0 & 1 \end{bmatrix}.$$

The result of one complete cycle of substitutions can be written

$$\mathbf{x}^{(4)} = \mathbf{T}_4\{\mathbf{T}_3[\mathbf{T}_2(\mathbf{T}_1 \mathbf{x}^{(0)})]\},$$

where the matrices $\mathbf{T}_3$ and $\mathbf{T}_4$ are of the same simple composition illustrated by $\mathbf{T}_1$ and $\mathbf{T}_2$. This same result will, of course, be obtained if we first calculate the matrix

$$\mathbf{T} = \mathbf{T}_4 \mathbf{T}_3 \mathbf{T}_2 \mathbf{T}_1$$

and then

$$\mathbf{x}^{(4)} = \mathbf{T}\mathbf{x}^{(0)}.$$

The advantage of writing the Gauss-Seidel procedure in this form is that the sequence of matrixes $\mathbf{T}^2$, $\mathbf{T}^4$, $\mathbf{T}^8$, $\mathbf{T}^{16}$, ... can be readily obtained. Thus, in our case, three matrix multiplications give $\mathbf{T}$ and four successive squarings followed by multiplication by the vector $\mathbf{x}^{(0)}$ will be equivalent to sixteen complete cycles of the Gauss-Seidel procedure. A further advantage is that the problem of solving a system of linear algebraic equations has been reduced to the problem of doing a sequence of matrix multiplications— a process for which a standard subroutine is available in most high-speed computer installations.

By writing the iteration in this matrix form we may observe that its convergence or divergence depends in no way on the initial vector $\mathbf{x}^{(0)}$. Thus we may take $\mathbf{x}^{(0)} = (1, 0, 0, 0)$. If the process is convergent, the first column of the matrices $\{\mathbf{T}^{2^n}\}$ will converge to the solution vector.

EXAMPLE 20.6. We apply the Gauss-Seidel-Hotelling iterative method to the system of equations of Example 20.4. We find

$$\mathbf{T} = \begin{bmatrix} 1 & 0 & 0 & 0 \\ 3.3 & 0 & -0.1 & -0.7 \\ 3.57 & 0 & 0.01 & -0.53 \\ 0.448 & 0 & 0.064 & 0.808 \end{bmatrix}.$$

Let

$$\mathbf{x}^{(2^i)} = (x_0^{(2^i)}, x_1^{(2^i)}\, x_2^{(2^i)}, x_3^{(2^i)})$$

be the vector formed from the first column of the matrix $\mathbf{T}^{2^i}$.

This sequence of vectors converges to the solution vector $(1, 1, 2, 3)$ as indicated by the following table:

i	$x_0^{(2^i)}$	$x_1^{(2^i)}$	$x_2^{(2^i)}$	$x_3^{(2^i)}$
1	1.000 000 000	2.629 400 000	3.368 260 000	1.038 464 000
2	1.000 000 000	1.942 817 046	2.804 129 764	1.857 550 209
3	1.000 000 000	1.319 447 433	2.272 479 238	2.612 899 254
4	1.000 000 000	1.036 675 039	2.031 282 726	2.955 557 837
5	1.000 000 000	1.000 483 407	2.000 412 332	2.999 414 216
6	1.000 000 000	1.000 000 084	2.000 000 072	2.999 999 898
7	1.000 000 000	2.000 000 000	2.000 000 000	3.000 000 000
. . . .				
20	1.000 000 000	1.000 000 000	2.000 000 000	3.000 000 000

(Machine time: 0 minutes, 41 seconds)

20.85 *OTHER ITERATIVE METHODS.* Although the iterative methods discussed in the preceding sections have the charm of appealing simplicity, they need not converge. In recent years there has been much research in the area of iterative procedures which converge for a larger class of linear systems and whose convergence is more rapid. Notable are the so-called *conjugate gradient* methods due to Hestenes and Stiefel [10,11]. These are suggested for consideration in a second course in numerical methods.

EXERCISES

1. Given the system:

$$2x_1 + x_2 + x_3 = 7$$

$$3x_1 - x_2 + 2x_3 = 7$$

$$x_1 + 3x_2 - x_3 = 4$$

(*a*) solve by Gauss's method of elimination; (*b*) solve by Jordan's method of elimination; (*c*) solve the three related systems discussed in Sec. 20.3; (*d*) obtain the solution of original system from solutions of (*c*); (*e*) write down the matrix **E**. Verify that it is the inverse of the coefficient matrix of our system.

2. Solve the system of Exercise 20.1 by the compact elimination method.

3. Use compact elimination method to find inverse of each of the following matrices:

$$(a) \begin{bmatrix} 2.89 & -1.34 & -0.67 & 3.25 \\ 1.35 & 2.87 & 5.43 & -0.89 \\ 1.96 & -1.75 & 3.49 & -5.41 \\ 2.34 & 3.37 & 1.38 & 4.09 \end{bmatrix} \qquad (b) \begin{bmatrix} 1 & 2 & 3 \\ 5 & 7 & 4 \\ 6 & 8 & 3 \end{bmatrix}$$

$$(c) \begin{bmatrix} 10 & 1 & 7 \\ 1 & 10 & 6 \\ 7 & 6 & 10 \end{bmatrix} \qquad (d) \begin{bmatrix} 10 & 1 & 7 \\ 1 & 10 & 8 \\ 7 & 8 & 10 \end{bmatrix}.$$

4. Solve the following system by the compact elimination method:

$$3.5x_1 + 2.5x_2 + 3x_3 = 6.5$$

$$7x_1 - 5x_2 + 6x_3 = 7$$

$$14x_1 + 5x_2 - 1.5x_3 = 5.$$

The exact solution vector is $(\frac{2}{7}, \frac{3}{5}, \frac{4}{3})$.

5. Use the method of Sec. 20.3 to find inverse of the matrix

$$\mathbf{A} = \begin{bmatrix} 2 & 1 & 1 \\ 3 & -1 & 2 \\ 1 & 3 & -1 \end{bmatrix}.$$

6. Verify that $(-48.6420,\ 52.1160,\ -25.0165)$ is the solution vector of the system

$$-36x_1 \qquad\qquad + 68x_3 = 50$$
$$-75x_1 - 70x_2 \qquad\qquad = 0$$
$$36x_2 + 71x_3 = 100$$

and that $(-95.84204,\ 101.27809,\ -28.55411)$ is the solution vector of the system

$$-35.6x_1 - 0.4x_2 + 68.4x_3 = 50.4$$
$$-74.6x_1 - 70.4x_2 + 0.4x_3 = 0.4$$
$$0.4x_1 + 35.6x_2 + 71.4x_3 = 100.4.$$

7. Show that $(2, 3)$ is the solution vector of the system

$$x_1 + 5 \quad x_2 = 17$$
$$1.500x_1 + 7.501x_2 = 25.503$$

while $(17, 0)$ is the solution vector of the system

$$x_1 + 5 \quad x_2 = 17$$
$$1.500x_1 + 7.501x_2 = 25.500.$$

Note the sensitivity of the solution vector to small variations in the coefficients. But note also that the slopes of the lines involved are almost identical.

Let

$$r_1(x_1, x_2) = \qquad x_1 + \qquad 5x_2 - 17$$
$$r_2(x_1, x_2) = 1.500x_1 + 7.501x_2 - 25.503.$$

Show that

$$r_1(1252.1, -247) = 0.1$$
$$r_2(1252.1, -247) = -0.1.$$

Here r_1 and r_2 are small for values of x_1 and x_2 very different from the solution $x_1 = 2$, $x_2 = 3$.

We have here a simple example of what are known as ill-conditioned equations [12].

8. Try to solve each of the following systems of equations using the Gauss-Seidel-Hotelling method:

$$(a) \quad 4x_1 - 5x_2 = -6 \qquad (b) \quad 10x_1 + 2x_2 = 14$$
$$x_1 - 1.1x_2 = 0 \qquad\qquad x_1 + 5x_2 = 11.$$

9. If all of the n systems of n equations in n unknowns

$$\mathbf{A}\mathbf{x}^{(i)} = \mathbf{k}^{(i)}, \qquad i = 1, 2, \ldots, n,$$

where $d(\mathbf{A}) \neq 0$, are solved simultaneously by Jordan elimination (Sec. 20.43), the matrix $\mathbf{E}$ of solution vectors is $\mathbf{A}^{-1}$ (Sec. 20.43); that is,

$$[\mathbf{x}^{(1)}, \mathbf{x}^{(2)}, \ldots, \mathbf{x}^{(n)}] = \mathbf{A}^{-1}.$$

Thus by applying a sequence of elementary transformations (B.11) to the rows of the $n \times 2n$ matrix $[\mathbf{A}, \mathbf{I}]$ we obtain the $n \times 2n$ matrix $[\mathbf{I}, \mathbf{A}^{-1}]$. This method was noted by A. A. Albert [15].

Use this method to invert the matrix

$$\mathbf{A} = \begin{bmatrix} -2 & 1 & 0 & 1 \\ 1 & 0 & 2 & -1 \\ -4 & 1 & -3 & 1 \\ -1 & 0 & -2 & 2 \end{bmatrix}.$$

REFERENCES

1. I. J. Paige and O. Taussky (eds.). *Simultaneous Linear Equations and the Determination of Eigenvalues*. National Bureau of Standards, Washington, D.C.: U.S. Government Printing Office, 1953.

2. O. Taussky (ed.). *Contributions to the Solution of Systems of Linear Equations and the Determination of Eigenvalues*. National Bureau of Standards, Washington, D.C.: U.S. Government Printing Office, 1954.

3. National Bureau of Standards. *Further Contributions to the Solution of Simultaneous Linear Equations and the Determination of Eigenvalues*. Washington, D.C.: U.S. Government Printing Office, 1958.

4. V. N. Faddeeva. *Computational Methods of Linear Algebra*. New York: Dover, 1959. Translated from the Russian edition of 1950.

5. P. S. Dwyer. *Linear Computations*. New York: Wiley, 1951.

6. E. Reich. "On the Convergence of the Classical Iterative Method of Solving Linear Simultaneous Equations," *Ann. Math. Statist.* **20**: 448–451 (1949).

7. K. S. Kunz. *Numerical Analysis*. New York: McGraw-Hill, 1957.

8. G. E. Forsythe. "Solving Linear Algebraic Equations Can Be Interesting," *Bull. Am. Math. Soc.* **59**: 299–329 (1953).

9. H. Hotelling. "Some New Methods in Matrix Calculations," *Ann. Math. Statist.* **14:** 1–34 (1943).

10. Hestenes and Stiefel. "Method of Conjugate Gradients for Solving Linear Systems," *J. Res. Nat. Bur. Standards* **49:** 409–436 (1952).

11. A. Ralston and H. S. Wilf (eds.). *Mathematical Methods for Digital Computers.* New York: Wiley, 1960.

12. R. G. Stanton. *Numerical Methods for Science and Engineering.* Englewood Cliffs, N.J.: Prentice-Hall, 1961.

13. J. H. Wilkinson. "Rounding Errors in Algebraic Processes," *Information Processing* 44–53 (1960), UNESCO, Paris.

14. J. H. Wilkinson. "Error Analysis in Floating-point Computation," *Num. Math.* **2:** 319–340 (1960).

15. A. A. Albert. "A Rule for Computing the Inverse Matrix," *Am. Math. Monthly* **48:** 198–199 (1941).

be a square matrix of order n. We say that the sequence

$$\mathbf{A}^{(1)}, \quad \mathbf{A}^{(2)}, \quad \mathbf{A}^{(3)}, \quad \ldots$$

21

MATRIX INVERSION

21.1 INTRODUCTION

In Sec. 20.3 we observed that if $\mathbf{x}^{(i)}$ is the solution vector of the system

$$\mathbf{A}\mathbf{x}^{(i)} = \mathbf{k}^{(i)}$$

where the components of the vector $\mathbf{k}^{(i)}$ are all 0 except its ith, which is equal to 1, and $\mathbf{E}$ is the matrix whose ith column is the vector $\mathbf{x}^{(i)}$, then $\mathbf{E} = \mathbf{A}^{-1}$. We then proceeded to describe a compact elimination method for producing the elements of $\mathbf{E}$. Owing, however, to the almost inevitable rounding, only an approximate inverse will be obtained. Of course, extra guard figures in the calculation could be used, but there seems to be no simple way of determining in advance how many will be needed. So it may be simpler to take the matrix obtained as a first approximation to the desired inverse and then use some iterative scheme for improving it. But before describing one such scheme, we first consider the concept of converging sequences of matrices.

21.2 SEQUENCES OF MATRICES

Let
$$\mathbf{A}^{(k)} = [a_{ij}^{(k)}]$$

183

be a square matrix of order n. We say that the sequence

$$\{\mathbf{A}^{(k)}\} \quad \text{or} \quad \mathbf{A}^{(1)}, \mathbf{A}^{(2)}, \ldots, \mathbf{A}^{(k)}, \ldots$$

of matrices converges to the matrix $\mathbf{A}$ if and only if the sequence $a_{ij}^{(1)}, a_{ij}^{(2)}, \ldots,$ $a_{ij}^{(k)}, \ldots$ converges to a_{ij} for all integers i and j between 1 and n.

The series

$$\mathbf{A}^{(1)} + \mathbf{A}^{(2)} + \cdots + \mathbf{A}^{(k)} + \cdots$$

is said to converge to a matrix $\mathbf{S}$ if and only if the sequence

$$\{\mathbf{S}^{(k)} = \mathbf{A}^{(1)} + \mathbf{A}^{(2)} + \cdots + \mathbf{A}^{(k)}\}$$

converges to $\mathbf{S}$.

21.3 MATRIX NORMS

A matrix *norm* is a measure of how well one matrix approximates another, or, more accurately, of how well their difference approximates the zero matrix. Any iterative procedure for inverting a matrix produces a sequence of approximate inverses. Since in practice such a process must be terminated, it is desirable to have some measure of the error of the approximate inverse.

Of the many norms that have been studied we shall use the following two norms for a square matrix $\mathbf{A}$ of order n:

Row norm: $\qquad N_r(\mathbf{A}) = \max_i \sum_{j=1}^{n} |a_{ij}|,$

Column norm: $\qquad N_c(\mathbf{A}) = \max_j \sum_{i=1}^{n} |a_{ij}|.$

Letting $N(\mathbf{A})$ denote either of these norms we note the following properties:

1. $N(\mathbf{A}) > 0, \quad \mathbf{A} \neq \mathbf{0}$
2. $N(\mathbf{O}) = 0$
3. $N(\mathbf{I}) = 1$
4. $N(\alpha\mathbf{A}) = |\alpha|\, N(\mathbf{A})$
5. $N(\mathbf{A} + \mathbf{B}) \leq N(\mathbf{A}) + N(\mathbf{B})$
6. $N(\mathbf{AB}) \leq N(\mathbf{A})N(\mathbf{B})$
7. $N(\mathbf{A} - \mathbf{B}) \geq |N(\mathbf{A}) - N(\mathbf{B})|.$

The first five of these properties follow at once from the definition of a matrix norm. The proof of Property 6 may be made as follows: Since the absolute value of a sum of real numbers cannot exceed the sum of their absolute values,

$$\left| \sum_{j=1}^{n} a_{ij} b_{jk} \right| \leq \sum_{j=1}^{n} |a_{ij}| \, |b_{jk}|.$$

Hence

$$\sum_{k=1}^{n} \left| \sum_{j=1}^{n} a_{ij} b_{jk} \right| \leq \sum_{j=1}^{n} \left\{ |a_{ij}| \sum_{k=1}^{n} |b_{jk}| \right\} \leq \left\{ \sum_{j=1}^{n} |a_{ij}| \right\} \left\{ \max_{j} \sum_{k=1}^{n} |b_{jk}| \right\}$$

and

$$N_r(\mathbf{AB}) = \max_{i} \sum_{k=1}^{n} \left| \sum_{j=1}^{n} a_{ij} b_{jk} \right| \leq N_r(\mathbf{A}) N_r(\mathbf{B}).$$

Similarly,

$$N_c(\mathbf{AB}) \leq N_c(\mathbf{A}) N_c(\mathbf{B}).$$

As for Property 7, we have but to observe that

$$N(\mathbf{A}) = N(\mathbf{A} - \mathbf{B} + \mathbf{B}) \leq N(\mathbf{A} - \mathbf{B}) + N(\mathbf{B}),$$

and hence

$$N(\mathbf{A}) - N(\mathbf{B}) \leq N(\mathbf{A} - \mathbf{B}).$$

But

$$N(\mathbf{A} - \mathbf{B}) = N(\mathbf{B} - \mathbf{A}) \geq N(\mathbf{B}) - N(\mathbf{A}),$$

and hence

$$N(\mathbf{A} - \mathbf{B}) \geq |N(\mathbf{A}) - N(\mathbf{B})|.$$

We now state three theorems about norms that will be needed in the sequel:

THEOREM 21.1. *The sequence* $\{\mathbf{A}^{(k)}\}$ *of matrices converges to the zero matrix if and only if the sequence* $\{N(\mathbf{A}^k)\}$ *of norms converges to the number* 0.

THEOREM 21.2. *If* $N(\mathbf{A}) < 1$, *then*

$$\mathbf{A}^n \xrightarrow[n \to \infty]{} \mathbf{0}.$$

THEOREM 21.3. *If* $N(\mathbf{A}) < 1$ *and* $d(\mathbf{I} - \mathbf{A}) \neq 0$, *then*

$$N[(\mathbf{I} - \mathbf{A})^{-1}] \leq \frac{1}{1 - N(\mathbf{A})}.$$

The first two theorems are obviously true and the third may be proved as follows: Since

$$(\mathbf{I} + \mathbf{A} + \mathbf{A}^2 + \cdots + \mathbf{A}^n)(\mathbf{I} - \mathbf{A}) = \mathbf{I} - \mathbf{A}^{n+1}$$

it follows that

$$(\mathbf{I} - \mathbf{A})^{-1} = \mathbf{I} + \mathbf{A} + \mathbf{A}^2 + \cdots + \mathbf{A}^n + \mathbf{A}^{n+1}(\mathbf{I} - \mathbf{A})^{-1}.$$

Taking norms of both sides and using the noted properties of norms, we have

$$N[(\mathbf{I} - \mathbf{A})^{-1}] \leq 1 + N(\mathbf{A}) + [N(\mathbf{A})]^2 + \cdots$$
$$+ [N(\mathbf{A})]^n + [N(\mathbf{A})]^{n+1} N[(\mathbf{I} - \mathbf{A})^{-1}].$$

Summing the geometric progression, we obtain

$$N[(\mathbf{I} - \mathbf{A})^{-1}] \leq \frac{[N(\mathbf{A})]^{n+1} - 1}{N(\mathbf{A}) - 1} + [N(\mathbf{A})]^{n+1} N[(\mathbf{I} - \mathbf{A})^{-1}] .$$

This holds for every positive integer n and hence in the limit we find that

$$N[(\mathbf{I} - \mathbf{A})^{-1}] \leq \frac{1}{1 - N(\mathbf{A})} .$$

21.4 HOTELLING'S METHOD

If an approximate inverse is available, an iterative scheme due to Hotelling [1] may be used to improve it. We suppose available an approximate inverse $\mathbf{E}_0$ of $\mathbf{A}$ such that $N(\mathbf{I} - \mathbf{A}\mathbf{E}_0) \leq k < 1$. We form the following sequences of matrices:

$$\begin{array}{ll}
\mathbf{E}_0 & \mathbf{F}_0 = \mathbf{I} - \mathbf{A}\mathbf{E}_0 \\
\mathbf{E}_1 = \mathbf{E}_0(\mathbf{I} + \mathbf{F}_0) & \mathbf{F}_1 = \mathbf{I} - \mathbf{A}\mathbf{E}_1 \\
\mathbf{E}_2 = \mathbf{E}_1(\mathbf{I} + \mathbf{F}_1) & \mathbf{F}_2 = \mathbf{I} - \mathbf{A}\mathbf{E}_2 \\
\cdot \quad \cdot \quad \cdot \quad \cdot \quad \cdot & \cdot \quad \cdot \quad \cdot \quad \cdot \quad \cdot \\
\mathbf{E}_{i+1} = \mathbf{E}_i(\mathbf{I} + \mathbf{F}_i) & \mathbf{F}_{i+1} = \mathbf{I} - \mathbf{A}\mathbf{E}_{i+1} \\
\cdot \quad \cdot \quad \cdot \quad \cdot \quad \cdot & \cdot \quad \cdot \quad \cdot \quad \cdot \quad \cdot
\end{array}$$

The error of a typical iterate $\mathbf{E}_i$ is

$$\mathbf{A}^{-1} - \mathbf{E}_i = \mathbf{A}^{-1}\mathbf{F}_i,$$

which is given approximately by $\mathbf{E}_i\mathbf{F}_i$. This latter quantity when added to $\mathbf{E}_i$ might be expected to give a better estimate $\mathbf{E}_{i+1}$ of $\mathbf{A}^{-1}$.

We shall show that the sequences defined above have the following properties:

1. $\mathbf{F}_i = \mathbf{F}_0^{2^i}$
2. $\mathbf{E}_i = \mathbf{A}^{-1}(\mathbf{I} - \mathbf{F}_0^{2^i})$
3. $N(\mathbf{E}_i - \mathbf{A}^{-1}) \leq N(\mathbf{E}_0)\dfrac{k^{2^i}}{1 - k} .$

Thus if $k \ll 1$ the sequence $\mathbf{E}_i$ converges rapidly to $\mathbf{A}^{-1}$.

The first property is a consequence of the fact that

$$\mathbf{F}_i = \mathbf{I} - \mathbf{A}\mathbf{E}_i = \mathbf{I} - \mathbf{A}\mathbf{E}_{i-1}(\mathbf{I} + \mathbf{F}_{i-1})$$
$$= \mathbf{I} - (\mathbf{I} - \mathbf{F}_{i-1})(\mathbf{I} + \mathbf{F}_{i-1}) = \mathbf{F}_{i-1}^2.$$

The second property follows from the first and the fact that

$$\mathbf{A}\mathbf{E}_i = \mathbf{I} - \mathbf{F}_i$$

and

$$\therefore \quad \mathbf{E}_i = \mathbf{A}^{-1}(\mathbf{I} - \mathbf{F}_i).$$

Property 3 may be established as follows:

$$N(\mathbf{E}_i - \mathbf{A}^{-1}) = N(-\mathbf{A}^{-1}\mathbf{F}_0^{2^i})$$
$$= N[-\mathbf{E}_0(\mathbf{I} - \mathbf{F}_0)^{-1}\mathbf{F}_0^{2^i}]$$
$$\leq N(\mathbf{E}_0)N[(\mathbf{I} - \mathbf{F}_0)^{-1}]N(\mathbf{F}_0^{2^i}).$$

By Theorem 21.3,

$$N[(\mathbf{I} - \mathbf{F}_0)^{-1}] \leq \frac{1}{1 - N(\mathbf{F}_0)}.$$

Hence

$$N(\mathbf{E}_i - \mathbf{A}^{-1}) \leq N(\mathbf{E}_0)\frac{[N(\mathbf{F}_0)]^{2^i}}{1 - N(\mathbf{F}_0)}$$

$$\leq N(\mathbf{E}_0)\frac{k^{2^i}}{1 - k}.$$

EXAMPLE 21.1.   The exact inverse of the matrix

$$\mathbf{A} = \begin{bmatrix} 1 & 2 & 3 \\ 5 & 7 & 4 \\ 6 & 8 & 3 \end{bmatrix} \quad \text{is} \quad \mathbf{A}^{-1} = \begin{bmatrix} -11 & 18 & -13 \\ 9 & -15 & 11 \\ -2 & 4 & -3 \end{bmatrix}.$$

However, if we use the procedure outlined in the introduction to this chapter we obtain the following approximate inverse:

$$\mathbf{E}_0 = \begin{bmatrix} -11.54 & 18.54 & -13.54 \\ 9.45 & -15.45 & 11.45 \\ -2.12 & 4.12 & -3.12 \end{bmatrix}.$$

Applying Hotelling's scheme to this initial approximation we obtain the following sequence of matrices (which is converging to the true inverse):

$$\mathbf{E}_1 = \begin{bmatrix} -10.9838 & 17.9838 & -12.9838 \\ 8.9865 & -14.9865 & 10.9865 \\ -1.9964 & 3.9964 & -2.9964 \end{bmatrix}$$

$$\mathbf{E}_2 = \begin{bmatrix} -11.0000 & 18.0000 & -13.0000 \\ 9.0000 & -15.0000 & 11.0000 \\ -2.0000 & 4.0000 & -3.0000 \end{bmatrix}.$$

EXERCISE

1. Use the Hotelling iterative scheme to improve the approximate inverses found for the matrices of Exercise 20.3, parts (c) and (d).

REFERENCE

1. H. Hotelling, "Some New Methods in Matrix Calculations," *Ann. Math. Statist.* **14**:1–34 (1943).

22

MATRIX CHARACTERISTIC

VALUE PROBLEMS

22.1 AN EXAMPLE

Systems of linear differential equations are one source of what are known as characteristic value problems. Consider, for example, a system of three homogeneous linear differential equations in three unknowns with constant coefficients. In matrix notation such a system can be written

$$\dot{\mathbf{x}} = \mathbf{A}\mathbf{x}, \tag{22.1}$$

where

$$\mathbf{A} = \begin{bmatrix} a_{11} & a_{12} & a_{13} \\ a_{21} & a_{22} & a_{23} \\ a_{31} & a_{32} & a_{33} \end{bmatrix}, \quad \mathbf{x} = \begin{bmatrix} x_1 \\ x_2 \\ x_3 \end{bmatrix}, \quad \dot{\mathbf{x}} = \begin{bmatrix} \dot{x}_1 \\ \dot{x}_2 \\ \dot{x}_3 \end{bmatrix}.$$

In analogy with a single third-order differential equation, it is reasonable to expect that the solution of the system of Eq. (22.1) might be obtained as a linear combination of solutions of the form

$$\mathbf{x} = \boldsymbol{\alpha} e^{\lambda t} \tag{22.2}$$

189

where $\boldsymbol{\alpha} = (\alpha_1, \alpha_2, \alpha_3)$ and λ a suitable scalar constant. Substitution of this into Eq. (22.1) leads to the equation

$$(\mathbf{A} - \lambda\mathbf{I})\boldsymbol{\alpha} = 0,$$

or   (22.3)

$$\mathbf{A}\boldsymbol{\alpha} = \lambda\boldsymbol{\alpha}.$$

This may be thought of as a system of three homogeneous linear algebraic equations in the three unknown components of the column matrix or vector $\boldsymbol{\alpha}$ which will have a nontrivial solution if and only if λ is chosen so that (D.1.3)

$$d(\mathbf{A} - \lambda\mathbf{I}) = 0,$$ (22.4)

that is, so that

$$\begin{vmatrix} a_{11} - \lambda & a_{12} & a_{13} \\ a_{21} & a_{22} - \lambda & a_{23} \\ a_{31} & a_{32} & a_{33} - \lambda \end{vmatrix} = 0.$$

This is a cubic polynomial equation in λ. The nature of the solutions of the original system of differential equations depends on the nature of the roots of Eq. (22.4). Suppose, for example, that it has three distinct roots $\lambda_1, \lambda_2, \lambda_3$. Corresponding to each λ_j is a solution $\boldsymbol{\alpha}^{(j)}$ of the system (22.3) of algebraic equations. Hence to each λ_j there corresponds a particular solution $\mathbf{x}^{(j)}$ of the system of differential equations. Then

$$\mathbf{x} = c_1\mathbf{x}^{(1)} + c_2\mathbf{x}^{(2)} + c_3\mathbf{x}^{(3)}$$

is a solution of Eq. (22.1). It can be shown that by taking all possible triples (c_1, c_2, c_3) of scalar constants we obtain all solutions of our system of differential equations.

The matrix $\mathbf{A} - \lambda\mathbf{I}$ is called the *characteristic matrix* of the matrix $\mathbf{A}$; the polynomial $d(\mathbf{A} - \lambda\mathbf{I})$ the *characteristic polynomial* of $\mathbf{A}$ and its zeros the *characteristic numbers* of $\mathbf{A}$. The vector $\boldsymbol{\alpha}^{(j)}$, the solution of Eq. (22.3) corresponding to λ_j is called a *characteristic vector* of $\mathbf{A}$. The problem of determining the characteristic numbers and corresponding vectors is referred to as a matrix *characteristic value problem*.

22.2   APPLICATIONS

One of the standard texts [1] on matrices and their applications lists the following examples of problems relating to small oscillations of dynamical systems. The mathematical formulation of each is that of a characteristic value problem.

1. Oscillations of a triple pendulum
2. Torsional oscillations of a uniform cantilever

3. Torsional oscillations of a multicylinder engine
4. Flexural oscillations of a tapered beam
5. Symmetrical vibrations of an annular membrane
6. Static twist of an aeroplane wing under aerodynamical load
7. Oscillations of a wing in an airstream

22.3 SIMILAR MATRICES

The matrix concepts introduced above can also be naturally evolved in connection with the idea of similar matrices (B.6). Recall that two n-square matrices **A** and **B** are said to be *similar* if there exists a nonsingular matrix **M** such that

$$\mathbf{B} = \mathbf{M}^{-1}\mathbf{A}\mathbf{M}.$$

Note that $\mathbf{B}^k = \mathbf{M}^{-1}\mathbf{A}^k\mathbf{M}$, $\quad k = 1, 2, 3, \ldots$, that **B** is nonsingular if **A** is nonsingular and that

$$\mathbf{B}^{-1} = \mathbf{M}^{-1}\mathbf{A}^{-1}\mathbf{M}.$$

Since powers of a diagonal matrix are easy to compute, it is natural to inquire whether or not a given matrix **A** is similar to some diagonal matrix **D**. Suppose such is the case. Then there exists a nonsingular matrix **M** such that

$$\mathbf{M}^{-1}\mathbf{A}\mathbf{M} = \mathbf{D}.$$

or

$$\mathbf{A}[\mathbf{m}_1, \ldots, \mathbf{m}_n] = [\mathbf{m}_1, \ldots, \mathbf{m}_n]\begin{bmatrix} \lambda_1 & 0 & \cdots & 0 \\ 0 & \lambda_2 & \cdots & 0 \\ \cdot & \cdot & \cdot & \cdot \\ 0 & 0 & \cdots & \lambda_n \end{bmatrix}$$

where $\mathbf{m}_i$ is the ith column of **M**. Equating the ith columns of the product matrices on the right and left of last equation we have

$$\mathbf{A}\mathbf{m}_i = \lambda_i\mathbf{m}_i, \qquad i = 1, 2, \ldots, n.$$

Thus the columns of **M** and the elements of **D** are in a relationship of same form found in Eq. (22.3). These equations suggest two basic concepts of matrix theory:

DEFINITION 21.1. Any nonzero column vector **x** is said to be a *characteristic vector* of the matrix **A** if there exists a number λ such that

$$\mathbf{A}\mathbf{x} = \lambda\mathbf{x}.$$

The number λ is called a *characteristic number* of **A** corresponding to the characteristic vector **x**, and conversely.

Characteristic vectors are often called *eigenvectors* and characteristic numbers *eigenvalues, proper numbers,* or *latent roots.*

Thus if a matrix **A** is similar to a diagonal matrix **D** then the diagonal elements of **D** are the characteristic numbers of **A** and the columns of **M** are the corresponding characteristic vectors of **A**.

In this connection we observe that the problem of simplification of quadratic forms is essentially the problem of reduction of the matrix of a quadratic form to a diagonal matrix by a similarity transformation.

Not every nonsingular matrix is similar to a diagonal matrix. (See Exercise 22.1.) But Jordan [2] has shown that every square matrix is similar to what is known as a quasi-diagonal matrix.

JORDAN CANONICAL FORM. If $\lambda_1, \lambda_2, \ldots, \lambda_n$ are the characteristic numbers of the square matrix **A** *of order n, then* **A** *is similar to the quasi-diagonal matrix*

$$\mathbf{A}_0 = \begin{bmatrix} \lambda_1 & k_1 & 0 & 0 & \cdots & 0 & 0 \\ 0 & \lambda_2 & k_2 & 0 & \cdots & 0 & 0 \\ 0 & 0 & \lambda_3 & k_3 & \cdots & 0 & 0 \\ \cdot & \cdot & \cdot & \cdot & \cdot & \cdot & \cdot \\ 0 & 0 & 0 & 0 & \cdots & \lambda_{n-1} & k_{n-1} \\ 0 & 0 & 0 & 0 & \cdots & 0 & \lambda_n \end{bmatrix}$$

where $\lambda_i \leq \lambda_{i+i}$ and all the k_i are either 0 or 1, and $k_i = 1$ only if $\lambda_i = \lambda_{i+i}$.

A more detailed description of the Jordan canonical form would involve the elementary divisors of the characteristic matrix **A** $-$ λ**I** and will not be given here.

22.4 CHARACTERISTIC NUMBERS OF POWERS OF MATRICES

If $\mathbf{x}_i$ is a characteristic vector corresponding to the characteristic number λ_i of the matrix **A**, then

$$\mathbf{A}\mathbf{x}_i = \lambda_i \mathbf{x}_i$$

and

$$\mathbf{A}^2\mathbf{x}_i = \lambda_i \mathbf{A}\mathbf{x}_i = \lambda_i^2 \mathbf{x}_i.$$

Thus $\mathbf{x}_i$ and λ_i^2 are characteristic vector and number of the matrix $\mathbf{A}^2$. Similarly $\mathbf{x}_i$ and λ_i^k are characteristic vector and number of $\mathbf{A}^k$, $k = 2, 3, 4, \ldots$. If the n characteristic numbers of **A** are distinct in absolute value then the numbers λ_i^k, $i = 1, 2, 3, \ldots, n$, are likewise distinct and hence give all the n characteristic numbers of the matrix $\mathbf{A}^k$. The result does not, however, depend on $|\lambda_i|$ being distinct. We shall prove

THEOREM 22.4. If $\lambda_1, \lambda_2, \ldots, \lambda_n$ are the characteristic numbers, distinct or not, of a matrix $\mathbf{A}$ of order n, then the characteristic numbers of $\mathbf{A}^k$ are $\lambda_1^k, \lambda_2^k, \ldots, \lambda_n^k$ for every positive integer k.

We are given that

$$d(\mathbf{A} - \lambda\mathbf{I}) = (-1)^n(\lambda - \lambda_1)(\lambda - \lambda_2) \cdots (\lambda - \lambda_n)$$

and we wish to prove that

$$d(\mathbf{A}^k - \lambda\mathbf{I}) = (-1)^n(\lambda - \lambda_1^k)(\lambda - \lambda_2^k) \cdots (\lambda - \lambda_n^k).$$

We set $\mathbf{A} = \mathbf{M}\mathbf{A}_0\mathbf{M}^{-1}$, where $\mathbf{A}_0$ is the Jordan canonical form. Then

$$\begin{aligned}
d(\mathbf{A}^k - \lambda\mathbf{I}) &= d(\mathbf{M}\mathbf{A}_0^k\mathbf{M}^{-1} - \lambda\mathbf{I}) \\
&= d[\mathbf{M}(\mathbf{A}_0^k - \lambda\mathbf{I})\mathbf{M}^{-1}] \\
&= d(\mathbf{M})d(\mathbf{A}_0^k - \lambda\mathbf{I})d(\mathbf{M}^{-1}) \\
&= d(\mathbf{A}_0^k - \lambda\mathbf{I}) \\
&= (-1)^n(\lambda - \lambda_1^k)(\lambda - \lambda_2^k) \cdots (\lambda - \lambda_n^k),
\end{aligned}$$

as was to be proved.

22.5 LEVERRIER-FADDEEV METHOD FOR OBTAINING CHARACTERISTIC POLYNOMIAL

Unless a matrix is of low order or has many zero elements it would be inefficient to obtain its characteristic polynomial by a direct expansion of the determinant defining it. The method of U. J. J. Leverrier (1840) and a modification of it by D. K. Faddeev (1949) are based on Newton's theorem (Sec. 5.3).

If $\lambda_1, \lambda_2, \ldots, \lambda_n$ are the characteristic numbers of the matrix $\mathbf{A}$, that is, the zeros of the polynomial

$$d(\mathbf{A} - \lambda\mathbf{I}) = (-1)^n[\lambda^n - p_1\lambda^{n-1} - p_2\lambda^{n-2} \cdots p_{n-1}\lambda - p_n], \quad (22.5)$$

and if

$$S_k = \sum_{i=1}^{n} \lambda_i^k, \qquad 1 \leq k \leq n, \tag{22.6}$$

then, according to Newton's theorem

$$kp_k = S_k - p_1S_{k-1} - \cdots - p_{k-1}S_1. \tag{22.7}$$

The coefficient of λ^{n-1} in the determinant expansion of left-hand member of Eq. (22.5) is $(-1)^{n-1}(a_{11} + a_{22} + \cdots + a_{nn})$ and on the right this coefficient is $(-1)^{n-1}p_1$. Hence

$$p_1 = a_{11} + a_{22} + \cdots + a_{nn}.$$

But $S_1 = p_1$ (Eq. (5.4)). The sum of the diagonal elements of a matrix $\mathbf{A}$ is known as the *trace* of the matrix $\mathbf{A}$, written $\operatorname{tr}(\mathbf{A})$. Thus

$$S_1 = \operatorname{tr}(\mathbf{A}).$$

That is, the sum of the characteristic numbers of a matrix $\mathbf{A}$ is equal to the trace of $\mathbf{A}$. Then, since the characteristic numbers of $\mathbf{A}^k$ are the kth powers of the characteristic numbers of $\mathbf{A}$.

$$S_k = \operatorname{tr}(\mathbf{A}^k).$$

Thus the numbers $S_1, S_2, \ldots, S_n$ are readily obtainable from the first n powers of $\mathbf{A}$. Then Newton's theorem Eq. (22.7), can be used to compute the coefficients of the characteristic polynomial. This is the method of Leverrier.

A modification due to Faddeev simplifies the calculation of the coefficients of the characteristic polynomial and produces also the characteristic vectors. Compute the following sequences of matrices:

$$\mathbf{A}_1 = \mathbf{A}, \qquad \operatorname{tr}(\mathbf{A}_1) = q_1, \qquad \mathbf{B}_1 = \mathbf{A}_1 - q_1\mathbf{I},$$

$$\mathbf{A}_2 = \mathbf{A}\mathbf{B}_1, \qquad \operatorname{tr}(\mathbf{A}_2) = 2q_2, \qquad \mathbf{B}_2 = \mathbf{A}_2 - q_2\mathbf{I},$$

$$\cdot \qquad \cdot \qquad \cdot \qquad \cdot \qquad \cdot \qquad \cdot$$

$$\mathbf{A}_{n-1} = \mathbf{A}\mathbf{B}_{n-2}, \quad \operatorname{tr}(\mathbf{A}_{n-1}) = (n-1)q_{n-1}, \quad \mathbf{B}_{n-1} = \mathbf{A}_{n-1} - q_{n-1}\mathbf{I},$$

$$\mathbf{A}_n = \mathbf{A}\mathbf{B}_{n-1}, \qquad \operatorname{tr}(\mathbf{A}_n) = nq_n, \qquad \mathbf{B}_n = \mathbf{A}_n - q_n\mathbf{I}.$$

We shall show by the use of mathematical induction that $q_i = p_i$, $i = 1, 2, \ldots, n$. Since $\mathbf{A} = \mathbf{A}_1$, $q_1 = p_1$. Suppose now that $q_i = p_i$ for $i = 1, 2, \ldots, k$. We prove that $q_{k+1} = p_{k+1}$. From the equations defining the $\mathbf{A}_i$ we have

$$\begin{aligned}
\mathbf{A}_{k+1} = \mathbf{A}\mathbf{B}_k &= \mathbf{A}(\mathbf{A}_k - q_k\mathbf{I}) \\
&= \mathbf{A}[\mathbf{A}(\mathbf{A}_{k-1} - q_{k-1}\mathbf{I}) - q_k\mathbf{I}] \\
&= \cdot \qquad \cdot \qquad \cdot \qquad \cdot \qquad \cdot \qquad \cdot \\
&= \mathbf{A}^{k+1} - q_1\mathbf{A}^k - q_2\mathbf{A}^{k-1} - \cdots - q_k\mathbf{A} \\
&= \mathbf{A}^{k+1} - p_1\mathbf{A}^k - p_2\mathbf{A}^{k-1} - \cdots - p_k\mathbf{A}.
\end{aligned}$$

Hence

$$\begin{aligned}
\operatorname{tr}(\mathbf{A}_{k+1}) &= \operatorname{tr}(\mathbf{A}^{k+1}) - p_1\operatorname{tr}(\mathbf{A}^k) - p_2\operatorname{tr}(\mathbf{A}^{k-1}) - \cdots - p_k\operatorname{tr}(\mathbf{A}) \\
&= S_{k+1} - p_1S_k - p_2S_{k-1} - \cdots - p_kS_1.
\end{aligned}$$

Thus, by Newton's theorem

$$\operatorname{tr}(\mathbf{A}_{k+1}) = (k+1)p_{k+1}.$$

But, by definition of q_{k+1},

$$\mathrm{tr}\,(\mathbf{A}_{k+1}) = (k + 1)q_{k+1}.$$

Hence

$$q_{k+1} = p_{k+1},$$

which completes the induction.

We now show for the case of distinct λ_i that each column of the matrix

$$\mathbf{Q}_i = \lambda_i^{n-1}\mathbf{I} + \lambda_i^{n-2}\mathbf{B}_1 + \cdots + \lambda_i\mathbf{B}_{n-2} + \mathbf{B}_{n-1}$$

is a characteristic vector corresponding to the characteristic number λ_i. For

$$(\lambda_i\mathbf{I} - \mathbf{A})\mathbf{Q}_i = \lambda_i^n\mathbf{I} + \lambda_i^{n-1}(\mathbf{B}_1 - \mathbf{A}) + \cdots + \lambda_i(\mathbf{B}_{n-1} - \mathbf{AB}_{n-2}) - \mathbf{AB}_{n-1}$$

$$= \lambda_i^n\mathbf{I} - p_1\lambda_i^{n-1}\mathbf{I} - p_2\lambda_i^{n-2}\mathbf{I} - \cdots - p_{n-1}\lambda_i\mathbf{I} - p_n\mathbf{I} = \mathbf{O}.$$

Thus

$$\mathbf{AQ}_i = \lambda_i\mathbf{Q}_i$$

and if $\mathbf{x}_i$ is any column of $\mathbf{Q}_i$, then

$$\mathbf{Ax}_i = \lambda_i\mathbf{x}_i,$$

and $\mathbf{x}_i$ is a characteristic vector corresponding to the characteristic number λ_i.

EXAMPLE 22.1. By direct calculation it is readily verified that for the matrix

$$\mathbf{A} = \begin{bmatrix} 1 & -2 \\ -2 & 1 \end{bmatrix}$$

we have the following:

characteristic polynomial: $\lambda^2 - 2\lambda - 3$

characteristic numbers: $3, -1$

characteristic vectors: $(1, -1), (1, 1).$

Using the method of Leverrier-Faddeev we find:

$$\mathbf{A} = \begin{bmatrix} 1 & -2 \\ -2 & 1 \end{bmatrix}, \qquad p_1 = 2, \qquad \mathbf{B}_1 = \begin{bmatrix} -1 & -2 \\ -2 & -1 \end{bmatrix}$$

$$\mathbf{A}_2 = \begin{bmatrix} 3 & 0 \\ 0 & 3 \end{bmatrix}, \qquad p_2 = 3, \qquad \mathbf{B}_2 = \begin{bmatrix} 0 & 0 \\ 0 & 0 \end{bmatrix}.$$

Hence the characteristic polynomial is $\lambda^2 - 2\lambda - 3$ and the characteristic numbers are 3, -1. Then

$$\mathbf{Q}_1 = \begin{bmatrix} 2 & -2 \\ -2 & 2 \end{bmatrix}, \qquad \mathbf{Q}_2 = \begin{bmatrix} -2 & -2 \\ -2 & -2 \end{bmatrix}$$

and it is seen that each column of $\mathbf{Q}_i$ is a characteristic vector corresponding to λ_i.

22.6   ITERATIVE METHODS

We shall describe a basic iterative method and one of its modifications for obtaining the dominant characteristic number and corresponding vector. These methods are sometimes referred to as matrix powering and are due to R. Von Mises (1929). We shall not consider the problem in complete generality. In particular, we shall not consider the case of complex characteristic numbers [5]. The case considered is, however of considerable practical interest since it is known that the characteristic numbers of a real symmetric matrix are all real [6].

22.61   *BASIC ITERATIVE METHOD FOR DOMINANT ZERO.* Let the characteristic numbers of the matrix $\mathbf{A}$ be real and ordered according to absolute value: $|\lambda_1| \geq |\lambda_2| \geq \cdots \geq |\lambda_n|$. We suppose that to each λ_i there corresponds a characteristic vector $\mathbf{x}_i$ such that the vectors $\mathbf{x}_i, \mathbf{x}_2, \ldots, \mathbf{x}_n$ are linearly independent. The matrix

$$\mathbf{X} = [\mathbf{x}_1, \mathbf{x}_2, \ldots, \mathbf{x}_n]$$

whose ith column is the characteristic vector $\mathbf{x}_i$, is nonsingular [B.8]. Then corresponding to any nonzero n-dimensional vector $\mathbf{y}_0$ there is a nonzero vector $\mathbf{a} = (a_1, a_2, \ldots, a_n)$ such that

$$\mathbf{y}_0 = \mathbf{Xa}.$$

The method to be described produces the characteristic number λ_1, the so-called dominant zero, and a corresponding vector $\mathbf{x}_1$.

Starting with an arbitrary nonzero vector $\mathbf{y}_0$ form the sequence of vectors

$$\mathbf{y}_1 = \mathbf{Ay}_0$$
$$\mathbf{y}_2 = \mathbf{Ay}_1$$
$$\cdot \ \cdot \ \cdot \ \cdot \ \cdot \ \cdot$$
$$\mathbf{y}_k = \mathbf{Ay}_{k-1}$$
$$\cdot \ \cdot \ \cdot \ \cdot \ \cdot \ \cdot \ \cdot$$

Then

$$\begin{aligned}
\mathbf{y}_k &= \mathbf{A}^k \mathbf{y}_0 = \mathbf{A}^k \mathbf{X} \mathbf{a} \\
&= \mathbf{A}^k [\mathbf{x}_1, \mathbf{x}_2, \ldots, \mathbf{x}_n] \mathbf{a} \\
&= [\mathbf{A}^k \mathbf{x}_1, \mathbf{A}^k \mathbf{x}_2, \ldots, \mathbf{A}^k \mathbf{x}_n] \mathbf{a}.
\end{aligned}$$

Thus, according to Sec. 22.4,

$$\begin{aligned}
\mathbf{y}_k &= [\lambda_1^k \mathbf{x}_1, \lambda_2^k \mathbf{x}_2, \ldots, \lambda_n^k \mathbf{x}_n] \mathbf{a} \\
&= \lambda_1^k a_1 \mathbf{x}_1 + \lambda_2^k a_2 \mathbf{x}_2 + \cdots + \lambda_n^k a_n \mathbf{x}_n.
\end{aligned}$$

We shall now examine two of several possibilities:

CASE I: $|\lambda_1| > |\lambda_2|$.

In this case we write

$$\mathbf{y}_k = \lambda_1^k \left\{ a_1 \mathbf{x}_1 + \left(\frac{\lambda_2}{\lambda_1} \right)^k a_2 \mathbf{x}_2 + \cdots + \left(\frac{\lambda_n}{\lambda_1} \right)^k a_n \mathbf{x}_n \right\}.$$

Thus

$$\mathbf{y}_k \doteq \lambda_1^k a_1 \mathbf{x}_1$$

for large values of k. More precisely, if

$$\mathbf{y}_k = (y_{1k}, y_{2k}, \ldots, y_{nk}),$$

then

$$\frac{y_{ik+1}}{y_{ik}} \xrightarrow[k \to \infty]{} \lambda_1, \qquad \frac{y_{ik}}{y_{1k}} \xrightarrow[k \to \infty]{} \frac{x_{i1}}{x_{11}}$$

provided $a_1 \neq 0$, that is, provided $\mathbf{y}_0$ has a component in direction of $\mathbf{x}_1$. If a choice of initial vector $\mathbf{y}_0$ had been made for which $a_1 = 0$, $a_2 \neq 0$, then the process would yield the characteristic number λ_2, provided $|\lambda_2| > |\lambda_3|$. Thus, unless an unusual choice for $\mathbf{y}_0$ has been made, the ratio of any component of $\mathbf{y}_{k+1}$ and corresponding component of $\mathbf{y}_k$ will converge to λ_1. Furthermore, for large k, two components of $\mathbf{y}_k$ will be in approximately same ratio as corresponding components of $\mathbf{x}_1$.

CASE II: $\lambda_2 = -\lambda_1$, $|\lambda_1| > |\lambda_3|$.

In this case we write

$$\begin{aligned}
\mathbf{y}_{2k} &= \{(a_1 \mathbf{x}_1 + a_2 \mathbf{x}_2) \lambda_1^{2k} + a_3 \mathbf{x}_3 \lambda_3^{2k} + \cdots + a_n \mathbf{x}_n \lambda_n^{2k}\} \\
\mathbf{y}_{2k+1} &= \{(a_1 \mathbf{x}_1 - a_2 \mathbf{x}_2) \lambda_1^{2k+1} + a_3 \mathbf{x}_3 \lambda_3^{2k} + \cdots + a_n \mathbf{x}_n \lambda_n^{2k+1}\}
\end{aligned}$$

and observe that

$$\begin{aligned}
\mathbf{y}_{2k} &\doteq \lambda_1^{2k} (a_1 \mathbf{x}_1 + a_2 \mathbf{x}_2), \\
\mathbf{y}_{2k+1} &\doteq \lambda_1^{2k+1} (a_1 \mathbf{x}_1 - a_2 \mathbf{x}_2)
\end{aligned}$$

for large values of k. Thus

$$\frac{y_{ij}}{y_{i,j+2}} \xrightarrow[j\to\infty]{} \lambda_1^2,$$

and for large values of k two components of $\mathbf{y}_k$ will be approximately in same ratio as corresponding components of $a_1\mathbf{x}_1 + a_2\mathbf{x}_2$, while two components of $\mathbf{y}_{2k+1}$ will be approximately in same ratio as corresponding components of $a_1\mathbf{x}_1 - a_2\mathbf{x}_2$. From these, $\mathbf{x}_1$ and $\mathbf{x}_2$ can be obtained.

22.62 *MODIFIED BASIC ITERATIVE METHOD.* The process described in the preceding section is somewhat simplified if at each stage the vector $\mathbf{y}_k$ is divided by its first nonzero component. Thus, starting with an arbitrary nonzero vector $\mathbf{y}_0$ we form the sequence

$$\begin{aligned}
\mathbf{y}_1 &= \mathbf{A}\mathbf{y}_0 & \mathbf{y}_1^\star &= \mu_1\mathbf{y}_1 \\
\mathbf{y}_2 &= \mathbf{A}\mathbf{y}_1^\star & \mathbf{y}_2^\star &= \mu_2\mathbf{y}_2 \\
&\cdots\cdots & &\cdots\cdots \\
\mathbf{y}_k &= \mathbf{A}\mathbf{y}_{k-1}^\star & \mathbf{y}_k^\star &= \mu_k\mathbf{y}_k \\
&\cdots\cdots & &\cdots\cdots
\end{aligned}$$

where μ_k is the reciprocal of the first nonzero component of $\mathbf{y}_k$. Then

$$\mathbf{y}_k^\star = \nu_k \mathbf{A}^k \mathbf{y}_0$$

where

$$\nu_k = \mu_1\mu_2\cdots\mu_k$$

and hence, as in preceding section,

$$\mathbf{y}_k^\star = \nu_k[\lambda_1^k a_1\mathbf{x}_1 + \lambda_2^k a_2\mathbf{x}_2 + \cdots + \lambda_n^k a_n\mathbf{x}_n]$$

and

$$\mathbf{y}_{k+1} = \nu_k[\lambda_1^{k+1} a_1\mathbf{x}_1 + \lambda_2^{k+1} a_2\mathbf{x}_2 + \cdots + \lambda_n^{k+1} a_n\mathbf{x}_n].$$

Henceforth we shall suppose that

$$\mathbf{y}_k^\star = (1, y_{2k}^\star, \ldots, y_{nk}^\star).$$

Again we consider the same cases as in the preceding section.

CASE I: $|\lambda_1| > |\lambda_2|$.
    In this case

$$\mathbf{y}_k^\star \doteq \nu_k \lambda_1^k a_1\mathbf{x}_1$$

and

$$\mathbf{y}_{k+1} \doteq \nu_k \lambda_1^{k+1} a_1\mathbf{x}_1$$

for large values of k. Thus

$$y_{1k+1} \xrightarrow[k\to\infty]{} \lambda_1$$

and

$$\mathbf{y}_k^\star \xrightarrow[k \to \infty]{} \mathbf{x}_1^\star,$$

provided $a_1 \neq 0$, where $\mathbf{x}_1^\star$ is $\mathbf{x}_1$ divided by its first nonzero component.

CASE II: $\lambda_2 = -\lambda_1, |\lambda_1| > |\lambda_3|$.

Here we find that for large values of k,

$$\mathbf{y}_{2k}^\star \doteq \nu_{2k}\lambda_1^{2k}(a_1\mathbf{x}_1 + a_2\mathbf{x}_2),$$

$$\mathbf{y}_{2k+1}^\star \doteq \nu_{2k+1}\lambda_1^{2k+1}(a_1\mathbf{x}_1 - a_2\mathbf{x}_2),$$

and

$$\mathbf{y}_{2k+2} \doteq \nu_{2k+1}\lambda_1^{2k+2}(a_1\mathbf{x}_1 + a_2\mathbf{x}_2).$$

Hence

$$y_{1,2k+2} \doteq \mu_{2k+1}\lambda_1^2,$$

$$\mathbf{y}_{2k}^\star \doteq c_1\mathbf{x}_1 + c_2\mathbf{x}_2,$$

and

$$\mathbf{y}_{2k+1}^\star \doteq (c_1\mathbf{x}_1 - c_2\mathbf{x}_2)\lambda_1\mu_{2k+1}.$$

From these $\mathbf{x}_1$ and $\mathbf{x}_2$ can be obtained.

EXAMPLE 22.2.   Let

$$\mathbf{A} = \begin{bmatrix} 1 & -2 \\ -2 & 1 \end{bmatrix}$$

as in Example 22.1. We let $\mathbf{y}_0 = (1, 0)$ and form the following sequences:

i	y_{1i}	y_{2i}	$y_{1i}^\star$	$y_{2i}^\star$
0	1	0		
1	1	-2	1	-2
2	5	-4	1	-0.8
3	2.6	-2.8	1	-1.0769
4	3.1538	-3.0769	1	-0.9756
5	2.9512	-2.9756	1	-1.0083
6	3.0166	-3.0083	1	-0.9972
7	2.9944	-2.9972	1	-1.0009
8	3.0018	-3.0009	1	-0.9997
9	2.9994	-2.9997	1	-1.0001
10	3.0002	-3.0001	1	-1.0000
11	3.0000	-3.0000	1	-1.0000
12	3.0000	-3.0000	1	-1.0000

Hence $\lambda_1 = 3.0000$, $x_1 = (1, -1.0000)$.

EXAMPLE 22.3. The characteristic numbers of the matrix

$$\mathbf{A} = \begin{bmatrix} 3 & 1 \\ -5 & -3 \end{bmatrix}$$

are found by direct calculation to be 2 and -2 with corresponding characteristic vectors $(1, -1)$ and $(1, -5)$. We let $\mathbf{y}_0 = (1, 0)$ and form the following sequences:

i	y_{1i}	y_{2i}	$y_{1i}^{\star}$	$y_{2i}^{\star}$
0	1	0		
1	3	-5	1	-1.6667
2	1.3333	0.0001	1	0.0001
3	3.0001	-5.0003	1	-1.6667
4	1.3333	0.0001	1	0.0001

Hence

$$1.333 \doteq \mu_3 \lambda_1^2 = \frac{1}{3.0001} \lambda_1^2$$

$$\therefore \ \lambda_1^2 \doteq 4.0000, \qquad \lambda_1 \doteq 2.0000, \qquad \lambda_2 \doteq -2.0000.$$

$$c_1 \mathbf{x}_1 + c_2 \mathbf{x}_2 = (1, 0.0001)$$

$$\frac{2}{3.0001} (c_1 \mathbf{x}_1 - c_2 \mathbf{x}_2) = (1, -1.6667)$$

$$\therefore \ c_1 \mathbf{x}_1 = (1.2500, -1.2500)$$

$$c_2 \mathbf{x}_2 = (-0.2500, 1.2500).$$

22.63 *SUBDOMINANT CHARACTERISTIC NUMBERS.* The methods of the preceding sections produce a dominant characteristic number, that is, one whose absolute value is not exceeded by that of any other. We now describe a procedure for obtaining a matrix $\mathbf{A}_1$ of order $n - 1$ whose characteristic numbers are in absolute value $|\lambda_2| \geq |\lambda_3| \geq \cdots \geq |\lambda_n|$. The remaining characteristic vectors of $\mathbf{A}$ will be shown to be obtainable from those of $\mathbf{A}_1$. The construction of the matrix $\mathbf{A}_1$ is of exceeding simplicity:

We suppose that the first component of the characteristic vector $\mathbf{x}_1$ is not zero and hence that the first component of $\mathbf{x}_1^{\star}$ is 1. Let

$$\mathbf{A}^{\star} = \mathbf{A} - \mathbf{x}_1^{\star} \mathbf{r}_1$$

where $\mathbf{r}_1$ is the row matrix formed from the first row of the matrix $\mathbf{A}$ (if the ith element of $\mathbf{x}_1$ were its first nonzero element, then a row matrix $\mathbf{r}_i$, formed from the ith row of $\mathbf{A}$, would be used). Then $\mathbf{A}_1$ is the matrix of order $n - 1$ formed by deleting the first row and first column of $\mathbf{A}^\star$.

For any integer i, between 2 and n inclusive,

$$\mathbf{A}^\star(\mathbf{x}_1^\star - \mathbf{x}_i^\star) = \mathbf{A}(\mathbf{x}_1^\star - \mathbf{x}_i^\star) - \mathbf{x}_1^\star \mathbf{r}_1(\mathbf{x}_1^\star - \mathbf{x}_i^\star)$$
$$= \lambda_1 \mathbf{x}_1^\star - \lambda_i \mathbf{x}_i^\star - \mathbf{x}_1^\star(\lambda_1 - \lambda_i)$$
$$= \lambda_i(\mathbf{x}_1^\star - \mathbf{x}_i^\star).$$

Thus λ_i, $i = 2, 3, \ldots, n$, is a characteristic number of $\mathbf{A}^\star$ and $\mathbf{x}_1^\star - \mathbf{x}_i^\star$ a corresponding characteristic vector. Clearly each element of the first row of $\mathbf{A}^\star$ is zero. Hence

$$d(\mathbf{A}^\star - \lambda\mathbf{I}) = -\lambda \, d(\mathbf{A}_1 - \lambda\mathbf{I})$$

and the characteristic numbers of $\mathbf{A}_1$ are $\lambda_2, \lambda_3, \ldots, \lambda_n$.

If $\mathbf{y}_2$ is a characteristic vector of $\mathbf{A}_1$ corresponding to λ_2 and $\mathbf{z}_2$ the n-dimensional vector whose first element is zero and whose next $n - 1$ elements form the vector $\mathbf{y}_2$, then $\mathbf{z}_2$ is a characteristic vector of $\mathbf{A}^\star$ corresponding to λ_2. Furthermore

$$\mathbf{x}_1^\star + \frac{\lambda_2 - \lambda_1}{\mathbf{r}_1\mathbf{z}_2} \mathbf{z}_2 = \mathbf{x}_2^\star.$$

For

$$\mathbf{A}\left(\mathbf{x}_1^\star + \frac{\lambda_2 - \lambda_1}{\mathbf{r}_1\mathbf{z}_2} \mathbf{z}_2\right) = \lambda_1\mathbf{x}_1^\star + (\mathbf{A}^\star + \mathbf{x}_1^\star\mathbf{r}_1)\frac{\lambda_2 - \lambda_1}{\mathbf{r}_1\mathbf{z}_2} \mathbf{z}_2$$

$$= \lambda_1\mathbf{x}_1^\star + \frac{\lambda_2 - \lambda_1}{\mathbf{r}_1\mathbf{z}_2}(\lambda_2\mathbf{z}_2 + \mathbf{x}_1^\star\mathbf{r}_1\mathbf{z}_2)$$

$$= \lambda_1\mathbf{x}_1^\star + (\lambda_2 - \lambda_1)\mathbf{x}_1^\star + \frac{\lambda_2 - \lambda_1}{\mathbf{r}_1\mathbf{z}_2}\lambda_2\mathbf{z}_2$$

$$= \lambda_2\left[\mathbf{x}_1^\star + \frac{\lambda_2 - \lambda_1}{\mathbf{r}_1\mathbf{z}_2}\mathbf{z}_2\right],$$

as was to be proved.

It should be noted that in this method the calculation of the characteristic number λ_2 and vector $\mathbf{x}_2$ both depend on λ_1 and $\mathbf{x}_1$. The almost inevitable rounding makes the calculated values of succeeding characteristic numbers and vectors less and less accurate. Wilkinson [5] has, however, shown that with proper care in programming the method can be effective through several such reductions.

EXAMPLE 22.4.   By direct calculation we find for the matrix

$$\mathbf{A} = \begin{bmatrix} 2 & -2 & 3 \\ 1 & 1 & 1 \\ 1 & 3 & -1 \end{bmatrix}$$

the following:

characteristic polynomial: $-\lambda^3 + 2\lambda^2 + 5\lambda - 6;$

characteristic numbers: $\lambda_1 = 3,$ $\lambda_2 = 1,$ $\lambda_3 = -2;$

characteristic vectors: $x_1 = (1, 1, 1),$ $x_2 = (-1, 1, 1),$

$$x_3 = (11, 1, -14).$$

We now suppose only λ_1 and $\mathbf{x}_1$ to be known and apply the method just described to find λ_2 and $\mathbf{x}_2$. We find

$$\mathbf{x}_1^{\star} = (1, 1, 1), \qquad \mathbf{r}_1 = [2, -2, 3],$$

$$\mathbf{A}^{\star} = \begin{bmatrix} 0 & 0 & 0 \\ -1 & 3 & -2 \\ -1 & 5 & -4 \end{bmatrix}, \qquad \mathbf{A}_1 = \begin{bmatrix} 3 & -2 \\ 5 & -4 \end{bmatrix}.$$

The dominant characteristic number and corresponding vector of $\mathbf{A}_1$ are

$$\lambda_2 = 1 \qquad \text{and} \qquad \mathbf{y}_2 = (1, 1).$$

Then

$$\mathbf{z}_2 = (0, 1, 1)$$

and

$$\mathbf{x}_2^{\star} = (1, 1, 1) + \left(\frac{-2}{1}\right)(0, 1, 1) = (1, -1, -1).$$

22.64   *OTHER METHODS.*   A method published by Jacobi in 1846 has been revived for digital computers [8]. In recent years there has been much research in the area of matrix characteristic value problems. Notable are the methods advanced by Givens [9] and Householder [10] for symmetric matrices. These are suggested as appropriate for consideration in a second course in numerical methods.

EXERCISES

1. Show that the methods of Secs. 22.61 and 22.62 will give λ_1 and a corresponding characteristic vector even if $\lambda_1 = \lambda_2 = \cdots = \lambda_r$ but $|\lambda_r| > |\lambda_{r+1}|.$

2. Extend the method of Sec. 22.63 to obtain λ_3 and $\mathbf{x}_3$ from a matrix of order $n - 2$.

3. Apply method of Sec. 22.62 to find λ_1 and $\mathbf{x}_1$ for the matrix of Example 22.4.

4. Find first two characteristic numbers and corresponding vectors of

$$\mathbf{A} = \begin{bmatrix} 2 & 3 & 2 \\ 10 & 3 & 4 \\ 3 & 6 & 1 \end{bmatrix}.$$

Check by direct calculation.

5. Find first two characteristic numbers and vectors of the matrix

$$\mathbf{A} = \begin{bmatrix} 4 & 2 & 2 \\ 2 & 5 & 1 \\ 2 & 1 & 6 \end{bmatrix}.$$

6. Another modification of the basic iterative method: Compute

$$\mathbf{A}^2, \mathbf{A}^4, \mathbf{A}^8, \ldots, \mathbf{A}^{2^k}, \mathbf{A}^{2^k+1}$$

and obtain λ_1 from

$$\mathbf{y}_{2^k} = \mathbf{A}^{2^k}\mathbf{y}_0, \qquad \mathbf{y}_{2^k+1} = \mathbf{A}^{2^k+1}\mathbf{y}_0.$$

We have here a fast way of obtaining the desirable high powers of $\mathbf{A}$. But compare number of multiplications required to obtain $\mathbf{A}^{2^k}\mathbf{y}_0$ by this method and by basic iterative method.

7. Show that the Leverrier-Faddeev iterative scheme described in Sec. 22.5 produces the inverse of any nonsingular matrix, namely,

$$\mathbf{A}^{-1} = \frac{1}{q_n} \mathbf{B}_{n-1}.$$

Note that $q_n = d(\mathbf{A})$.

HINT: Use Cayley-Hamilton theorem and recall the procedure of nested multiplication for evaluation of polynomials.

8. Use method of preceding exercise to invert the coefficient matrices of Examples 20.4 and 20.5. Use inverses thus obtained to solve the given linear systems of equations.

9. Let

$$f(x) = x^n + a_1 x^{n-1} + a_2 x^{n-2} + \cdots + a_{n-1}x + a_n$$

and

$$\mathbf{A} = \begin{bmatrix} -a_1 & -a_2 & \cdots & -a_{n-1} & -a_n \\ 1 & 0 & \cdots & 0 & 0 \\ 0 & 1 & \cdots & 0 & 0 \\ \cdot & \cdot & \cdot & \cdot & \cdot \\ 0 & 0 & \cdots & 1 & 0 \end{bmatrix}.$$

Show that

$$d(\mathbf{A} - x\mathbf{I}) = -f(x).$$

Thus the zeros of $f(x)$ are the characteristic numbers of $\mathbf{A}$, which can be found by iterative methods. The matrix $\mathbf{A}$ is known as the *companion matrix* of the polynomial $f(x)$.

HINT: In the determinant of the matrix $\mathbf{A} - x\mathbf{I}$ multiply the elements of the first column by x and add to corresponding elements of the second column. Multiply the elements of the new second column by x and add to the corresponding elements of the third column, etc.

10. If $\mathbf{a} = (a_1, a_2, \ldots, a_n)$ and $\mathbf{b} = (b_1, b_2, \ldots, b_n)$ are any two column matrices (vectors) of the same order let

$$(\mathbf{a}, \mathbf{b}) = a_1 b_1 + a_2 b_2 + \cdots + a_n b_n$$

denote their *inner product*. Show that under the hypotheses of Case I, Sec. 22.61, λ_1 may be calculated as follows:

Given an arbitrary nonzero vector $\mathbf{y}_0$ calculate the sequence of vectors $\{\mathbf{y}_{k+1} = \mathbf{A}\mathbf{y}_k\}$. Show that

$$\frac{(\mathbf{y}_{k+1}, \mathbf{y}_k)}{(\mathbf{y}_k, \mathbf{y}_k)} \xrightarrow[k \to \infty]{} \lambda_1.$$

REFERENCES

1. R. A. Frazer, W. J. Duncan, and A. R. Collar. *Elementary Matrices and Some Applications to Dynamics and Differential Equations.* Cambridge: Cambridge U.P., 1950.

2. W. V. Parker, and J. C. Eaves. *Matrices.* New York: Ronald, 1960.

3. National Physical Laboratory. *Modern Computing Methods.* London: Her Majesty's Stationery Office, 1957; revised and enlarged 1961.

4. V. N. Faddeeva. *Computational Methods of Linear Algebra.* New York: Dover, 1959; translated from the Russian edition of 1950.

5. J. H. Wilkinson. "The Calculation of the Latent Roots and Vectors of Matrices on The Pilot Model of A.C.E.," *Cambridge Phil. Soc. Proc.* **50:** 536–566 (1954).

6. F. E. Hohn. *Elementary Matrix Algebra*. New York: Macmillan, 2nd ed., 1964.

7. E. Bodewig. *Matrix Calculus*. Amsterdam: North Holland Pub. Co., 1959.

8. A. Ralston, and H. S. Wilf (eds.), *Mathematical Methods for Digital Computers*. New York: Wiley, 1960.

9. W. Givens. "Computation of Plane Unitary Rotations Transforming a General Matrix to Triangular Form," *J. Soc. Indust. Appl. Math.* **6:** 26–50 (1958).

10. A. S. Householder, and F. L. Bauer. "On Certain Methods for Expanding the Characteristic Polynomial," *Numerische Math.* **1:** 29–37 (1959).

APPENDIX A

SOME THEOREMS ABOUT

REAL FUNCTIONS

A.1 MEAN VALUE THEOREM FOR DERIVATIVES

Let $f(x)$ be continuous for $x_0 \leq x \leq x_1$ and differentiable for $x_0 < x < x_1$. Then there exists at least one number ξ between x_0 and x_1 such that

$$f'(\xi) = \frac{f(x_1) - f(x_0)}{x_1 - x_0}.$$

A.2 ROLLE'S THEOREM

Let $f(x)$ be continuous for $x_0 \leq x \leq x_1$ and differentiable for $x_0 < x < x_1$. If $f(x_0) = f(x_1)$ then there exists at least one number ξ between x_0 and x_1 such that $f'(\xi) = 0$.

A.3 GENERALIZATION OF ROLLE'S THEOREM

Let $f(x)$ be continuous for $a \leq x \leq b$ and such that $f^{(n)}(x)$ exists for $a < x < b$ and that $f(x_i) = 0$ with $a \leq x_0 < x_1 < \cdots < x_n \leq b$. Then there exists at least one number ξ between a and b such that $f^{(n)}(\xi) = 0$.

A.4 FIRST THEOREM OF THE MEAN FOR INTEGRALS

If $f(x)$ is continuous for $x_0 \leq x \leq x_1$ then there exists at least one number ξ between x_0 and x_1 such that

$$\int_{x_0}^{x_1} f(x) \, dx = (x_1 - x_0) f(\xi).$$

A.5 SECOND THEOREM OF THE MEAN FOR INTEGRALS

If $f(x)$ is continuous for $x_0 \leq x \leq x_1$ and $g(x)$ does not change sign there, then there exists at least one number ξ between x_0 and x_1 such that

$$\int_{x_0}^{x_1} f(x) g(x) \, dx = f(\xi) \int_{x_0}^{x_1} g(x) \, dx,$$

provided only that $g(x)$ be integrable on (x_0, x_1).

A.6 TAYLOR'S FORMULA

If $f^{(n+1)}(x)$ exists and is continuous throughout an interval including x_0, then in that interval

$$f(x) = T_n(x) + R_{n+1}(x),$$

where

$$T_n(x) = f(x_0) + f'(x_0)(x - x_0) + \cdots + \frac{f^{(n)}(x_0)}{n!}(x - x_0)^n$$

and

$$R_{n+1}(x) = \frac{1}{n!} \int_{x_0}^{x} (x - s)^n f^{(n+1)}(s) \, ds.$$

Furthermore, there exists at least one number ξ between x_0 and x such that

$$R_{n+1}(x) = \frac{f^{(n+1)}(\xi)}{(n+1)!}(x - x_0)^{n+1}.$$

A.7 THEOREM

If $f(x)$ is continuous for $\xi_1 \leq x \leq \xi_2$ and λ_1, λ_2 are constants of like sign, then there exists at least one number ξ between ξ_1 and ξ_2 for which

$$\lambda_1 f(\xi_1) + \lambda_2 f(\xi_2) = (\lambda_1 + \lambda_2) f(\xi).$$

A.8 THEOREM

A continuous function attains a maximum and a minimum value, as well as every value in between, on any finite closed interval.

That is, if $f(x)$ is continuous on the closed interval $[a, b]$ then that interval contains two numbers x_0 and x_1 such that

$$f(x_0) \le f(x) \le f(x_1)$$

for all x with $a \le x \le b$. Furthermore, if η is any number between $f(x_0)$ and $f(x_1)$ then there exists a number ξ between a and b for which $f(\xi) = \eta$.

A.8.1 *THEOREM.* A continuous function which assumes values of opposite sign on an interval must vanish somewhere on that interval.

A.9 TAYLOR'S QUADRATIC FORMULA IN TWO VARIABLES

If $f(x, y)$ has continuous third-order partial derivatives in a circle with center at (x_0, y_0), then in that circle

$$f(x, y) = T_2(x, y) + R_3(x, y)$$

where

$$
\begin{aligned}
T_2(x, y) = {} & f(x_0, y_0) + f_x(x_0, y_0)(x - x_0) + f_y(x_0, y_0)(y - y_0) \\
& + \tfrac{1}{2} f_{xx}(x_0, y_0)(x - x_0)^2 + f_{xy}(x_0, y_0)(x - x_0)(y - y_0) \\
& + \tfrac{1}{2} f_{yy}(x_0, y_0)(y - y_0)^2
\end{aligned}
$$

and

$$
\begin{aligned}
R_3(x, y) = {} & \tfrac{1}{6} [f_{xxx}(\xi, \eta)(x - x_0)^3 + 3 f_{xxy}(\xi, \eta)(x - x_0)^2(y - y_0) \\
& + 3 f_{xyy}(\xi, \eta)(x - x_0)(y - y_0)^2 + f_{yyy}(\xi, \eta)(y - y_0)^3].
\end{aligned}
$$

The point (ξ, η) lies on the line joining (x_0, y_0) and (x, y).

APPENDIX B

MATRICES

A BRIEF SUMMARY OF ELEMENTARY MATRIX ALGEBRA

B.1 DEFINITION

A rectangular table of $m \times n$ elements arranged in m rows and n columns

$$
\begin{bmatrix}
a_{11} & a_{12} & \cdots & a_{1n} \\
a_{21} & a_{22} & \cdots & a_{2n} \\
\cdot & \cdot & \cdot & \cdot \\
a_{m1} & a_{m2} & \cdots & a_{mn}
\end{bmatrix}
$$

will be called an $m \times n$ matrix.

It will be sufficient for our purposes to consider only matrices whose elements are real numbers.

Two matrices are *equal* if and only if their corresponding elements are equal.

B.2 ADDITION OF MATRICES

The *sum* of two $m \times n$ matrices **A** and **B** is a matrix **C** such that

$$
c_{ij} = a_{ij} + b_{ij}, \qquad
\begin{aligned}
i &= 1, 2, \ldots, m. \\
j &= 1, 2, \ldots, n.
\end{aligned}
$$

Matrix addition is both *associative* and *commutative*, that is,

(1) $$\mathbf{A} + (\mathbf{B} + \mathbf{C}) = (\mathbf{A} + \mathbf{B}) + \mathbf{C}$$

(2) $$\mathbf{A} + \mathbf{B} = \mathbf{B} + \mathbf{A}.$$

B.3 MULTIPLICATION BY A NUMBER

The matrix obtained by multiplying *all* the elements of a matrix $\mathbf{A}$ by a number α is called the *product* of the number α and the matrix $\mathbf{A}$.

Multiplication of matrices by numbers obeys two forms of the *distributive* law:

(1) $$\alpha(\mathbf{A} + \mathbf{B}) = \alpha\mathbf{A} + \alpha\mathbf{B}$$

(2) $$(\alpha + \beta)\mathbf{A} = \alpha\mathbf{A} + \beta\mathbf{A}.$$

B.4 MULTIPLICATION OF MATRICES

The homogeneous linear transformation

$$
\begin{aligned}
a_{11}x_1 + a_{12}x_2 + \cdots + a_{1n}x_n &= y_1 \\
a_{21}x_1 + a_{22}x_2 + \cdots + a_{2n}x_n &= y_2 \\
\cdot \quad \cdot \quad \cdot \quad \cdot \quad \cdot \quad \cdot \quad \cdot \quad \cdot \quad \cdot \quad \cdot \\
a_{m1}x_1 + a_{m2}x_2 + \cdots + a_{mn}x_n &= y_m
\end{aligned}
\tag{1}
$$

can be written in matrix form

$$\mathbf{A}\mathbf{x} = \mathbf{y} \tag{1$'$}$$

where $\mathbf{A}$ is the matrix of coefficients and $\mathbf{x}$ and $\mathbf{y}$ are *column matrices* or *vectors*:

$$
\mathbf{x} = \begin{bmatrix} x_1 \\ x_2 \\ \cdots \\ \cdots \\ x_n \end{bmatrix}, \qquad
\mathbf{y} = \begin{bmatrix} y_1 \\ y_2 \\ \cdots \\ \cdots \\ y_m \end{bmatrix},
$$

provided that we agree that $\mathbf{A}\mathbf{x}$ is the column matrix whose elements are

$$\sum_{j=1}^{n} a_{ij}x_j, \qquad i = 1, 2, \ldots, m.$$

Consider now a second homogeneous linear transformation

$$b_{11}y_1 + b_{12}y_2 + \cdots + b_{1m}y_m = z_1$$
$$b_{21}y_1 + b_{22}y_2 + \cdots + b_{2m}y_m = z_2$$
$$\cdot \ \cdot \ \cdot \ \cdot \ \cdot \ \cdot \ \cdot \ \cdot \ \cdot \ \cdot$$
$$b_{p1}y_1 + b_{p2}y_2 + \cdots + b_{pm}y_m = z_p$$

$$(2)$$

which, in matrix form, is

$$\mathbf{By} = \mathbf{z}. \tag{2'}$$

If the expressions for the y's from (1) are substituted into (2) we obtain

$$c_{11}x_1 + c_{12}x_2 + \cdots + c_{1n}x_n = z_1$$
$$c_{21}x_1 + c_{22}x_2 + \cdots + c_{2n}x_n = z_2$$
$$\cdot \ \cdot \ \cdot \ \cdot \ \cdot \ \cdot \ \cdot \ \cdot \ \cdot \ \cdot$$
$$c_{p1}x_1 + c_{p2}x_2 + \cdots + c_{pn}x_n = z_p$$

$$(3)$$

or

$$\mathbf{Cx} = \mathbf{z}$$

where

$$c_{kj} = \sum_{i=1}^{n} b_{ki}a_{ij}, \qquad \begin{array}{l} k = 1, 2, \ldots, p \\ j = 1, 2, \ldots, n. \end{array} \tag{4}$$

On the other hand, Eqs. (1') and (2') imply

$$\mathbf{B(Ax)} = \mathbf{z}.$$

But

$$\mathbf{Cx} = \mathbf{z}.$$

We are thus motivated to define the *product* **BA** as the $p \times n$ matrix **C** whose elements are defined by Eq. (4). Note that **C** has the same number of rows as **B** and columns as **A**. Furthermore, the product **BA** can be formed only if the number of columns of **B** equals the number of rows of **A**.

Even square matrices of the same order (both having n rows and n columns) need not commute. For example:

$$\begin{bmatrix} 1 & 2 \\ 3 & 4 \end{bmatrix}\begin{bmatrix} 1 & 1 \\ 0 & 1 \end{bmatrix} = \begin{bmatrix} 1 & 3 \\ 3 & 7 \end{bmatrix}$$

while

$$\begin{bmatrix} 1 & 1 \\ 0 & 1 \end{bmatrix}\begin{bmatrix} 1 & 2 \\ 3 & 4 \end{bmatrix} = \begin{bmatrix} 4 & 6 \\ 3 & 4 \end{bmatrix}.$$

Matrix multiplication does, however, have the following properties:

(1) $A(BC) = (AB)C$

(2) $\alpha(AB) = (\alpha A)B = A(\alpha B)$

(3) $(A + B)C = AC + BC$

(4) $C(A + B) = CA + CB$

where **A, B, C** are matrices for which the indicated operations are possible and α a number.

If **A** and **B** are square matrices of same order then

$$d(AB) = d(A)\ d(B),$$

where $d(A)$ denotes the determinant of the matrix A.

B.5 SPECIAL MATRICES

(a) DIAGONAL: A square matrix whose only nonzero elements lie on its main diagonal. Thus

$$D = \begin{bmatrix} \alpha_1 & 0 & \cdots & 0 \\ 0 & \alpha_2 & \cdots & 0 \\ . & . & . & . \\ 0 & 0 & \cdots & \alpha_n \end{bmatrix} = \lceil \alpha_1, \alpha_2, \ldots, \alpha_n \rfloor$$

is a diagonal matrix. Note that

$$d(D) = \alpha_1 \alpha_2 \cdots \alpha_n$$

and

$$D^k = \lceil \alpha_1^k, \alpha_2^k, \ldots, \alpha_n^k \rfloor.$$

If all the α_i are different from zero then

$$\lceil \alpha_1, \alpha_2, \ldots, \alpha_n \rfloor \lceil 1/\alpha_1, 1/\alpha_2, \ldots, 1/\alpha_n \rfloor = \lceil 1, 1, \ldots, 1 \rfloor.$$

(b) SCALAR: A diagonal matrix having diagonal elements all the same.

Note that if **A** is a square matrix of order n and $S = \lceil \alpha, \alpha, \ldots, \alpha \rfloor$ a scalar matrix of order n, then

$$SA = AS = \alpha A.$$

(c) IDENTITY: A diagonal matrix having ones down the main diagonal. We denote it by **I**, letting the context indicate its order.

There is no matrix **B** other than **I** such that

$$AB = BA = A.$$

(d) SYMMETRIC: A matrix for which $a_{ij} = a_{ji}$.

(e) SKEW-SYMMETRIC: A matrix for which $a_{ij} = -a_{ji}$.
A skew-symmetric matrix is necessarily square with zeros down the main diagonal.

(f) ZERO: A matrix each element of which is zero. We denote it by **0**, letting context indicate its order.
For any square matrix **A**,

(1) $$\mathbf{A} + \mathbf{0} = \mathbf{0} + \mathbf{A} = \mathbf{A}$$

(2) $$\mathbf{A0} = \mathbf{0A} = \mathbf{0}.$$

Note, however, that the product of two nonzero matrices can be the zero matrix. For example:

$$\begin{bmatrix} 1 & 0 \\ 1 & 0 \end{bmatrix} \begin{bmatrix} 0 & 0 \\ 1 & 1 \end{bmatrix} = \begin{bmatrix} 0 & 0 \\ 0 & 0 \end{bmatrix}.$$

(g) VECTORS: Matrices having a single row or a single column (but not both).
We shall use the notation $[x_1, x_2, \ldots, x_n]$ to designate a row vector and $(x_1, x_2, \ldots, x_n)$ a column vector. A vector having n elements is said to be n-dimensional.

(h) SINGULAR: Square matrix whose determinant is zero

(i) TRIANGULAR: A square matrix having either all elements above or below the main diagonal equal to zero.
Note that the determinant of a triangular matrix is equal to product of its diagonal elements.

B.6 RELATED MATRICES

(a) TRANSPOSE: Matrix obtained from a matrix **A** by interchanging its rows and columns.
We shall use $\mathbf{A}^\mathsf{T}$ to designate the transpose. The transpose has the following properties:

(1) $$(\mathbf{A}^\mathsf{T})^\mathsf{T} = \mathbf{A}$$

(2) $$(\mathbf{A} + \mathbf{B})^\mathsf{T} = \mathbf{A}^\mathsf{T} + \mathbf{B}^\mathsf{T}$$

(3) $$(\mathbf{AB})^\mathsf{T} = \mathbf{B}^\mathsf{T}\mathbf{A}^\mathsf{T}$$

(4) $$(\alpha\mathbf{A})^\mathsf{T} = \alpha\mathbf{A}^\mathsf{T}.$$

(b) MATRIX OF COFACTORS: Matrix obtained from a square matrix by replacing each element by its cofactor. (See C.4).

(c) ADJOINT: Transpose of the matrix of cofactors.

We shall use $\mathbf{A}^{\mathbf{A}}$ to designate the adjoint.

(d) INVERSE: Adjoint of $\mathbf{A}$ divided by determinant of $\mathbf{A}$. We shall designate the inverse by $\mathbf{A}^{-1}$. For any nonsingular matrix $\mathbf{A}$

$$\mathbf{A}^{-1}\mathbf{A} = \mathbf{A}\mathbf{A}^{-1} = \mathbf{I}.$$

There is no matrix $\mathbf{B}$ other than $\mathbf{A}^{-1}$ for which

$$\mathbf{A}\mathbf{B} = \mathbf{B}\mathbf{A} = \mathbf{I}.$$

The inverse of a product also follows a reversal rule:

$$(\mathbf{A}\mathbf{B})^{-1} = \mathbf{B}^{-1}\mathbf{A}^{-1}.$$

(e) MINOR OR SUBMATRIX: A matrix formed from the elements of a given matrix situated at the intersections of some of its rows and columns, in their natural arrangement. That is, the residual matrix obtained by striking out some of the rows and columns of a given matrix.

(f) SIMILAR MATRICES: Two square matrices $\mathbf{A}$ and $\mathbf{B}$ of same order are said to be *similar* if there exists a nonsingular matrix $\mathbf{M}$ such that

$$\mathbf{B} = \mathbf{M}^{-1}\mathbf{A}\mathbf{M}.$$

Note that for any positive integer n,

$$\mathbf{B}^n = \mathbf{M}^{-1}\mathbf{A}^n\mathbf{M}.$$

This relationship holds also for negative integers provided $\mathbf{A}$ is nonsingular.

B.7 LINEARLY DEPENDENT VECTORS

Any k n-dimensional vectors $\mathbf{a}_1, \mathbf{a}_2, \ldots, \mathbf{a}_k$ are called *linearly dependent* if constants $c_1, c_2, \ldots, c_k$ exist, not all zero, such that

$$c_1\mathbf{a}_1 + c_2\mathbf{a}_2 + \cdots + c_k\mathbf{a}_k = \mathbf{0}.$$

Otherwise the vectors are called *linearly independent*.

Note that in the case of linearly dependent vectors, at least one will be a linear combination of the others. For example, if $c_k \neq 0$, then

$$\mathbf{a}_k = -\frac{c_1}{c_k}\mathbf{a}_1 - \frac{c_2}{c_k}\mathbf{a}_2 - \cdots - \frac{c_{k-1}}{c_k}\mathbf{a}_{k-1}.$$

B.8 RANK OF MATRICES

The order of the nonsingular minor of largest order is called the *rank* of the matrix—that is, the rank r of a matrix is an integer such that there exists a nonsingular minor of order r, but all minors of higher order, if such exist, are singular.

The concept of rank is useful in connection with systems of linear equations.

The maximum number of linearly independent rows of a matrix equals the maximum number of linearly independent columns equals the rank of the matrix.

B.9 POLYNOMIAL FUNCTIONS OF MATRICES

If

$$f(x) = a_0 x^k + a_1 x^{k-1} + \cdots + a_{k-1} x + a_k$$

is a polynomial of degree k and $\mathbf{A}$ is a square matrix of order n we define

$$f(\mathbf{A}) = a_0 \mathbf{A}^k + a_1 \mathbf{A}^{k-1} + \cdots + a_{k-1} \mathbf{A} + a_k \mathbf{I}.$$

Polynomials in matrices have the following properties:

1. If

$$f(x) + g(x) = s(x)$$

and if

$$f(x)g(x) = p(x),$$

then

$$f(\mathbf{A}) + g(\mathbf{A}) = s(\mathbf{A})$$

and

$$f(\mathbf{A})g(\mathbf{A}) = p(\mathbf{A}).$$

2. If

$$f(x) = a_0(x - x_1)(x - x_2) \cdots (x - x_k),$$

then

$$f(\mathbf{A}) = a_0(\mathbf{A} - x_1 \mathbf{I})(\mathbf{A} - x_2 \mathbf{I}) \cdots (\mathbf{A} - x_k \mathbf{I}).$$

Polynomials of degree k in the matrix $\mathbf{A}$ may have more than k zeros. For example, the polynomial

$$f(\mathbf{A}) = \mathbf{A}^2 + \mathbf{I}$$

has (among others) the zeros

$$\begin{bmatrix} i & 0 \\ 0 & i \end{bmatrix}, \quad \begin{bmatrix} -i & 0 \\ 0 & -i \end{bmatrix} \quad \text{and} \quad \begin{bmatrix} 1 & 2 \\ -1 & -1 \end{bmatrix}.$$

B.10 THE CAYLEY-HAMILTON THEOREM

If

$$d(\mathbf{A} - \lambda \mathbf{I}) = (-1)^n \{\lambda^n - p_1 \lambda^{n-1} - p_2 \lambda^{n-2} - \cdots - p_{n-1} \lambda - p_n\} = \phi(\lambda)$$

then

$$\phi(\mathbf{A}) = (-1)^n \{ \mathbf{A}^n - p_1 \mathbf{A}^{n-1} - p_2 \mathbf{A}^{n-2} - \cdots - p_{n-1} \mathbf{A} - p_n \mathbf{I} \} = \mathbf{0},$$

that is, a matrix satisfies its own characteristic equation.

B.11 ELEMENTARY TRANSFORMATIONS OF A MATRIX

By an *elementary row transformation* of a matrix is meant one of the following:
1. The interchange of two rows.
2. The multiplication of all the elements of a row by a number $k \neq 0$.
3. The addition to the elements of one row of the products of the corresponding elements of another row by the same number k.
Elementary column transformations are defined similarly.

REFERENCES

1. G. C. Best. "Two Theorem Tables of Matrix Algebra," *Math. Comput.* **15**: 19–22 (1961).

2. M. Marcus. *Basic Theorems in Matrix Theory*. Washington, D.C.: National Bureau of Standards, U.S. Government Printing Office, 1960.

3. F. E. Hohn. *Elementary Matrix Algebra*. New York: Macmillan, 2nd ed., 1964.

4. R. Bellman. *Introduction to Matrix Theory*. New York: McGraw-Hill, 1960.

5. F. R. Gantmacher. *The Theory of Matrices*. New York: Chelsea, 1959. Translated from the Russian and German editions.

APPENDIX C

DETERMINANTS

A determinant is a number associated with a square array (matrix) of numbers arranged in n rows and n columns. It is thus a function on the set of square matrices to the set of numbers (real or complex). Although a determinant can be defined in several equivalent ways, we shall make the definition in terms of the concepts of permutations and inversions, which we now define.

C.1 PERMUTATION

Any ordered listing of all the first n integers $1, 2, 3, \ldots, n$ is said to be a *permutation* of these integers.

There are $n! = n(n-1)(n-2) \cdots 3\ 2\ 1$ distinct permutations of the first n integers.

C.2 INVERSION

If in a given permutation an integer precedes a smaller integer, we say the permutation contains an *inversion*.

The total number of inversions in a permutation is the sum of the numbers of smaller integers following each integer of the permutation. Thus the permutation 5 7 1 2 6 4 3 has twelve inversions.

217

C.3   DETERMINANT

Let **A** denote the matrix

$$
\begin{bmatrix}
a_{11} & a_{12} & \cdots & a_{1n} \\
a_{21} & a_{22} & \cdots & a_{2n} \\
\cdot & \cdot & \cdot & \cdot \\
a_{n1} & a_{n2} & \cdots & a_{nn}
\end{bmatrix}.
$$

The determinant of **A**, written $d(\mathbf{A})$, is the sum of $n!$ signed products:

$$
d(\mathbf{A}) = \sum (-1)^k a_{i_1 1} a_{i_2 2} \cdots a_{i_n n}
$$

where the summation is over the $n!$ permutations of the first n integers and k is the number of inversions in the permutation $i_1, i_2, \ldots, i_n$.

C.4   MINORS AND COFACTORS

The determinant M_{ij} of the matrix formed by deleting all the elements of the ith row and jth column of a matrix **A** is called the *minor* of the element a_{ij} of **A**. Then

$$
A_{ij} = (-1)^{i+j} M_{ij}
$$

is called the *cofactor* of a_{ij}.

We now state a useful result about expansions of determinants using cofactors:

$$
\sum_{i=1}^{n} a_{ij} A_{ik} = \delta_{jk} \, d(\mathbf{A}),
$$

$$
\sum_{j=1}^{n} a_{ij} A_{kj} = \delta_{ik} \, d(\mathbf{A}),
$$

where

$$
\delta_{ij} = \begin{cases} 1 & \text{if } i = j \\ 0 & \text{if } i \neq j. \end{cases}
$$

C.5   DIFFERENTIATION

If the elements of the square matrix **A** are differentiable functions of a variable x then the derivative of $d(\mathbf{A})$ may be calculated as follows:

Let $\mathbf{A}_i'$ denote the matrix formed from the matrix **A** by replacing the elements of its ith row (column) by their derivatives. Then

$$
d'(\mathbf{A}) = \sum_{i=1}^{n} d(\mathbf{A}_i').
$$

C.6 VANDERMONDE'S DETERMINANT

One determinant of special interest is that discussed by Vandermonde in 1770. He showed that the matrix

$$\mathbf{X} = \begin{bmatrix} 1 & x_1 & x_1^2 & \cdots & x_1^{n-1} \\ 1 & x_2 & x_1^2 & \cdots & x_2^{n-1} \\ \cdot & \cdot & \cdot & \cdot & \cdot \\ 1 & x_n & x_n^2 & \cdots & x_n^{n-1} \end{bmatrix},$$

now known as the *Vandermonde matrix*, has determinant

$$d(\mathbf{X}) = \prod_{1 \le j < i \le n} (x_i - x_j),$$

where the symbol on the right means the product of all factors of the type indicated. It cannot be zero if the numbers $x_1, x_2, \ldots, x_n$ are all distinct.

REFERENCES

1. H. B. Fine. *College Algebra*. Boston: Ginn, 1905, reprinted by Dover (New York) 1961.
2. L. E. Dickson. *New First Course in Theory of Equations*. New York: Wiley, 1952.
3. A. C. Aitken. *Determinants and Matrices*. Edinburgh: Oliver & Boyd, 1939.
4. H. W. Turnbull. *The Theory of Determinants, Matrices, and Invariants*. London: Blackie, 1928, 1945, reprinted by Dover (New York) 1960.

APPENDIX D

SYSTEMS OF LINEAR

EQUATIONS

D.1

The system of m linear equations in n unknowns

$$a_{11}x_1 + a_{12}x_2 + \cdots + a_{1n}x_n = a_1$$
$$a_{21}x_1 + a_{22}x_2 + \cdots + a_{2n}x_n = a_2$$
$$\cdot \quad \cdot \quad \cdot \quad \cdot \quad \cdot \quad \cdot \quad \cdot \quad \cdot \quad \cdot \quad \cdot \quad \cdot$$
$$a_{m1}x_1 + a_{m2}x_2 + \cdots + a_{mn}x_n = a_m$$

has a *coefficient matrix*

$$\begin{bmatrix} a_{11} & a_{12} & \cdots & a_{1n} \\ a_{21} & a_{22} & \cdots & a_{2n} \\ \cdot & \cdot & \cdot & \cdot \\ a_{m1} & a_{m2} & \cdots & a_{mn} \end{bmatrix}$$

and an *augmented matrix*

$$\begin{bmatrix} a_{11} & a_{12} & \cdots & a_{1n} & a_1 \\ a_{21} & a_{22} & \cdots & a_{2n} & a_2 \\ \cdot & \cdot & \cdot & \cdot & \cdot \\ a_{m1} & a_{m2} & \cdots & a_{mn} & a_m \end{bmatrix}.$$

A system that has at least one solution is said to be *consistent*.

If $a_1 = a_2 = \cdots = a_m = 0$, the system is called *homogeneous*. The basic classical theorems for linear systems are:

D.1.1.   A system of m linear equations in n unknowns is consistent if and only if the coefficient and augmented matrices are of equal rank r. Then some r of the equations determine uniquely r of the unknowns as linear functions of the remaining $n - r$ unknowns. The resulting expressions for these r unknowns also satisfy the remaining $m - r$ equations.

D.1.2.   Any system of $n + 1$ linear equations in n unknowns is inconsistent if the determinant of the augmented matrix is not zero.

D.1.3.   A necessary and sufficient condition that n linear homogeneous equations in n unknowns have a solution, other than the trivial one in which each unknown is zero, is that the determinant of the coefficients be zero.

D.2   CRAMER'S RULE

The rule of G. Cramer, dating from 1750, is concerned with n linear equations in n unknowns:

Let D denote the determinant of the coefficient matrix **A**, and let D_i, $i = 1, 2, 3, \ldots, n$ denote the determinant of the matrix formed by replacing the ith column of **A** by the vector $(a_1, a_2, \ldots, a_n)$. Then

$$Dx_i = D_i, \qquad i = 1, 2, 3, \ldots, n.$$

If $D \neq 0$,

$$x_i = D_i/D, \qquad i = 1, 2, 3, \ldots, n,$$

is the unique solution of the given linear system.

REFERENCE

1. L. E. Dickson. *New First Course in Theory of Equations*. New York: Wiley, 1952.

APPENDIX E

INTERPOLATION

COEFFICIENTS

Table I

NEWTON'S INTERPOLATION COEFFICIENTS

U	$\binom{U}{2}$	$\binom{U}{3}$	$\binom{U}{4}$
0.1	−0.045	0.028 5	−0.020 66
0.2	−0.080	0.048 0	−0.033 60
0.3	−0.105	0.059 5	−0.040 16
0.4	−0.120	0.064 0	−0.041 60
0.5	−0.125	0.062 5	−0.039 06
0.6	−0.120	0.056 0	−0.033 60
0.7	−0.105	0.045 5	−0.026 16
0.8	−0.080	0.032 0	−0.017 60
0.9	−0.045	0.016 5	−0.008 66
1.0	−0.000	0.000 0	−0.000 00

Table II

STIRLING'S INTERPOLATION COEFFICIENTS

U	S_2	S_3	S_4	S_5
0.0	0.000	−0.000 0	−0.000 000 0	0.000 000
0.1	0.005	−0.016 5	−0.000 412 5	0.003 292
0.2	0.020	−0.032 0	−0.001 600 0	0.006 336
0.3	0.045	−0.045 5	−0.003 412 5	0.008 952
0.4	0.080	−0.056 0	−0.005 600 0	0.010 752
0.5	0.125	−0.062 5	−0.007 812 5	0.011 719
$-U$	S_2	$-S_3$	S_4	$-S_5$

Table III

BESSEL'S INTERPOLATION COEFFICIENTS

U	B_2	B_3	B_4	B_5
0.0	−0.000	0.000	0.000 00	−0.000 00
0.1	−0.045	0.006	0.007 84	−0.000 63
0.2	−0.080	0.008	0.014 40	−0.000 86
0.3	−0.105	0.007	0.019 34	−0.000 77
0.4	−0.120	0.004	0.022 40	−0.000 45
0.5	−0.125	0.000	0.023 44	−0.000 00
0.6	−0.120	−0.004	0.022 40	0.000 45
0.7	−0.105	−0.007	0.019 34	0.000 77
0.8	−0.080	−0.008	0.014 40	0.000 86
0.9	−0.045	−0.006	0.007 84	0.000 63
1.0	−0.000	−0.000	0.000 00	0.000 00

Table IV

EVERETT'S INTERPOLATION COEFFICIENTS

t	E_2	E_4
0.0	−0.000 0	0.000 00
0.1	−0.016 5	0.003 29
0.2	−0.032 0	0.006 34
0.3	−0.045 5	0.008 90
0.4	−0.056 0	0.010 75
0.5	−0.062 5	0.011 72

Table IV (*continued*)

t	E_2	E_4
0.6	—0.064 0	0.011 65
0.7	—0.059 5	0.010 44
0.8	—0.048 0	0.008 06
0.9	—0.028 5	0.004 55
1.0	—0.000 0	0.000 00

Table V

EVERETT'S CUBIC INTERPOLATION COEFFICIENTS

t	$-E_2$	t	$-E_2$	t	$-E_2$	t	$-E_2$
0.00	0.0000	0.25	0.0391	0.50	0.0625	0.75	0.0547
1	17	6	404	1	629	6	535
2	33	7	417	2	632	7	522
3	50	8	430	3	635	8	509
4	67	9	443	4	638	9	495
0.05	0.0083	0.30	0.0455	0.55	0.0639	0.80	0.0480
6	100	1	467	6	641	1	464
7	116	2	479	7	641	2	448
8	132	3	490	8	641	3	430
9	149	4	501	9	641	4	412
0.10	0.0165	0.35	0.0512	0.60	0.0640	0.85	0.0393
1	181	6	522	1	638	6	373
2	197	7	532	2	636	7	352
3	213	8	542	3	633	8	331
4	229	9	551	4	630	9	308
0.15	0.0244	0.40	0.0560	0.65	0.0626	0.90	0.0285
6	260	1	568	6	621	1	261
7	275	2	577	7	615	2	236
8	290	3	584	8	609	3	209
9	305	4	591	9	602	4	182
0.20	0.0320	0.45	0.0598	0.70	0.0595	0.95	0.0154
1	335	6	604	1	587	6	125
2	349	7	610	2	578	7	96
3	363	8	616	3	568	8	65
4	377	9	621	4	558	9	33
0.25	0.0391	0.50	0.0625	0.75	0.0547	1.00	0.0000

Table VI

LAGRANGIAN INTERPOLATION COEFFICIENTS

THREE-POINT INTERPOLATION COEFFICIENTS

U	A_{-1}	A_0	A_1	U	A_{-1}	A_0	A_1
0.1	−0.045	0.990	0.055	0.5	−0.125	0.750	0.375
0.2	−0.080	0.960	0.120	0.6	−0.120	0.640	0.480
0.3	−0.105	0.910	0.195	0.7	−0.105	0.510	0.595
0.4	−0.120	0.840	0.280	0.8	−0.080	0.360	0.720
0.5	−0.125	0.750	0.375	0.9	−0.045	0.190	0.855
$-U$	A_1	A_0	A_{-1}	$-U$	A_1	A_0	A_{-1}

FOUR-POINT INTERPOLATION COEFFICIENTS

U	A_{-1}	A_0	A_1	A_2	
0.1	−0.0285	0.9405	0.1045	−0.0165	0.9
0.2	−0.0480	0.8640	0.2160	−0.0320	0.8
0.3	−0.0595	0.7735	0.3315	−0.0454	0.7
0.4	−0.0640	0.6720	0.4480	−0.0560	0.6
0.5	−0.0625	0.5625	0.5625	−0.0625	0.5
1.1	0.0165	−0.0945	1.0395	0.0385	−0.1
1.2	0.0320	−0.1760	1.0560	0.0880	−0.2
1.3	0.0455	−0.2415	1.0465	0.1495	−0.3
1.4	0.0560	−0.2880	1.0080	0.2240	−0.4
1.5	0.0625	−0.3125	0.9375	0.3125	−0.5
	A_2	A_1	A_0	A_{-1}	U

FIVE-POINT INTERPOLATION COEFFICIENTS

U	A_{-2}	$-A_{-1}$	A_0	A_1	$-A_2$	U
0.1	0.007 8375	0.059 85	0.987 525	0.073 15	0.008 6625	0.1
0.2	0.014 4000	0.105 60	0.950 400	0.158 40	0.017 6000	0.2
0.3	0.019 3375	0.136 85	0.889 525	0.254 15	0.026 1625	0.3
0.4	0.022 4000	0.153 60	0.806 400	0.358 40	0.033 6000	0.4
0.5	0.023 4375	0.156 25	0.703 125	0.468 75	0.039 0625	0.5
0.6	0.022 4000	0.145 60	0.582 400	0.582 40	0.041 6000	0.6
0.7	0.019 3375	0.122 85	0.447 525	0.696 35	0.040 1625	0.7
0.8	0.014 4000	0.089 60	0.302 400	0.806 40	0.033 6000	0.8
0.9	0.007 8375	0.047 85	0.151 525	0.909 15	0.020 6625	0.9
$-U$	A_2	$-A_1$	A_0	A_{-1}	$-A_{-2}$	$-U$

SUPPLEMENTARY

BIBLIOGRAPHY

NUMERICAL ANALYSIS
1. A. S. Householder. *Principles of Numerical Analysis*. New York: McGraw-Hill, 1953.
2. G. E. Forsythe, and W. R. Wasow. *Finite-Difference Methods for Partial Differential Equations*. New York: Wiley, 1960.
3. L. V. Kantorovic, and V. I. Krylov. *Approximate Methods of Higher Analysis*. The Netherlands: Noordhoff, 1958, translated from the Russian edition of 1952.
4. J. Todd (ed.). *Survey of Numerical Analysis*. New York: McGraw-Hill, 1962.
5. R. E. Langer (ed.). *Frontiers of Numerical Mathematics*. Madison: Wisconsin U.P., 1960.
6. G. E. Forsythe. "A Numerical Analyst's Fifteen-foot Shelf," *Math. Tables Aids Comput.* **7**: 221–228 (1953).
7. Sh. E. Mikeladze. *Numerical Methods of Mathematical Analysis*. Washington, D.C.: Office of Technical Services, Department of Commerce (AEC-tr-4285), 1961. Translated from Russian edition of 1953.
8. A. S. Householder. "Bibliography on Numerical Analysis," *J. Assoc. Comput. Mach.* **3**: 85–100 (1956).

MATHEMATICAL TABLES
1. L. J. Comrie (ed.). *Barlow's Tables of Squares, Cubes, Square Roots, Cube Roots and Reciprocals*. New York: Chemical Pub. 1944.
2. L. J. Comrie. *Chamber's Six-Figure Mathematical Tables*. London: Chambers, 1949.

DIGITAL COMPUTERS
1. F. L. Alt. *Electronic Digital Computers*. New York: Academic, 1958.
2. D. D. McCracken. *Digital Computer Programming*. New York: Wiley, 1957.

226

JOURNALS
1. *The Computer Journal.*
2. *Journal of the Association for Computing Machinery.*
3. *Journal of Research of the National Bureau of Standards.*
4. *Journal of the Society for Industrial and Applied Mathematics.*
5. *Mathematical Reviews.*
6. *Mathematics of Computation.*

ANSWERS TO SELECTED EXERCISES

Chapter 2

1. $-37, 48$
2. $-1 + 36i,$ $20 + 50i$

Chapter 3

1. $0.450\ 64,$ $0.451\ 08$
2. $2.094,$ -0.006
3. $(41 \times 10^{-5}, 47 \times 10^{-5}),$ $0.000\ 44$
4. 4×10^{-5}
5. 11×10^{-9}
6. $0.6822x + 0.0452$
7. $\pm\frac{1}{2}\sqrt{2}$

Chapter 4

4. (a) $1.806\ 37$ (b) $1.806\ 37$

Chapter 5

1. $2,$ $-6,$ $-22,$ -14
2. $2.5 \pm 3.2i,$ 0.5
6. ± 0.8

Chapter 6

9. $0.373\ 125$

Chapter 8

1. $1.214\ 91,$ $1.214\ 91$
3. $2.7 \times 10^{-7} < R < 1.2 \times 10^{-6}$
4. $3 - 3x + 4x(x - 1) + 2x(x - 1)(x - 3)$
6. $2.094\ 54$

Chapter 9

  6. 1.247 032

  7. $1 + 2x + \frac{1}{2}x(x - 1)$

16. 0.438 371

Chapter 11

2. $\frac{1}{48}h^3 M_3^\star$

3. 0.099

Chapter 14

  2. 1552

  5. 0.694 44,   0.693 25,   0.693 15,   0.693 15

  6. 0.785 40,   0.784 98,   0.785 40

10. 0.470 19,   0.470 09,   0.470 00

11. 578,   24

12. 1.089 55,   1.089 41

Chapter 16

3. 0.693 121 7

Chapter 17

3. $\dfrac{u^2}{2}(1 - u)f_{-1} + (1 - u^2)f_0 + \dfrac{u^2}{2}(1 + u)f_1 + hu(1 - u^2)f_0'$

Chapter 18

6. (0.2, 1.000 068)

8. $m_{n+1} = p_{n+1} + \frac{28}{29}(c_n - p_n)$

    $y_{n+1} = c_{n+1} - \frac{1}{29}(c_{n+1} - p_{n+1})$

Chapter 19

1. $\frac{5}{14}$

Chapter 20

9. $\begin{bmatrix} 2 & -6 & -2 & -3 \\ 5 & -13 & -4 & -7 \\ -1 & 4 & 1 & 2 \\ 0 & 1 & 0 & 1 \end{bmatrix}$

Index

229

SOCIAL SCIENCE LIBRARY

Manor Road Building
Manor Road
Oxford OX1 3UQ
Tel: (2)71093 (enquiries and renewals)
http://www.ssl.ox.ac.uk

This is a NORMAL LOAN item.

We will email you a reminder before this item is due.

Please see http://www.ssl.ox.ac.uk/lending.html
for details on:

- loan policies; these are also displayed on the notice boards and in our library guide.

- how to check when your books are due back.

- how to renew your books, including information on the maximum number of renewals.
  Items may be renewed if not reserved by another reader. Items must be renewed before the library closes on the due date.

- level of fines; fines are charged on overdue books.

Please note that this item may be recalled during Term.